EMERGING STRATEGIES IN EARLY CHILDHOOD EDUCATION

Edited by

J. Wesley Little
University of Tulsa

Arthur J. Brigham
Carroll College

MSS Information Corporation
655 Madison Avenue, New York, N. Y. 10021

This is a custom-made book of readings prepared for the courses taught by the editors, as well as for related courses and for college and university libraries. For information about our program, please write to:

MSS INFORMATION CORPORATION
655 Madison Avenue
New York, New York 10021

MSS wishes to express its appreciation to the authors of the articles in this collection for their cooperation in making their work available in this format.

Library of Congress Cataloging in Publication Data

Little, J   Wesley, comp.
    Emerging strategies in early childhood education.

    1.   Education, Preschool--Addresses, essays, lecture
I.   Brigham, Arthur J., joint comp.   II.   Title.
[DNLM: 1.   Child, Preschool--Collected works.   2.   Edu
cation--Collected works.   3.   Psychology, Education--
In infancy & childhood--Collected works.
LB 1140 L778e   1973]
LB1140.2.L57 1973   372.21   73-99
ISBN 0-8422-0285-4

CONTENTS

IV. APPROACHES TO EARLY CHILDHOOD EDUCATION

PREFACE

Interest in the area of Early Childhood Education is not peculiar to this decade. For nearly two hundred years, pioneers in this field have contributed invaluable research, theories, methods and records. Without the work done by such people as Froebel, Schurz, Peabody, Montessori, Piaget, and many others, we could not look to the future of Early Childhood Education with such great expectation.

One can certainly expect significant changes to take place during the next decade. New interest and concern in Early Education has prompted a renewed dedication to this field by thousands of educators, parents, politicians, and interested citizens across the land. The area of Early Childhood Education has caused such a high degree of interest and concern, we now have millions, if not billions, of dollars being directed into a variety of programs in Early Education. Research has shown that "Early Childhood Education" actually begins at birth as the child begins to interact with his environment. Therefore, the concept of kindergarten education as the focal point in Early Education has been modified to be more inclusive.

Researchers the world over are working to find better ways of working with young children. By integrating new strategies with those developed by the early pioneers in the field, one can expect to see an increasing number of approaches to Early Education. Hopefully, program developers will consider all possible sources of research relating to the total development of young children. Strategies should embrace not only the theories of our culture and political system, but also the theories of other cultures and political systems.

It is the intent of the editors of this book of readings to provide the student with a variety of articles that reflect the diversified programs, models and strategies in existence at this time. This book should provide the student with a basic background of information that encompasses many of the major issues and concerns in the field of Early Childhood Education. In conjunction with guided discussion, the editors feel that this book of readings can serve as a basic reference tool to help the student broaden his understanding of the emerging strategies in Early Childhood Education.

I. AN INTRODUCTION

EDWARD ZIGLER

Contemporary Concerns in Early Childhood Education[1]

Every speaker always says: "It's such a pleasure to be with you today." But I think many of you appreciate the sincerity with which I make that statement to this particular group. Getting together with NAEYC and so many of my old friends is always a very warm and gratifying experience to me.

It is, however, more than personally gratifying to be with you today. Once I had agreed to go to Washington, I asked myself just what in the world do they expect me to do? Naturally, I was quite apprehensive, and it dawned on me that exactly the wrong thing for me to do was to pretend to be some super-intellectual, in possession of all the wisdom in the world about children. Not only would that be erroneous, it would be presumptious.

However, it seemed to me that what I could do, and what the Office of Child Development could do, would be to act as a conduit between the wisdom and knowledge that we have in this nation about children, and social action programs for children. A great deal of that knowledge and wisdom about children is represented in this room, and my office intends to channel your wisdom to the social action programs that we are presently mounting for children.

[1] Address presented at the 1970 Conference of the National Association for the Education of Young Children, Boston, Mass., November 21.

YOUNG CHILDREN, 1971, Vol. 26, No. 3, pp. 141-156.

Now the Office of Child Development is still a relatively new office, and people are still having considerable difficulty in defining it. Exactly what is the Office of Child Development? Well, if everyone promises not to tell anybody, I'll confess that I'm really not sure!

I have been given, I think, three major charges and a corollary, and it's these three charges and corollary that ·will define the Office of Child Development. The charges are as follows:

1. Operating quality programs for children.

2. Coordinating children's services and programs at the national level.

3. Advocacy and innovation.

In addition to these three major charges, I see a function that cuts across all of them; namely, rigorous research and evaluation. We must continue to discover more about children, we must discover what works and what doesn't. We must have some assurance, even in our advocacy efforts, that we are on the right track.

Today, I'd like to speak primarily about OCD's responsibility in operating programs.

When one thinks of the programs under the aegis of the Office of Child Development, one thinks immediately of the Head Start effort. I do remember 1965; I do remember when a group of people sat down with a dream, and I can think of nothing more gratifying in my professional career than the role I played in conceptualizing Head Start.

However, I am very troubled with respect to what's happened to the Head Start program over the very short period of five years. We all remember the first summer, when everyone was convinced that if we just gave a child six or eight weeks of Head Start in the summertime, at the very least he would become President of the Chase National Bank, and he would never have a cavity again and so forth and so on. It was a period when we were unduly optimistic, and we didn't really appreciate the kind of effort and the amount of dollars that it takes to intervene effectively in the life of a child.

Head Start was then riding a crest of popularity. Well, in five short years we have witnessed a change in this attitude, not in your association, but in the nation at large—a change which I think is very dangerous for the future of our nation's children, especially those that need our help the most. Thus, along with taking on the operation of the Head Start program, I've also had to take on the honest battle of trying to convince the decision makers that Head Start is a successful program.

It is not an easy battle, and I need your help. We all remember the Westinghouse Report; I shall not use this platform to reiterate my scientific opinion that this report is a rather shallow and poorly done evaluation of Head Start. I've made this point on numerous occasions and in some detail.

What troubles me now is not so much the report, but the way it's been accepted to justify an attitude toward Head Start which is totally inappropriate.

I have before me this week's *U.S. News and World Report*, which notes the views of an unnamed person at the White House, and the reforms that are

Dr. Edward Zigler, currently Director of the Office of Child Development, Dept. of Health, Education, and Welfare, was formerly a professor in the Dept. of Psychology, Yale University, New Haven, Conn.

to come, and I would just like to quote a couple of sentences. All of the story isn't about Head Start, but the point of view expressed is becoming an accepted attitude.

It says: "One report after another shows that compensatory education programs for the underprivileged do not do any good. It is questionable whether the Head Start preschool training program is anything more than a babysitter service for welfare mothers."

Now, it is exactly this kind of attitude that I find damnable, irresponsible and one which you and I must speak out against. I think that we made a very serious error, and journalists compounded it, in trying to convince people that Head Start was essentially a program to produce a homogeneous group of intellectual paragons. In presenting the goals of the program this way, we allowed the "know-nothings" in the area of childhood education to paint us into a totally inappropriate IQ corner, so that Head Start has continuously been evaluated in terms of whether we could produce four or five magic IQ points.

As I have said before, we have literally crucified the needy children of this nation on a cross of IQ!

We must now educate people. I will educate the decision-makers in Washington. You must educate people in your communities to the fact that Head Start is a comprehensive program, as all early childhood programs should be, and that what we are interested in is not programming tiny computers, but producing healthy, whole, wonderful human beings.

We do not have to engage in rhetoric to make our point, but the goals and accomplishments of Head Start have yet to be made clear to either decision-makers or to the American public. What can we say?

Let us talk about the accomplishments of the Head Start program. Let us take one very tangible area: physical health and well-being. Why has no one spoken up and said over and over, that the Head Start program remains the single largest health services delivery system to needy children in this nation? Of the children that come to our Head Start centers in the full-year programs about 36 percent have an identifiable physical problem. In our summer programs, that number jumps to 43 percent. We have screened these children; and we are now talking about literally hundreds of thousands of children with health problems—and of those children with health problems, roughly 75 percent of them have had their defects corrected or helped.

Let us go beyond health. I am convinced, as I've said to so many groups, that what childhood education and all education is all about is not to produce only physicists and professors for Yale and Harvard, but to produce that heterogeneous group of people with various types of abilities and skills and interests to do the kinds of jobs that are necessary to keep a country going.

Now, when you approach it this way, what we're interested in is not the production of intelligence only; we're interested in the production of social competence in every developing child. Study after study indicates that if you're interested in the social competence of the child, you should be just as interested in that child's attitudes about himself, about others, about his society, his sense of autonomy, his sense of purpose, his sense of industry; you must be just as concerned with developing his curiosity, developing the sense that this world is one in which he can achieve.

These are the motivational factors which are just as important in determining whether a child is to develop into a competent individual as is any IQ measure. But these motivational factors have not been measured. By concentrating on IQ we have indicted poor children in this nation needlessly. Many of us have convinced the nation that poor children are stupid children; untrue! *Untrue!*

You will find in the economically disadvantaged segment of our population, every IQ represented from the retarded to the genius. The basic problem that I have found in these children has not been a problem of IQ or stupidity, but that this group of children has had those experiences, usually of a depriving economic sort, that have caused them to develop a motivational system in which they cannot use the intelligence that they have.

In fact, one of the most obvious phenomena to the student of childhood behavior is the difference in our ghetto children in terms of their performance in school and their performance out of school, where they're back in the milieu in which they feel comfortable and for which they feel some sense of identification.

Our problem is that we haven't explicitly directed and measured the kinds of changes that we could produce through preschools and through the early education efforts in the very crucial motivational system of such children. It is still my contention that if we did the proper kinds of evaluations, we could demonstrate convincingly that compensatory education will probably make its most important and most practical contribution to the lives of poor children in changing their attitudes so they all can

use all of the intelligence they have and operate in an optimal manner.

Now, I would like to point out another accomplishment of Head Start, and that is the change in family and community.

One of the first things I did after being sworn in as Director of the Office of Child Development was to hold a press conference to acquaint the press of this nation with the glory and accomplishments of Head Start. At that time, I unveiled the Kirschner Report, which is in my estimation a very impressive social study. What it indicates is that in 58 communities where there is a full year Head Start, there were 1,500 identifiable changes in two very important social systems that are crucial to the life of a child; namely, the educational system and the health delivery system of those communities. You can look at the specific things that were accomplished as a result of Head Start being there, and see that this is how the lives of children may be changed.

Parent Satisfaction

I would like to go on to two other accomplishments of Head Start, which seem never to get enough attention.

It seems that in Washington in any Administration people are very fond of what we call "cost-benefit analysis." I find it a rather empty game; the problem with cost-benefit analysis is that somebody has to designate finally the variables that go into the equation; and what I find in respect to Head Start is that some of the key variables are invariably left out!

For instance: there is one bit of evidence that I have also yet to see quoted as hard empirical evidence supporting a social action program in this nation, and

10

that is the satisfaction that the parents of Head Start children have with the program.

Certainly, one of the criteria of a program for children is whether the parents of those children step forward and say: "I like this program. I can see what it's doing for my child, and I want it." To me, that is one component of an evaluation of a program. When you look at that kind of data you invariably find that the percentage of Head Start parents that like this program, that want this program, that see this program as helping them and their children, is approximately 95 percent! I can think of no other social action program that gets more support from its primary beneficiaries.

Now, I want to go one step further and raise with you a point that I've heard Dr. Julius Richmond make very eloquently, and which I would like to underline, namely, our concern with the quality of the lives of our nation's children.

I agree with Dr. Urie Bronfenbrenner, that we pride ourselves on our child-orientedness in this country, and that pride is misplaced. We do not do well by children in this nation, as compared to the achievements and accomplishments, and the dedication and commitment of resources that other nations have displayed.

I think one evidence of this is in the Head Start program and its evaluation. I've heard the President of the United States speak to the importance of the quality of human life; I've heard the Secretary of Health, Education, and Welfare support this view. Any Administration is dedicated to improving the quality of human life. But unfortunately, most people think—when they think about the quality of human life—only about the quality of *adult* human lives. If you have a program for a child, the only way they believe you can assess it is to see whether that program makes some differences four years later, 10 years later or 15 years later, when that child becomes an adult.

When you walk into a Head Start center, you may see a child who has come from a horribly deprived surrounding, such as a shack in Alabama with an over-burdened mother, with nine siblings, with the problem of subsistence essentially eroding that child's life; and you see that same child in a Head Start center, with air and light; you see that child interacting with other children with a concerned human being; you see that child laughing, and you see that child having an nutritious lunch. I say to you that for that day, in the life of that child, you have improved the quality of his life, and that in itself is enough to justify programs such as Head Start.

Now, after indicating to you that we have nothing to be ashamed about concerning our five years' accomplishment with Head Start, I must say to you that we must be hardheaded about Head Start; there are problems and we must not ignore them.

Head Start is still a young program. It is not yet a program of homogeneously high quality. That's why when people say they're evaluating Head Start, I'm never really sure what it is that they're talking about; Head Start varies in its quality and in its style all across this nation.

There are many, many excellent Head Start centers. There are also many Head Start centers where honest evaluation leads me to conclude that the best that could be said of them is that they are mediocre. We owe deprived children, needy children, who have suffered enough at the hands of society, the best! *The best!* And one of my first courses of action was to underline an effort that I found already underway in my excellent Washington staff; namely, the development of a monitoring system, so that the dream of Head Start can finally be actualized all over this country.

That dream, one that I dedicate my office to, is to see that every Head Start center in this country has every component of Head Start, without which it isn't Head Start; and that not only is every component there, but that every component meets a high level of quality.

I've had to make one very difficult decision and I hope I did the right thing. I think that I did; if I had it to do over again, I would not do it any differently. What I am alluding to here is that when confronted with a potential cut in the Head Start program I went forward to the Secretary and said: "We have one of two courses of action. One is to try to spread the dollars over the same number of children." It was my opinion down that road lay destruction; that is, if you take in a period of inflation the same amount of dollars, or less dollars, and try to spread them, thinner and thinner and thinner, you will finally have a kind of token program that is, I think, far less than what anybody has in mind for Head Start.

The decision that I made was that if we are confronted with cuts, we will not cut the quality of the program for any child. We will, of course, try to take all the fat that we can find out of every program, but after we've done that, then we will fulfill our promise to those children in our charge. Every child that comes to Head Start will get a Head Start program, but we will not water down the program by trying to serve the same number of children with ever-lessening numbers of dollars.

It's hard to cut children out of a program; I know it is. But the way things have worked out, I think it was just that possibility, and the decision to stand firm and fulfill our commitment to children, that made people realize that you just couldn't keep giving fewer and fewer dollars and expect to spread it ever thinner and really do the job that we're dedicated to do for young children in this nation. Once the public became aware of this fact, Congress responded with a new appropriations figure which, if passed, will be adequate to maintain the program at the present level of enrollment.

Planning for Day Care

I want to go on to another program that is of great concern to my office; namely, Day Care. We have a planning group, and a very hard-working group it is, at the Office of Child Development, concerned with Day Care. I know the Family Assistance Plan is having trouble with Congress but I still hope that some form of the plan will be passed. In that plan there is a Day Care component that is of the magnitude of $386,000,000 in its first year. What that means is that there will be a major new thrust in Day Care in this nation.

I'm not a political pundit; maybe Day Care will not come through FAP. But you know, there are ideas whose time has come, and that must certainly be the case with Day Care. Unless I'm a very bad prognosticator, we will see a massive increase in Day Care in this nation. If nothing else, women's liberation will impose it upon us!

Now I must say, if I may be permitted

an aside without being tarred and feathered and called a male chauvinist pig—I am a little bit troubled by the women's liberation effort in Day Care. What I see is that when they put forth a platform, Day Care is always included, but they are surprisingly quiet about the quality of Day Care that they want.

Again, I must reiterate Dr. Urie Bronfenbrenner's theme: Who speaks for children?! It's one thing to say that you want Day Care for your children; but if you think that the primary purpose of day care is to permit a lady to do her thing, then you have again sold out the children of this nation.

Now, in this respect, I'm also troubled by things that I hear in Washington, because there again—and I don't see these people as villainous, any more than I see women's lib people as villainous—it's a question of where their priorities seem to be. And what I'm talking about here is, even with the FAP Day Care plan, I hear too many people saying: "Gee, this is a means for mothers to go to work." Well, if a mother would like to work, and she gets a sense of dignity and accomplishment therefrom, by all means let's have day care for her children. The nation needs it; the nation wants it. The day care that we establish must be just as concerned with the development of the child as it is concerned with the opportunity it gives the mother to go to work.

Now, there is a jargon developing in Washington, and you're probably apprised of it; if not, let me inform you. I can see the battle lines beginning to shape up. It's the battle between something or other called "custodial care," which is better called, I guess, peanut butter and jelly sandwich care, and what's come to be known as developmental day care.

Now, developmental day care is nothing but a fancy word for good quality day care that takes into consideration what children are all about and surrounds them with the developmental services that have characterized Head Start.

My office stands for developmental day care.

What this nation cannot tolerate, at this particular juncture of its history, is the establishment of warehouses for children. I will fight against "custodial" care, and I expect this organization and you as individuals to fight this battle. Otherwise, we will all be a party to a conspiracy against children.

I do have a very strong ally in this matter, and that ally is the President of the United States. He has spoken eloquently on this point in his message to Congress in which FAP was described. In speaking about the Day Care component of the Family Assistance Plan, the President was specific in saying that the cycle of poverty in this nation can be broken by enhancing the lives of children, and that what we need is high-quality day care for children, not custodial day care, and that day care and the services it performs for children will be considered an end in and of itself.

The Office of Child Development is committed to the President's view, and we are now anticipating some legislation for Day Care, setting the standards, developing policies and moving ahead. We have made two efforts that I should call to your attention. One is what will, I guess, some day be known as "the Airlie House effort" of the summer of 1970. Many of you participated in that effort, and the nation is grateful to you. What we in essence said to ourselves, with a little prodding from the President's

Scientific Advisory Council, and from the Office of Economic Opportunity, is that if you are going to have a major new thrust in day care in this nation, why not anticipate it? Why not prepare models? Why not help people to set up Day Care around the nation, give them the information, and the know-how put in simple language, that would help them?

I've been speaking to people here at these meetings who are always struck when they go into a bad Day Care center, not by the villainy of the people—they tend to be warm people who love children too—but by the fact that they simply do not know what it takes, what they are supposed to do.

So what we decided to do was to bring together approximately 120 of the most knowledgeable people about day care in this nation; academics, very practical operators of day care and the whole spectrum of those concerned with day care activities. What we said to them was "This is a task that confronts the country. Help us." Again, I felt I was fulfilling the primary principle of OCD; namely, to be a conduit between good thinkers, good workers and government efforts for children. These people worked hard, not only at Airlie House, but before Airlie House, and after. We will have ready for the nation, hopefully by the first of the year, a number of models and techniques for every age child in day care which will actually help somebody who'd like to set up a Day Care center in Keokuk. Many of you don't need these kinds of materials, but day care will be in the hands of many people who do; and we will have materials that will tell them specifically about programs for infants, programs for preschool children, and programs for the school-age child. Across all these programs there will be a comprehensive rubric. There will be nutrition; there will be health; there will be parental involvement; there will be the social services component, and I hope to have these materials ready to coincide with the passage of FAP.

Staffing the Day Care Center

I want to point out one other concern that we're moving ahead on and that must be of major concern to NAEYC. That concern is where are we to get the cadre of workers to man Head Start and Day Care and all of what I consider to be the burgeoning development of comprehensive children's centers which we will see in this nation over the next decade or two?

Well, I think there are two extremes, for both of which I have little sympathy. One extreme is that the only person qualified to care adequately for the young child is the well-trained M.A. level worker in child development. The problem here is not with their training; the problem here is not with their knowledge, and not with their wisdom. The basic problem is of their scarcity. To say that the professionals will handle the problems of child care in this nation is akin to saying that psychoanalysts will handle the mental health needs of this nation. It's simply impossible in terms of numbers. Therefore, I think that a nation cannot plan to staff day care centers with those kinds of workers, because we must fail; numbers alone will defeat us.

There is another point of view which was very prominent some five years ago—I think it's a little bit on the wane as people have learned from experience—but it was a kind of a naive romanticism; that is, that any person who had a good heart was a wonderful caretaker for children. This is also not true. There is knowledge about children, there is much in the experience and the learning; there is much that has to be known in order to handle a child and interact with him in a way that is conducive to his growth.

What this nation must do is develop a cadre of workers very much like those that we find in other nations, but that have no counterpart in this country. I'm thinking about the "Upbringer" in Russia, the "Child Nurse" in Denmark, the "Childrens-House worker" in Israel. These are neither top-level professionals, nor are they people who haven't had much experience or instruction about children. Rather, they are people who have very circumscribed training. Okay; so they may not know much about Einstein's theory of relativity, but so what?! What we have to do is develop in this nation a course or courses which produce a new type of child-care worker, somewhere between the unknowledgeable and the very highly trained. They would get sufficient training, and they would get a great deal of that training in the centers themselves.

I have talked long and hard with people like Eveline Omwake and Barbara Biber, and I don't really see any argument. Everybody's aware that we have to produce this kind of person if we are to surround children with agents for their growth. The problem is: how do we do it? How do we get on with it? I think that another aspect of this development that is terribly important is that these people must have status. They must be certified, as they are in other nations. They must have a salable commodity! My national office people, under the direction of Jenny Klein are now working with many of you and other workers in other fields to see how the Office of Child Development can move in this direction. This will be a major goal.

I want to end by discussing the newspaper stories about my stance on integrating children of various socioeconomic classes in the type of child centers that I would like to see in this nation. Somehow or other that was interpreted by the *New York Times* and other papers as meaning that Ed Zigler was in favor of taking away from the poor and giving to the rich, a principle that made our country great, but really not one that I espouse!

What I actually had in mind is: let us have vision; let us not think that Head Start is the final solution to the problems confronting needy children of this nation. Head Start today serves no more than 10 to 15 percent of the children eligible for the program. We must expand these programs, but they should be expanded thoughtfully and with a view to the optimal development of children.

When the children's centers I envision are set down in this nation, I believe they must be totally integrated, or as integrated as we can make them, racially and socioeconomically. And I say this for two reasons.

The first, I will confess to you, is pragmatic and political. I must defend Head Start. I must see that it prospers and grows, yet I am continuously confronted by the onslaught on this program. Why have people soured on Head Start in such a short time? I think part of it is sour grapes. I think that when you tell a family very little removed from the poverty level themselves that their child can't go to Head Start, all you're saying to them is that some child is getting something their child can't have. All Head Start means to that family is that some child is getting a head start over their children; and this makes for antagonism and resentment. When it comes time to get the dollars to expand Head Start, if people feel they're not getting something—in fact, their child may even be damaged because, after all, some other child is getting a head start and that means your child is falling behind—then you get either hostility or, at best, antipathy towards a program that needs all the support it can get.

But again, my real motivation for advancing what I consider to be the ideal of children's centers in this nation in the future is not so much political and pragmatic as it is based upon what I consider to be sound developmental and sociopsychological principles. The first of these is that if you want to help children grow, you do not isolate them along any kind of group lines. What children need for their optimal development are many, many models. White children should see black children, and black children should see white children. People from different cultures should see each other, and people from different socioeconomic classes should mingle. If we are going to demarcate this society, please let us not demarcate it at the age of children six months or three years of age!

We know that seeing many types of peer and adult models optimizes the development of children—and understand me clearly—I am not talking about one-way street models. It is not just that children from economically disadvantaged homes, the child of poverty, can learn from the middle-class child. Sure, the middle-class child, in attitude and certain behavior styles would be worth modeling; but it works in reverse, too.

What we have not yet appreciated fully, is that the middle-class child is himself handicapped since he doesn't have the opportunity to interact with children from other cultures and other socioeconomic groupings. Children from poverty have certain skills that I wish middle-class children had. Again, one does not have to be ephemeral about this. I'm talking about very concrete behaviors, such as earlier independence; how many middle-class seven-year-olds manage to get on a bus, go downtown and make three dollars a day shining shoes? Do you know what that demands? That's independence! Not that I say this is what children should do, but what I'm talking about is that you have in these children a strength, a quality, an independence, and now there's some evidence of even greater creativity that would be very beneficial for middle-class children to see and model themselves after.

Now I come to the second reason, which is more sociopsychological than it is developmental, but clearly important if what we're interested in is not just total IQ development, but the kind of development and type of citizens that I want the nation to have. I am troubled, and have been long troubled, about the state of our society. It is full of conflict; it is full of hatred; it is full of violence. I see our society polarized at every turn, the old against the young, the black against the white, the academician against the hard-hat. How much longer can we have a society that keeps becoming more and more fragmented, fractionated? How much longer can we survive as a nation if we are at each other's throats? What we must do in this nation is develop those institutions in which people of varying cultures and milieus learn respect and learn tolerance for one another. Granted, it's not just a matter of teaching. It's a matter of every group earning the right to respect, and our society acting in the appropriate manner; but by and large, I say to you that everything I know about psychology leads me to conclude that if you separate groups, and they do not intermingle, and they do not interact, what you will develop is a great amount of in-group feeling but out-group hatred. It's almost a sociopsychological law; and we can see this hatred now developing. We must develop social institutions that get people in this nation back together. The place where I feel we must start is with children.

If we cannot tolerate, or if we cannot begin constructing or even planning for delivery of services to children in a totally integrated way, and if we insist on dividing children up, in terms of color, or in terms of socioeconomic class, I think that all we will be doing is adding to the very serious problems that are already confronting this nation.

In conclusion, let me say I'm optimistic; I have very high hopes. I do believe that with the kind of support I'm getting in Washington, the kind of support I'm getting around the nation, the tremendous job I see my national staff and my regional staff doing in behalf of children, the Office of Child Development can become a major social institution and a major force for the children of this nation. But I am not totally sanguine, because the political world and the world of changing institutions, especially in the times in which we're living does not allow me to be sanguine.

It is possible that if we do not move forward, if we do not produce the kinds of institutions for children or provide the kinds of advocacy for children, the kinds of coordination that we need for children, if we don't manage pretty quickly to convince the nation that children are important, it may well be that OCD could be a passing fad in the history of the American social scene. Whether it goes on to do the job that all of us want done for children, or whether it becomes just a footnote in the history of this nation, will depend on the efforts of all of us, and I'm asking you at this point for your support.

Questions from the Floor
Immediately Following Dr. Zigler's Address

STATEMENT FROM THE FLOOR. *Dr. Zigler, and members of the National Association for the Education of Young Children, I stand before you as a mother, as a black woman, a teacher and as a Director of the Orange Community School, which is partially funded by Head Start. I also stand before you as a member of the United Parents for Child Development of New Jersey and as an active participant of the Steering Committee of the Proposed National Parent Policy Board formed last year at the 1969 Head Start Conference.*

I also stand before you as a person with a piece of paper which states that I have an M.A. degree in Childhood Education, but I do not feel that I am the only qualified person by virtue of that piece of paper to teach young children.

I worked with parents when I finished school. I worked very closely with parents in my classroom, and I saw in them competencies that I had not gained as a result of the experiences and tasks that were provided for me or that I was exposed to in my training. So I cannot accept that people with M.A. degrees are the only people qualified.

17

We have seen too much in the educational system of this country, that there are people with the certification who don't have the competency. There is something in the process of learning that we have not understood.

I just had to respond to that, because competency in guiding children to learn involves something more than gaining a piece of paper which states that you have an M.A. degree.

CHAIRMAN: I think she said that for many of us.

QUESTION: *Dr. Zigler, I come before you because I'm somewhat confused with the message you brought to us this morning. You started out by glorifying the accomplishments of Head Start; you mentioned that your office is committed to the program, the Administration is committed to the program, and then you alluded to the fact that we are confronted with the possibility of a cut. Recently, the Administration convinced me that they are committed to the foreign aid program, because President Nixon asked for an increase of 50 percent in his foreign aid appropriations, amounting to billions of dollars.*

Now, I cannot reconcile the fact that the Administration, and your office, is committed to child development programs, when you are talking in terms of cuts in funds that are already mediocre.

DR. ZIGLER: Sure doesn't make much sense, does it?

Well, let me respond—there has been no cut in Head Start. The cut was an anticipated cut which was not a product of Administration action.

Now, since the anticipated cut was announced, a bipartisan group in the Senate led by a Republican and a Democrat, Cranston and Mondale, passed an amendment to the appropriations bill, and my reading of the newspaper this morning is that now the total Senate appropriations bill has passed, in which Head Start would receive—remember, we need $350,000,000 to maintain the program with absolutely no cuts—that Head Start will receive $398,000,000.

However, we have been disappointed in the past. This appropriation now must go to a House Conference, but all I can say at this point is that given these figures, and the current thinking, it would be my expectation, with the evidence that we have before us now and the Senate action yesterday, that Head Start children in this country will experience no cuts. [Subsequent to this address, the House and Senate agreed on a funding level for Head Start of $360,000,000 for 1971.]

QUESTION: *I was a Head Start parent in the Boston program from July of 1966 through June of 1970, and I am now a very interested former Head Start parent. I have read some statements that Doctor Zigler has made as far as parent participation, his concern, and would like some clarification on one of them.*

"Teaching parents community organization is beyond the mission of Head Start" is a statement that I have read that he has made. I have had quite a few changes made in my life because of the Head Start program in Boston, and because of the feeling of our former director that one of the very most important things in changing the lives of our low-income children was to change the lives of those families in those parents directly.

Now, in order to do this you have to train parents who, because we've been told so often that there was nothing we could do to change the community and change the system, just sat home and let someone else do it. Through Head Start I've learned that I have got just as big a mouth as anybody else with money! And therefore, I should have just as much say in what's going to happen to my child. This has been through organizing in the community, and I got trained in Head Start to do it.

DR. ZIGLER: I don't remember saying that community organization was beyond the ken of Head Start. What I have said, and what I will continue to say, is something of the following sort.

Head Start has something very important to do with children. I'm concerned about these children, and as long as I am the Director of the Office of Child Development, the primary concern that I will have will be with the development of the children in our care.

Now, after having said this, and after pointing with pride to my role as an original architect of parental involvement in Head Start, I will say that my position boils down to a matter of priorities. If you're going to organize, first organize your Head Start center. Make sure that that is of a quality you want for your children and for the children following your children in that setting.

I do not want to see Head Start ever become simply a take-off point to do something else. I think that parental involvement should work in the following direction, and it's simply reasserting the original ideas of Head Start.

First, the parental involvement should be such that will immediately influence the life of that child. Next, it ought to be very, very heavily involved in making sure that the Head Start Center itself is of such a quality that it's conducive to the growth of the child.

Now, if these kinds of goals are met, there is nothing in any change to OCD guidelines that stops parents from doing exactly what you are talking about. As I have said, I take great pride in the Kirschner Report, that has shown the changes that have been brought about in communities.

We must change the total lives of these children, and I am in favor of parents doing that. The question I have raised is, what are the priorities?

Head Start is a limited program with limited dollars, and I just want to make sure that we do our primary things first, and if there's still energy and effort and ability and funds to do more than that, my feeling is, great—let's get it done. There are many community action programs in addition to Head Start, and I think, realistically, you're not going to change this entire society on the backs of four-and five-year-old children.

I want the society changed in ways that you want it changed, that are conducive to growth and development. But I have a responsibility to the Head Start children and that responsibility will always take precedence. There's nothing in OCD that opposes community organization, especially that organization that improves the life span of children; but what must be paramount in our concern is to do a good job with the parents and children that are in our care.

QUESTION: *I'm sorry, but I'm going to have to say something. You can't put a kid in a classroom setting for four hours a day and expect some miraculous change. You're going to have to change that whole family to do it, and the only way you can do it is by really involving the parents, so that the priorities should be child and family together, because four hours in a classroom isn't going to do it.*

DR. ZIGLER: You know, we're going to have so many things that we can legitimately disagree on, I hate to disagree when there's really no argument. I couldn't agree any more with the statement that I've just heard.

Now, I think that somehow or other there's a confrontation shaping up on this issue which I really don't feel. All I'm talking about is priorities. If you're going to change the life of a child, it may be necessary to change society. The question you have to ask, as taxpayers and as mothers of Head Start children is—what do you want me to do? What priorities do you want me to have?

I still think, as I said before, that everything you're saying is true, all I committed myself to do is to simply make sure that we spend our money and our energies and our efforts in ways that centrally converge on the child and his family. So I really don't see a great argument on this point.

QUESTION: *On my way over here today I heard on the radio that the government granted $6,000,000 to an historical society for a monument.*

Now, I feel that our children should come first, and this monument is something that could possibly wait. Why can't we do something about the money that they're giving to them, and get more money for our children and parent-participation in this program that we need?

DR. ZIGLER: Again, I like children a lot better than I like monuments, too. The fact of the matter is, there are people in this nation who like monuments. The government budget is like a pie, and everybody tries to get the biggest piece for his own interest.

One thing I guarantee you, that when it comes time to divide up that pie, I'm going to be there fighting hammer and tongs with the monument-putter-uppers. That's why it is so necessary to get all the support that we can get at every level.

I still have a lot of confidence in this country. If we want to go to the moon, we're going to go to the moon. If we want to put up monuments, we'll put up monuments. And if we want to take care of children, and we really let people in Washington know we want to take care of children, then we will take care of children.

QUESTION: *I'm a Head Start teacher from East Boston, and I'm interested in knowing whether Dr. Zigler's office is in favor of private enterprise running day care centers, running large chains of day care centers across the country, or in community controlled day care centers that are run and controlled by the parents of the children who are in the centers?*

I want to know where the government plans to put its money?

DR. ZIGLER: The government has no final plan on where it's going to put its money. According to the guidelines we now have, no day care center would be considered an adequate day care center without considerable parental involvement.

Now, on the business of the private versus public day care, the wonderful talk we had by our first questioner, I think said pretty much where I stand.

There's nothing magic in public day-care, there's nothing magic in private day-care.

The thing that OCD will be terribly concerned about will be what happens to a child in the day care center. Right now, it's a very open ballgame; whoever can produce quality developmental day care for these children be it public, be it private-for-profit, (providing of course, by developmental that you mean parental involvement), can get a piece of the action.

The need is going to be so great that it's much too early in the game to say that just because somebody thinks that they could make a profit, that they should not even be considered. What my office will look at is not the profit or nonprofit aspect; it will be the quality of day care provided the children.

QUESTION: *I'm a Head Start parent of Boston, and have been a parent from 1966, in Head Start, up until now.*

I would like Doctor Zigler to tell me what his feelings are about the parent and child relationship pertaining to Head Start; and you were talking about some of the accomplishments and goals that Head Start has made in the previous years. And I would like for you to clarify that a little bit.

DR. ZIGLER: Well, that would call for another 45-minute address; all I can say is that with other people who have asked questions and made comments, I believe that really the most important socializing agent in the life of a child remains the mother, the father and the family.

And that for this reason, Head Start centers must be very concerned about the nature of the relationship between family and child, particularly mother and child; considerable energy should be given towards helping mothers, instructing mothers, in what types of interactions with children are more conducive to their growth and development; (again with growth and development being defined very broadly as both intellectual, motivational and personal growth and development).

Now, many of the people in the Head Start centers have these skills, have this knowledge, and they should immediately share them with parents so that Head Start can in many places not only be Head Start, but home start.

LILIAN G. KATZ

Early Childhood Education as a Discipline[1]

Most readers of *Young Children* are familiar with the ERIC Clearinghouse on Early Childhood Education at the University of Illinois. ERIC/ECE,[2] as we call it, is one of 20 clearinghouses in the national clearinghouse system, each focused on collecting, storing and disseminating information in its own field. Organizing and analyzing the information gathered at ERIC/ECE has raised some interesting questions concerning the scope and definition of what is encompassed by the term *early childhood education*. In the following discussion, a tentative definition of the discipline of early childhood education is presented, and some suggestions of how it can be used are offered.

Definition of Early Childhood Education

It is common to speak of early education as an interdisciplinary field encompassing the interests of specialists in developmental psychology, pediatrics, social work, anthropology, elementary education and other fields. Specialists from these many fields have strong scientific interests in the young child. While young children have been the subjects of disciplined inquiry for more than a half century, their *education* has not. A distinct disciplinary approach to their education has been neglected in favor of problem-oriented investigations designed to discover the most powerful way to offset the ill effects of poverty. For the purposes of discussion, it is proposed that the referent for the

[1] Supported in part by a contract with the U.S. Office of Education, Contract OEC-0-70-2623 (519), Project No. 0-0288.
[2] Educational Resources Information Center/Early Childhood Education. Funded by the U.S. Office of Education, Contracts and Grants Div.

YOUNG CHILDREN, 1970, Vol. 26, No. 2, pp. 82-89.

term *early childhood education* be stated as follows:

> Group settings which are deliberately intended to effect developmental changes in children in the age range from birth up to the age of entering the first grade.

With this definition, education rather than child development or child rearing becomes the point of entry into the field, thus giving early childhood education disciplinary status in its own right. From this definition, the parameters of the field can be derived, and can then provide a basis for the development of the branch of knowledge called *early childhood education*.

Before we explore the parameters of the field, some comments on the definition are in order. First, the cutoff point at the age of entrance into the first grade seems to draw an undesirable division between preschool and primary education, a division that the profession has been striving to reduce. However, this delimitation of scope is suggested only in order to facilitate organizing our information. The complex and crucial issues surrounding the problem of continuity of experience, learning and education, into the primary grades cannot be taken up here. Thorough analysis and discussion of those issues is greatly needed. A second point is that there are a number of projects and programs in early childhood education which are not in fact "group settings," but which properly fall into our domain. Included here are programs in which mothers in their homes are given assistance with

Lilian G. Katz, Ph.D., is Director of the ERIC Clearinghouse on Early Childhood Education, University of Illinois, Urbana-Champaign. Dr. Katz is also Associate Professor of Education at the University of Illinois.

the stimulation of their infants' learning and development.

Parameters of Early Childhood Education

The term *parameter* is used broadly here to indicate a superordinate category of variables which applies to *all* early educational settings, and which typically remains constant during a given study or a given event which we might call an *early childhood program*. That is to say, a parameter describes a class of phenomena in which every early childhood education program must have an entry, even though the entries of different programs vary. For example, every program must have clients (i.e., children), but the children of different programs may vary in age or in socioeconomic status; every program must have a physical location, but these locations may vary from quonset huts in a downtown area to elegant university laboratory settings in a comparatively rural setting.

The set of parameters presented here is suggested by two major research projects reported during the 1960s. John Pierce-Jones and his associates at the University of Texas conducted a large study of Project Head Start Centers in Texas in 1965 (Pierce-Jones, 1966, p. 6). The Texas group identified teacher and child antecedent variables which interacted, producing a variety of classroom "inputs," which in turn resulted in differential changes in the Head Start children. In 1967, Prescott and Jones (1967) reported a study of group day care in the Los Angeles area using a similar but more comprehensive framework. Prescott and Jones studied all of the same variables the Pierce-Jones group had examined, such as characteristics of children, teachers, classroom "input," and in addition examined variables of physical space, size of center, types of sponsorship, and other administrative factors.

The present state of the art does not permit us to look at the parameters of early childhood education, and ascertain the extent to which they are either independent of, or compounded with each other. The following descriptive outlines of the parameters are not intended to be exhaustive, but merely to suggest some of the variables within each parameter which have been or could be used to form guidelines for review and future research.

Parameter Descriptions

A. *Characteristics of clients.* Within this parameter are included variable characteristics of both the children and parents served by any given early childhood program. Examples of these variables are age, socioeconomic background and status, ethnicity, sex, physical and mental health, mother tongue, second language, urban/rural background, the goal orientation of parents, father absence, age and number of siblings, and other child rearing variables.

B. *Characteristics of teachers and other assisting adults.* This parameter includes variations in teacher characteristics such as teacher behavior, teacher role prescriptions, teacher performance, teaching styles, teacher attributes such as age, experience, sex, attitudes and beliefs, teacher self-concept, teachers' goals, ethnicity, training, satisfaction; teacher recruitment, occupational status, relationship with assistants, and credentialing patterns.

C. *Program organization.* Included in this parameter are such variables as the variety and quantity of stimulation in a program, the temporal organization of classroom activities, the lessons "taught" and not "taught," the materials available, the control of activity selection, the inclusion of rest time, storyreading, formal group instruction organized by ability groups, autotelic materials, etc. This group of variables is commonly referred to as the *curriculum.*

D. *Philosophical orientation and historical factors.* This parameter refers to the school of thought adhered to in any given early childhood program representing a range of values, goals and objectives; it includes also the learning theory "used." The philosophical orientation may be explicit or implicit, or it may vary on these two levels. Examples of programs with diverse philosophical orientation are Montessori Schools, and models such as Bank Street, the Behavior Analysis program, or the British Infant School. Historical factors may include remote or immediate antecedents of contemporary program operation.

E. *Parent power.* This parameter refers to variations in the extent to which parents participate in central or peripheral decision-making concerning the operation of early childhood education programs for their children. There are, for instance, parent cooperatives, where parents participate fully in program operations, and there are also university laboratory schools where parent participation and decision-making is minimal or peripheral. There are Head Start programs where parents select curriculum and staff, Head Start programs where parents are only consulted, and others where they are passive recipients of services. The extent to which parents pay for services rendered for a preschool

Figure I: Schematic Representation of Parameters of Early Education

Parameters	A. Clients	B. Teachers	C. Program	D. Philosophy	E. Parents	F. Administration	G. Length	H. Physical
A. Characteristics of clients (children and parents)	A	A→B						
B. Characteristics of teachers and other assisting adults	B→A	B	B→C					
C. Program organization (curriculum)		C→B	C					
D. Philosophical orientation and historical factors		D→B		D				
E. Parent power		E→B			E			
F. Administrative factors and sponsorship		F→B				F		
G. Length of program		G→B					G	
H. Physical plant and climate		H→B						H

program also represents a variation in their power.

F. *Administrative factors and sponsorship.* This parameter refers to variables associated with program administration such as size of program, distribution of authority, division of labor (maintenance, personnel, curriculum, etc.), staff morale, staff leadership, staff coordination, and staff cooperation versus staff friction. Also included in this parameter are the variety of public and private sponsoring agencies such as public school systems, community centers, churches, Office of Child Development, university laboratory schools, mental health departments, franchise entrepreneurs, parent cooperatives, and one-shot demonstration projects.

G. *Length of program.* Variables within this parameter include the length of the school day, and the number of school days. Examples are all-day daily care; two and one-half hours per day, morning or afternoon sessions; two, three, or four days per week and eight-week Head Start programs.

H. *Physical plant and climate.* This parameter includes variables in the amount of space, the type of space, outdoor/indoor facilities and their accessibility, neighborhood location, the number of classrooms per site, and regional climate (Head Start in Alaska as compared to Head Start in Hawaii).

A Matrix for Early Childhood Education

Figure 1 is a schematic representation showing how a matrix can be generated from the parameters of early childhood education proposed above. First, let us look in turn at each cell falling into the diagonal of the matrix and marked A, B, C, etc. In reviewing research on early childhood education each of these diagonal cells requires comprehensive analysis of all of the knowledge within itself. The within-parameter knowledge indicated by the diagonal cells focuses on those studies in which the cell's variables constitute both the dependent and independent variables. For example, in cell A, comprehensive analysis is needed of all of the literature related to child development and child rearing. Such a complete analysis would represent an encyclopedia of the developmental literature with special emphasis, of course, on the young child. In the cell marked B, where Parameter B intersects with itself, we need a comprehensive analysis of all of the knowledge related to these within-parameter variables, namely to teachers. The use of the matrix for analyzing problems of early childhood education and for reviewing research can be illustrated by looking at Parameter B (Characteristics of teachers) and moving down the column, (we will speak of horizontal *rows* and vertical *columns*). Beginning with the first cell in Column B, (marked A→B) it can be seen that one set of questions concerns the effect of A variables on B variables. Examples of the type of question which might be asked in this cell are: What characteristics of children influence the teacher behavior in what ways? What effect does the age range of the children in a given class have on the teacher's behavior? If a teacher has 15 or 20 three-year-olds in her class, then she is likely to be working with a smaller range of social and intellectual maturity than if the age range were from three to five years old. How does this age range composition affect the teacher's definition of her role? Or we could ask: What are the effects of the sex distribution of the class membership upon the teacher? Compare for example, a class consisting of two-thirds boys with one consisting of two-thirds girls, or with classes of one sex only.

It is important to note, at this point, that questions concerning "effects" reflect an idealized conception of research on teaching. In general, research findings suggest relationships between co-occurring events. For example, returning to the effects of child variables on teachers (A→B), Dorothy Haupt reported (1966) differences between boys and girls in the content of the questions they asked their nursery school teachers. Haupt also found differences in the way teachers responded to the questions of boys and girls. These findings represent co-occurring events. It is difficult at our present stage of knowledge to separate cause from effect.

As already indicated, the cell marked B in Column B reflects the need for within-parameter knowledge and reviews. Moving down to the cell where Row C intersects with Column B (C→B), we can ask questions concerning the effects of program organization variables upon teachers, although again these are more likely to be co-occurring events than causes and effects. For example, let us suppose that a program is organized in such a way that children are obliged to attend to a group storyreading activity and that no alternative behavior is permitted during this activity. One might ask: How does such a programmatic constraint affect teachers? Or, which teachers are affected or troubled by such a program variable? Let us suppose, for example, that a particular curriculum model specifies that children should have water play regularly. Undoubtedly some teachers welcome this activity, and others do not. In a Behavior Modification approach to preschool programs, teachers are expected to ignore children when they cry. How does this program specification affect teachers? We may be wise to ask which programs are congenial to which kind of teachers, and how we can facilitate matching program design with variation among teachers.

In Row D (D→B), information is sought pertaining to the relationships between and effects of philosophies (values, goals, and objectives, etc.) upon teacher performance and attitudes. Let us take for example the observation reported by Sears and Dowley (1963, p. 857) that there are teachers who have "child-centered *theory* and authoritarian practice." One could ask, at least theoretically: Can the reverse be true? That is, it may be that some teachers who describe themselves and their classrooms as open and flexible may in fact have classrooms which are restrictive and closed. Perhaps one of the most important questions to be answered in early childhood education is: What are the elements which account for the gap between rhetoric and performance? It is commonly assumed for example, that when teachers can embrace the "philosophy" of the British Infant School, their classrooms will become open. However, it may be that embracing the philosophy is a necessary step but an insufficient one. Because of the way the British Infant School curriculum is organized, a teacher probably must also have the capacity for fluency and for flexibility to generate ideas about extending and elaborating children's spontaneously expressed interests.

Historical factors, namely a program's past experiences, may be causally related to teacher variables. Let us suppose, for example, that a Head Start program has had a history of threats of nonrefunding. In what ways might such a history affect teachers' commitment or their op-

timism about the future and their work?

In Row E (E→B), questions can be asked about the relationships between variables of parent power and teacher variables. For example, when parents pay high fees for an early childhood program, are teachers likely to experience pressure to interact with children in ways that they would otherwise not choose? How do teachers feel about being hired (or fired) by parents? One of the fundamental tenets of Head Start is that parents be involved in every part of Head Start operation. Parent involvement in Head Start includes making policy decisions that affect their children's growth and learning and participating in the development of the program (Office of Economic Opportunity, 1969). Among the questions raised here is: To what extent is there consensus between parents and teachers in Head Start on how their programs should be organized and implemented? And how are teachers affected by this high level of parent power?

In Row F (F→B), we pose questions concerning administrative factors and their impact or relationship to variables in Parameter B. For instance, Alexanian (1967, p. 1) reported that "in some instances, the administrative problems of Head Start centers were so overwhelming that the very survival of the program was the all-important focus." Almost anyone with Head Start experience can verify the observation that administrative factors can have a consuming effect on the energy of teachers and other staff members. Questions about the uncertainties associated with year-to-year funding belong in this cell. Similarly, questions concerning the way equipment and supplies are secured be-

27

long here. It has also been observed in some Head Start programs that giving equal pay to teachers with widely different training and experience contributes to staff friction and unrest. It would be interesting to know to what extent administrative factors contribute to the total impact of a preschool program on children's development.

In Row G (G→B), questions concerning the relationship between the length of the program and teacher variables can be posed. One can ask, at least theoretically, whether teaching a whole day is characterized by twice as much of whatever characterizes a half-day? Obviously factors like fatigue should be considered. The management of naptimes in all-day programs frequently induces stresses and strains in teachers as well as children. In an interesting study comparing long- vs. short-day preschool programs, Handler (1970) proposed several important differences between the long- and short-day relating to teachers. For example, she stated that children are more dependent upon teachers in long- than in short-day schools (p. 38) and the teachers are more emotionally involved with children in the long- than in the short-day schools (p. 38). In what other ways do these length-of-day variables affect teachers?

In Row H, physical plant and climate (H→B), we pose questions concerning the relationship between the physical plant variables and the teacher variables. For example, in some physical facilities children can move freely from indoors to outdoors without encountering potential physical danger. In other places, all children must be visible and accounted for because the plant borders on a major highway, or because there are stairways or long corridors to consider. Similarly, in some geographical climates weather is congenial for outdoor activity only half of the school year—the proverbial rainy days affect the teachers as well as children.

The intersections between Column B variables, characteristics of teachers, and each of the parameters in the rows have been examined, and some questions have been raised concerning what effect the row variables have on column variables, namely on teachers and teaching. The use of the matrix can also be illustrated by taking Parameter B in the row (characteristics of teachers and other teaching adults), and examining the intersection of the row with each of the columns. Beginning with Row B, and going to the first column (B→A), questions concerning the effect of given teacher characteristics on child variables can be raised. Questions like the effect of the teacher's ethnic group on children's self-concepts, or the impact of teacher praise on children's motivation for learning, are examples of types of questions which belong in the cell marked B→A.

At the intersection of Row B with Column C (B→C), questions can be raised concerning the "effects" of teacher variables on program organization. For example, the organization of the Montessori classroom requires teachers to be fairly unobtrusive. One might ask: What personal attributes of teachers make the Montessori requirement for unobtrusiveness a more or less congenial one?

Continuing across the rows, questions concerning the relationships between characteristics of teachers and philosophy, parent power, administrative factors, length of program, physical plant and climate variables can be raised and the relevant research summarized. In addition to the information available or needed for each of these cells, a wide range of combinations of cells can be studied. For example, an important question for early childhood education is: What is the role of charismatic leaders (historically and contemporaneously) in program development? Or to what extent are effective programs, even though of widely different types, associated with leader evangelism? These questions fall into the intersection of cells B and C and D and F. Similarly, other groups of cells can be taken for inspection.

Summary

In summary, the parameters of early childhood education have been proposed and outlined above. Some ways in which the matrix generated from these parameters can be used have been illustrated. The major purpose of setting out the matrix is to emphasize that early childhood education is a complex domain which deserves extensive analysis which takes the complexities into full account. A major portion of the activity in early childhood education today is focused on either characteristics of clients (parameter A) or program organization (parameter C). (See also Scott et al., 1969.) There appears to be an assumption that it is possible to transport a carefully derived and "packaged" early childhood education program from one context to another, and to expect positive outcomes. The point here is not to deny the centrality of questions in these two parameters, but rather to emphasize that knowledge of the complex events in any given context, the gap between our rhetoric and our practice, and knowledge of the relative influence of all of the other parameters may enhance our power to predict and replicate the findings of current research and development, and deepen our understanding of the complex issues in the discipline of early childhood education.

References

Alexanian, Sandra. *Teacher Seminar.* Head Start Evaluation and Research Center, Office of Economic Opportunity. Available as ED 022567 from ERIC Document Reproduction Service. 1967.

Handler, Ellen O. *The professional self-image and the attributes of a profession: An exploratory study of the preschool teacher.* Unpublished paper. Urbana: University of Illinois, 1970a.

———— *Preschools and their graduates.* Unpublished paper. Urbana: University of Illinois. Available as PS 003800 from ERIC/ECE. 1970b.

Haupt, Dorothy. *Children's questions: Teacher response.* Unpublished doctoral dissertation. Detroit: Wayne State University, 1966.

Office of Economic Opportunity. *Parent involvement: A Workbook of Training Tips for Head Start Staff* (Rainbow Series Packet No. 10A) Washington, D.C. 1969.

Pierce-Jones, John. *Outcomes of Individual and Programmatic Variations Among Project Head Start Centers. Final Report, Office of Economic Opportunity.* Austin: University of Texas. Available as ED 014325 from ERIC Document Reproduction Service. 1966.

Prescott, E. & Jones, E. *Group Day Care as a Child Rearing Environment: An Observation Study of Day Care Programs.* Pasadena: Pacific Oaks College. Available as ED 024453 from ERIC Document Reproduction Service. 1967.

Scott, M., Eklund, S. J. & Miller, J. O. Analysis of Early Childhood Education Research and Development. National Laboratory on Early Childhood Education, 1969.

Sears, Pauline S. & Dowley, Edith M. Research on teaching in the nursery school. In Gage, N. L. (ed.), *Handbook on Research on Teaching.* Chicago: Rand McNally, 1968, pp. 814-864.

EARLY CHILDHOOD EDUCATION:
THE SCENE THEN & NOW

MARGARET LAY

Those who received their training in the field of early childhood education during the fifties must at times shake their heads in dismay over the rapidity with which the avant-garde practices of those days have become labeled *traditional*. They occasionally even find themselves viewed derisively as "warm puppyish" by some who consider themselves the avant-garde of today.

In the "olden days" of the fifties, the nursery school was rather universally expected to provide a child-size world in which home experiences were supplemented by opportunities to work and play with peers in a relatively unstructured atmosphere. Learning was considered to be the natural concomitant of the development of positive attitudes in a setting that provided toys, manipulative materials, expressive media, and extensive opportunities for social interaction and exploration.

The child's own powers of self-selection were said to provide an optimal learning environment as long as the school provided numerous choices and no adult tried to manipulate the direction of the child's inherent strivings. Nursery school teachers gave repeated anecdotal evidence of how effective these "permissive" and "child-centered activity" programs were for individual children. There was indeed a near consensus as to what constituted appropriate teaching behavior in the early childhood field.

During the sixties, a series of events and educational trends significantly disrupted the previous consensus about early childhood education. First came the ideas popularized by Bruner—that the structural dimensions of any subject discipline were basically similar

TODAY'S EDUCATION, 1970, Vol. 59, No. 4, pp. 37-38.

at all levels and that appropriate perspectives gained at early levels would facilitate later functioning in these disciplines. Some reexamination of the "play world" of nursery school resulted from the accompanying view that children cannot discover the basic principles of each discipline for themselves without the minimal requirement of an environment in which appropriate discoveries would occur.

A second influence came with the realization among educators that the "intelligence" that they had considered to be an inborn constant was being theoretically and empirically described as depending largely upon the child's early experience. As a result, educators rushed to structure environments experimentally to enhance early learning.

Foundation and federal funding during the sixties spurred an unprecedented expansion of programs for the young child, tremendously intensifying the debate about what was appropriate experience for him. The funding came unexpectedly to most educators, and far too few early childhood specialists were available to advise these programs. In addition, Head Start was meant to compensate for severe lacks in the home experiences rather than to provide an enriching supplement. This created a substantially new situation that demanded new perspectives on early childhood education.

In the spring of 1965, people from all backgrounds became involved in setting up Head Start programs under community action agencies. Professionals from the related fields of elementary education, psychology, sociology, health, and others became immediately involved in advising and evaluating the new programs. Their commitment was not necessarily to permissive, play-oriented programs. In fact, some of the innovators from outside the early education field constructed programs of intensive direct instruction and began referring to previous nursery programs as "traditional." At this point a complete about-face had occurred regarding what was *new* and what was *traditional*— and all within the space of a few years.

Diversity is the keynote in early childhood education today. Many current programs have specific and highly varied aims, such as to develop academic readiness, attentional processes, good work habits and categorization skills; to improve or standardize language usage; to train for logical thinking; to teach phonics and/or reading; to increase positive self-identification; and to enhance achievement motivation. Practices, equipment, characteristics of program personnel, and

31

program settings are also quite varied.

Clearly, this is an age of questioning and "trying." From some sources comes the fear that for young children trying may indeed be very trying. Some even express fears that children are being robbed of their childhood because of adult overeagerness to demonstrate early learning.

It is worth noting, however, that few of the publicized "prototypic" programs for the young children that have specifically focused on cognitive learning have simply taken existent elementary school materials and practices and used them earlier. Instead, they have employed special techniques—highly active games, manipulative equipment, diversity of media, low pupil-teacher ratios, varieties of teaching strategies. (If all the furor over new programs for early learning has misguided some teachers into acting toward three- and four-year-olds—or even younger— as though they were in the traditionally conceived first grade class, some children may well have suffered as a result.)

Many educators continue to insist that a rich environment with opportunity for the child to explore, to play, to interact with his peers with a minimum of adult-imposed structure results in optimal development of all kinds. These persons point out that even though the research to date seems to support the effectiveness of direct instruction for precise cognitive goals, whether or not gains are long-term is in doubt. And we have little evidence about other broader aspects of development.

We need to obtain final answers to these arguments. We should not do so by means of global comparisons of one kind of representative program with another but rather through comparisons of a gamut of programs from which we have gathered and analyzed, in relation to a variety of outcomes for children, data on such questions as the following:

• To what extent does the program indicate when certain kinds of behavior are considered appropriate?

• How much variety in terms of equipment, settings, peers, and teachers does a child encounter?

• What allowance is made for diversity in behavior and progress?

• To what extent does the program environment encourage and respond to child initiations and explorations?

• To what extent are experiences presented in a logical sequence and simplified with the child in mind?

This kind of specific research would have greater effectiveness in restoring consensus than the studies more usually undertaken of contrasting total programs.

Until we have clearer research evidence and some kind of consensus among professionals on how various parts of the program affect various kinds of development, we will have to continue implementing programs according to carefully considered hunches about what is most desirable. The following items exemplify the level of abstraction at which such hunches might well be stated. Some educators (including this writer) would favor these conditions:

• A regular daily pattern of program offerings, of snack, rest, outdoor play, story, and so on, but with a minimum of coercion to participate in these activities

• Considerable space and/or time with a minimum of adult restriction on exploratory and motor behavior

• Diverse use of space to provide the greatest amount of freedom for children to move from one kind of in-school setting to another—that is, from expressive and divergent play space to organized and convergent work space, from active group interaction to quiet individual activity

• A variety of materials and equipment that (a) provide opportunity for manipulation and experimentation, (b) offer multisensory experiences, (c) are "responsive" in that the child receives some information as to the effectiveness of his actions, and (d) can be used by the child with a minimum of adult assistance

• Frequent adult verbal interaction with individual children about their ongoing activities that will include relevant comparisons between current encounters and prior experiences

• A gradual increase, not only in kinds of equipment and materials but also in the number of adults and peers the child encounters

• Specialized programs (direct instruction, special facilities, simplified and/or sequenced encounters) for children with diagnosed developmental deficiencies, with a very small group of children for each adult.

Although early childhood educators would be unlikely to reach a consensus on the value of the above conditions as opposed to others, clarification of areas of agreement/disagreement on dimensions such as these would seem to provide a basis for understanding and communication. We need these today in the field of nursery and kindergarten education. □

Constructing a Model for a Teacher Education Program In Early Childhood Education*

By
Bernard Spodek

A RECENT article in **Young Children,** entitled "Teachers of Young Children Need Basic Inner Qualities," lists the prerequisites for becoming a teacher of young children. The first prerequisite, it states, is that the teacher should enjoy learning. "Clearly if we wish our children to love learning we must provide them with teachers who love learning." The second prerequisite is the teacher's ability to distinguish between her personal needs and the children's needs. The author's implication is that the teacher who makes a clear distinction between the two is less likely to use the children to satisfy her need for affection and more likely to plan a suitable curriculum for them. The third and fourth prerequisites are that the teacher "must know appropriate materials and how to create curriculum" and that he "must have a personality that is comfortable with open-endedness." Finally, the article states, the teacher must take pleasure in working with parents.[1]

In many ways, this article represents the traditional approach to the preparation of teachers of young children. It assumes that there is only one kind of educational program for young children and that there is only one kind of teacher that is suitable for teaching in that program. It further assumes that personality factors are the most important attributes of

good teachers and that teacher competency is relatively unimportant. Finally the article reflects little concern for any kind of evidence to support the assertions made or to test ideas about what really makes a good teacher. Recourse to conventional wisdom provides the only support for the author's assertions.

An even more significant problem with this article and the viewpoint it represents is that even if the arguments presented were valid, and they may well be, the guidelines presented are not useful in developing programs to prepare early childhood personnel. Since "basic inner qualities" are not taught, at least in the conventional sense within conventional institutions, teacher preparation would become more a matter of selection of persons who manifest these qualities than of educating persons and providing them with an appropriate body of significant knowledge and competencies. Formal college instruction does not create "basic inner qualities," especially among those women who become teachers of young children. Clearly the traditional rhetoric of early childhood education provides a poor foundation for developing a teacher education program in early childhood education.

Assumptions Upon Which to Base a Teacher Education Program

One must, therefore, look elsewhere for the basis for a program to prepare teachers of young children. The foundations of such a program, as a matter of fact, need to extend beyond the content of early childhood education. I would suggest the following assumptions be used:

1. **What it takes to be a teacher is teachable.** The primary assumption is that good teaching can be a function of a teacher

---

DR. SPODEK *is Professor of Early Childhood Education, University of Illinois.*

*Based upon a presentation made at the Bank Street College Colloquium on The Professional Development of Early Childhood Personnel, March 15, 1968.

[1]Dorothy Weisman Gross, "Teachers of Young Children Need Basic Inner Qualities," **Young Children.** Vol. 23, No. 2. November 1967. Pp. 107-110.

CONTEMPORARY EDUCATION, 1969, Vol. 40, No. 3, pp. 145-149.

education program. Unless we can assume that a program can make a difference, there is little reason to operate any program. While there is little evidence that present teacher education programs do make a difference, our knowledge of the modifiability of human behavior suggests that some effective programs could make a difference. Teaching is not solely a function of teacher personality. Teachers can be made.

2. **What goes into a teacher preparation program should be related to what the teacher will do.** The content of a teacher education program needs to be determined by its relevancy to the teaching act. No course content should be included within the profession preparation simply because it is significant child development knowledge or important historical fact. Teachers teaching in different kinds of early childhood programs might have significantly different programs of teacher preparation.

3. **A program of teacher preparation should be based on what the preparing institution can do.** A college of education is a place where persons are educated. Teacher preparation programs in such institutions should use an education model in designing their programs. Neither a therapeutic model nor a personality development model is appropriate. Also institutions that do not have within them the competencies needed to fully prepare teachers should look elsewhere to provide that necessary competency. Thus it is possible that a good program of teacher preparation would not be the responsibility of a college of education alone, but would be a joint effort involving many diverse institutions.

4. **A sound program of teacher preparation needs to take into account the learning patterns of its client as well as the bureaucratic structure of its sponsoring institution.** Young adults differ as individuals just as young children do. We need to differentiate organizational structures, grouping patterns, learning pace, and scope for persons preparing to teach. To require all students to spend the same amount of time learning the same content, and participate in the same experiences is to deny individual differences. Differentiation needs to occur, however, in ways that institutions can support. But just as people change, institutions can change.

5. **A broad range of teaching types needs to be developed in a program.** Individuals differ in style of behavior, pace of activity, amount of energy available, value system, and even sex. There is no evidence that one style of teaching is more effective than any other. Diversity ought to be nurtured. Too often we have taken the sweet-voiced, charming, feminine teacher as the perfect model of a teacher of young children. This is not the only model possible, and it may not even be the most effective model. Men whose behavior is not in accord with this model have been known to be effective teachers.

6. **A program of teacher education cannot be conceived as a tightly wrapped package.** The idea that all that needs to be known about teaching can be transmitted into a four-year program which immunizes the teacher from any future need for learning is obsolete. Programs of education and knowledge about children are changing at a rapid rate. Teachers need to be continually involved in teacher education programs as part of their professional development.

The Content of a Teacher Education Program

Building up from these assumptions one must determine what elements to include in a program for teacher preparation and how these elements could best be organized and presented. Our second assumption states that the criterion for inclusion must be relevancy to the teaching act. Philip Jackson has separated the teaching act into the preactive stage and the interactive stage.[2] The preactive stage consists of acts that occur prior to the time the teacher is directly involved with children. This would include such activities as planning, organizing, and accumulating resources. The interactive stage is the stage in which the teacher is actually working with the children. During the preactive stage the

[2]Philip W. Jackson, "The Way Teaching Is," in The Way Teaching Is. Washington, D.C.: Association for Supervision and Curriculum Development, 1966.

teacher's behavior includes much conscious decision making. During the interactive stage the interactions between teacher and child occur at such a rapid rate that little intellectualization and deliberate actions occur. Most of the interactions involve teachers' intuitive reaction to the children's behavior.

One might also add a third stage, the **post active** stage. This would include the period after the teacher has interacted with the child and would involve recalling occurrences, interpreting behavior, evaluating learning and accumulating the data to be used for future planning.

Traditionally teacher education programs in college have dealt mainly with the preactive stage of teaching. We **talk about** methods, we **talk about** curriculum, we **talk about** discipline problems. We seldom go beyond the **talking about** stage. We need to include opportunity to practice for only as teachers practice behavior will they have the appropriate patterns available to them to use intuitively.

Components of a Teacher Education Program

What would characterize a good teacher education program? Such a program should consist of a series of guided experiences (not necessarily traditional courses) through which students would attain the knowledge and competencies deemed necessary and appropriate for teachers of young children. The goals of the program would be mastery of technique as well as accumulation of knowledge and the program would include doing as well as talking about. Preteachers would be guided through a series of successive approximations of the teaching act in which they could master technique. The program would be flexible enough to allow students to enter it at various points and would allow students to use evidence of proficiency to meet any program requirement. A range of options would be available within the program and elements in the program could be completed at different paces by different students. Flexibility must be characteristic of such a program.

As components in the program, it is possible to suggest the following:

1. **A selection and recruitment component** — Most teacher education programs select students on the basis of scholastic competence alone. This, however, is not the most appropriate means of selection. While basic intelligence and academic competence are important, it is doubtful that once beyond a minimal point such selection really results in providing better teachers for the field. A whole range of other selection criteria could be included.

One of these might be selection based upon "basic inner qualities" as suggested above. Other possibilities are also available. We need to look at interpersonal skills as well as intellectual skills in selecting prospective teachers of young children.

Recruitment needs to go hand-in-hand with selection. Teacher education programs assume that there will be an adequate self-selection and self-recruitment of candidates from among college-age women. This is inadequate. Candidates for programs need to be as actively recruited as candidates for teaching positions. Different populations need to be attracted into programs. The young college graduate often spends only two or three years actively teaching before marrying and raising a family. The attrition rate of young teachers is high enough to begin to question the appropriateness of leaving selection to chance. We need to recruit men as well as more mature women who are beyond the point of initial child-rearing. Programs designed for such people will necessarily differ from traditional teacher education programs both in organization and content.

2. **A broad base of general education** — All teachers ought to be well-educated persons. The scope of the content of programs for young children is so broad that a sound general education is a professional as well as a personal requirement. Just what constitutes such an education, however, is a controversial question. Certainly the present student unrest would suggest that traditional college requirements are inadequate. A good general education should be substantive but relevant to current life as well.

3. **A professional foundations compon-**

ent—This component would include knowledge that is not immediately transferable to teacher behavior, yet is relevant to the basic decision-making process of teaching. Some of the content of the behavioral and social sciences fit this category. This ought not to be the traditional introductory course in sociology, psychology, anthropology, or philosophy, but rather, elements from these fields presented so that their relevancy to education is apparent.

4. **An instructional knowledge component**—This would include much from present "curriculum" and "methods" courses in education. This component will deal directly with the knowledge teachers must use in classroom practice and in planning for and evaluating classroom practice.

5. **A practice component** — This would be a series of components rather than a single independent component. The two components above would have related opportunities for practice. Knowledge in child development and behavior would be gained through course work, observation and interaction with children. Visits to school board meetings, conferences with officials of teachers' unions, and meetings with parents and members of civil rights groups could be related to traditional foundations components. In many communities, teacher strikes and parent boycotts provide ample opportunity for direct practice experience related to the social foundations of education.

Student teaching has long been considered an important practice component of teacher education programs. Often it is the only opportunity for practice in a program. Student teaching, however, is not the only way and possibly not even the best way, to acquire the necessary behaviors. A creative use of observation, in simulation and small groups as well as full-class practice situations, could lead to the assumption of full responsibility for the total learning experiences of a class. Simulation and microteaching techniques could also be used as "practice tutoring" situations, allowing teachers to work on specific problem areas. Each of these practice situations should provide the student with feedback for analyzing and modifying behavior.

This practice component should go beyond the traditional termination of a teacher preparation program. Graduation, certification and employment do not signify total teacher competence. Teachers need continued help in their beginning years, and such aid should become an integral part of the teacher education program. With graduates of college programs scattering to the four winds this presents some difficulties. But current technology suggests some ways that can overcome these difficulties. Conference telephone calls and the exchange of film clips or videotapes of teaching could provide long range consultation related to practice.

6. **An evaluation and program modification component** — An important part of any teacher education program is its assessment. Generally we use a student's performance within a program to predict his effectiveness as a teacher. Seldom is the effectiveness of a total program or program components for producing competent teachers evaluated.

We use paper and pencil tests or written essays to assess knowledge, and supervisory observation and judgments to assess performance. Seldom are there clear criteria upon which to base judgment, nor do we make much use of these judgments. We record a letter grade, fail a student, or write a recommendation, but we seldom change a student's program. Decisions based upon evaluation of students' performances should provide for differentiation of experiences. Time allotments could be varied so that some students are given more time to successfully master elements of the program. Other students may have portions of the program waived for them when diagnostic assessment suggests they have already achieved mastery.

In addition, the program's effectiveness in producing competent teachers of young children needs to be assessed. Built into the program should be the means for its modification. Unfortunately too often we find that college-based programs are the most conservative and the most difficult to change.

CONCLUSIONS

A new era in early childhood education seems to be dawning. Great interest on the part of the public has led to the extension of programs for young children across the nation. It has also led to increased questioning regarding the nature of educational programs offered young children. A range of alternatives is becoming available. This renaissance in early childhood education has led to an increased concern for the preparation of teachers to staff these programs. Innovation should be paralleled by innovation and inquiry in supporting teacher education programs. Otherwise there will be little net gain for the children resulting from current improvements and extensions. This is a danger we must guard against.

II. RATIONALE AND CONCERNS

WHEN SHOULD SCHOOLING BEGIN?

Burton White
John Brademas
Wilson Riles

Among interested professionals and many parents, the topic of pre-school education is a sure bet to arouse emotion. Especially during the last decade, when a good deal of attention has been focused on the issue, we have heard one strident voice after another. In this *Kappan*, Moore, Moon, and Moore present a provocative but reasonable analysis of the problem which to me merits serious consideration. Put simply, they claim that the recommendation of the California Report* that *all* children four years of age and older receive formal schooling is based on a seriously erroneous interpretation of research evidence, and indeed is directly contradicted by that evidence. The authors would rather

*California Task Force Report, "Report of the Task Force on Early Childhood Education." Sacramento, Calif.: Wilson Riles, State Superintendent of Public Instruction, and the State Board of Education, November 21, 1971.

see more public support go toward preparing people to become effective parents and for programs for early detection and treatment of educational deficits. As for children without obvious difficulties, they would have the reader consider the idea that formal schooling ought to begin no sooner than the ninth year of life.

My colleagues and I have been studying the development of infants and young children for over 14 years. For the last seven, the work has been pursued at a graduate school of education. We have been continuously aware of the fact that though humans begin to learn at least as early as birth, most societies do not provide organized educational support until a child is six or seven years old. This has been the case for Western civilization for all its recorded history. It is my guess that the major reason for this tradition is that at six or seven years of age most children can be taught (in

PHI DELTA KAPPAN, 1972, Vol. 53, pp. 610-614.

groups) to read without great difficulty. Substantial numbers of students of child development (including myself) are totally convinced that all children are being "educated" in areas of profound importance during the first six years of life. This education takes place mostly in the home. Too many children are failing this course of study, and failure at this stage apparently usually means failure throughout life. Until very recently, educators have paid relatively slight attention to questions of the curriculum, the staff, and the methods of the "informal schooling" of the first six years of a child's life. But, whether educators examine the process or not, it goes on for all children, and many of us believe that our current professional neglect of the educational developments of the first six years is a serious disservice to most children, including many we consider perfectly normal.

I believe that within a few decades most Western societies will assume public responsibility for guiding the educational development of all children from birth. I do not mean to say that all infants and toddlers will attend schools, although a minority may in cases where a child needs remedial treatment; or where a family (even with outside support) cannot provide minimally acceptable educational experiences for a baby.

If public responsibility for pre-school education does not mean formal schools, what does it mean? My ideas are quite compatible with those of Moore *et al.*

First of all, parents need to be educated for parenthood. If there are better and poorer ways to rear young children, we have to identify them and make them a serious part of our public education curriculum. Over and above knowledge, families will often need other kinds of support. Parents we work with seem to need someone to talk with during more stressful periods, such as during an infant's second year of life when he becomes both more accident-prone and more negativistic.

Second, we do not currently know much about sensory development in the first years of life. The consequences of untreated sensory defects, especially in the areas of hearing and vision, can be devastating to a child, yet in most cases any but the grossest defects of this sort are not discovered until a child is six or seven years of age. We now have usable techniques for detecting most significant handicaps during the first three years. Each community will someday use these techniques in systematic ways.

Third, once a handicap is identified in an infant, we should treat it. In the case of a hearing deficit, hearing aids can be used, apparently with infants as young as six months of age. How can we tolerate letting children pass through the first three years of life, the period of language acquisition and primary socialization, with an undetected hearing loss? We are allowing this to happen every day to thousands of young children.

Here at Harvard we have been studying how some families provide remarkably effective early education for their young children. These families, affluent and poor, from many different backgrounds, are rearing children who at three years of age are remarkably competent. They not only score at about 140 on a standard I.Q. test, but they are equally impressive in their social abilities. In addition, they are not fragile or precocious little geniuses, but instead seem secure, independent, and happy. We have been trying to discover what role the family's educational practices play in such beneficial outcomes. Though we do not have all the answers, we believe we have acquired much practical information. Studies such as ours can lead to a better-informed public, to better child-rearing practices, to better early education in the home, and to better development of children.

In Brookline, a suburb of Boston, we have begun a five-year test of the feasibility of a public school system assuming a formal professional role in guiding the educational development of children from birth. The plan has the following major features:

1. Strengthening each family's ca-

40

pacity to rear young children through provision of parent education, professional consultation, and support and materials when needed.

2. Identification of educationally relevant handicaps as early as possible through a systematic medical and psychological diagnostic program administered continuously from before the child is born on through the preschool years.

3. Treatment of identified handicaps such as sensory deficits, language acquisition and other learning difficulties, mental retardation, etc., beginning at birth.

4. A high likelihood of continuity with elementary educational experiences by virtue of the fact that the school system is the initiator and director of this experimental venture.

Currently, we spend comparatively little public money on the education of children until they are six years of age. Subsequently, we tend to spend more and more each year as children move through the system. There is good reason to question the wisdom of this arrangement. It may turn out to be more sensible to invest heavily in the first years of a child's life and spend less as he moves through elementary and secondary education. Such a shift of resources would be sure to meet resistance, but I believe it is inevitable.

–Burton L. White

BURTON L. WHITE is director of the Pre-School Project, Laboratory of Human Development, Graduate School of Education, Harvard University.

In February, 1969, President Nixon told Congress, "So critical is the matter of early growth that we must make a national commitment to providing all American children an opportunity for healthful and stimulating development during the first five years of life."

In December, 1971, President Nixon vetoed a measure passed by both houses of Congress, the Comprehensive Child Development Bill, aimed at achieving precisely this goal. Between the President's eloquent statement in 1969 and his veto message in 1971, the Select Education Subcommittee, which I have the honor to chair, the House Committee on Education and Labor, and a Senate subcommittee headed by Senator Walter F. Mondale (D.-Minnesota) conducted the most extensive hearings Congress has ever held on early childhood programs. Last month, in May, the Senate Labor and Public Welfare Committee favorably reported a modified version of the vetoed bill. Even as I write, members of both the House and the Senate are continuing this bipartisan effort to write legislation that would provide opportunities for health, nutrition, education, and other services for pre-school children, not only of families of the poor, as with Head Start, but for children of all income groups.

I recite this background in response to the request of *Kappan* editors for comment on the essay, "The California Report: Early Schooling for All?," prepared by the Hewitt Research Center, because the authors, who complain of a drive for earlier and earlier schooling which appears to be either overlooking or ignoring many of the most important findings of development research, appear either to be overlooking or ignoring the history of this major legislation. Indeed, only a few weeks ago, one of the authors of the Hewitt Report told me, to my astonishment, that he had not even read the Select Education Subcommittee hearings on the Comprehensive Child Development Bill.

When, therefore, we are told that "the Hewitt Research Center has involved leading educators, legislators, scholars, and researchers at local, state, and national levels from coast to coast in a review of early childhood research," we must ask if we are being subjected to Chamber of Commerce-style rhetoric boosting the home-town product, or a scholarly effort to increase our knowledge about an important problem. For, although strongly identified with child development legislation over the last two and a half years, neither I nor any member of my subcommittee staff was consulted by the Hewitt Center; nor, I find on inquiry, was the principal Senate sponsor of the Child Development Bill, Senator Mondale.

My point is certainly not wounded pride. It is simply the accuracy of the pretensions of Messrs. Moore, Moon, and Moore. Who are the "leading legislators at national levels" who were "involved" in the Hewitt Center review of early childhood research?

But I believe that the Hewitt report raises more important points and causes of concern for those of us who have for some time been toiling in the vineyard of early childhood programs. The authors appear either to have overlooked or ignored the distinction between the phrases "early schooling" and "childhood development." There was a reason that the sponsors of the Comprehensive Child Development Bill called it that and not the "Early Schooling Bill." The reason is that our measure went beyond providing opportunity for cognitive growth for children. We included health, nutrition, and other services (hence "comprehensive") that affect the growth of the child (hence "development").

Messrs. Moore, Moon, and Moore appear to oscillate in their awareness of this distinction or, if they are aware of it, in their appreciation of its significance. Their paper seems to focus on the education in formal schools of very young children. Yet they contend that the "principal questions" they propose to treat are 1) "the best kind of intervention or care for young children" and 2) "the best and most financially feasible environment for early childhood development." The content of their paper reflects this continuing ambiguity of purpose. Does the Hewitt Center report pretend to address itself to the cognitive growth of young chil-

dren in formal schools? Or does it seek as well to answer questions about the noncognitive aspects of the growth of young children? It is also unclear whether the authors intend to consider learning or development only as it takes place in formal schools. Do they include other settings as well?

What must in any event be clear is that the Hewitt writers have failed to make good on their own promise to treat their two "principal questions, the best kind of intervention or care for young children, and the best environment for early childhood development."

Although President Nixon broke his word on his 1969 commitment, he at least appears to have understood the differences between early schooling and childhood development. Moreover, the 1970 White House Conference on Children (which, I cannot resist noting, "involved leading educators, legislators, scholars, and researchers at local, state, and national levels from coast to coast") recommended as its number one priority "that the federal government fund comprehensive child-care programs, including health, early childhood education, and social services."

As I have been invited to comment on the significance of the Hewitt Center essay to the child development legislation now under consideration in Congress, I have not attempted to analyze the paper as it relates to the California proposal. In this connection I think it is essential that the reader have an opportunity to read both the report of the California Task Force on Early Childhood Education and the master plan in order to judge the accuracy and scholarship of both the California proposal and the Hewitt Report.

The Hewitt essay does, however, lead me to this general observation: Researchers who expect their work to be taken seriously must make a serious effort to be precise about their objectives. As I have indicated, ambiguity about whether they are studying early schooling or child development runs throughout the Moore, Moon, Moore report, making it difficult to evaluate their evaluations and, for those of us who are deeply desirous of as much scholarly evidence as we can get about the lives of children, rendering the Hewitt Center findings of little use. Based on the evidence presented to congressional committees over the last two and a half years, there is ample justification for President Nixon's 1969 call for "a national commitment to providing all American children an opportunity for healthful and stimulating development during the first five years of life."

I have sent the authors of the Hewitt Report a copy of our subcommittee hearing.

—John Brademas

JOHN BRADEMAS (D.-Indiana) is chairman of the House Select Education Subcommittee and sponsor of the Comprehensive Child Development Bill now before Congress. He was first elected to Congress in 1957 after serving as executive assistant to presidential nominee Adlai Stevenson. A Harvard graduate, magna cum laude, *he is a former Rhodes Scholar.*

The schools as they presently operate are failing many of our children. Everyone knows that. We all want to change it, but we know we cannot change it all at once. What we must do is find the best place to begin making the necessary changes, and I believe that early childhood is the best place to start.

Soon after I took office as California's state superintendent of public instruction, I appointed a group of distinguished researchers and experts to an *ad hoc* task force on early childhood education, with a mandate to rethink the education of primary children in this state. The task force was broadly representative, multi-ethnic, both men and women, and included parents, teachers, and experts from early childhood education, medicine, sociology, home economics, psychology, business, and architecture.

From the report of that task force came a declaration of priority from the California State Board of Education. The report became the framework for an implementation plan which is the basis for early childhood proposals now being considered by the state legislature.

In this brief article I can mention only some of the highlights of the current thrust for improvement of primary education in California.

Task Force Philosophy

The following passages drawn from their report summarize the philosophy of the *ad hoc* task force:

> The Task Force on Early Childhood Education hereby dedicates itself to the proposition that since all men and women of every race and creed indeed do have inalienable rights to life, liberty, and the pursuit of happiness, it is the business of society to assure these rights for every child. He is, we emphasize, tomorrow's adult.
>
> The past decade has produced a new body of educational, psychological, and medical research documenting the crucial importance of the first eight years of life.* And we are convinced that these early years are critical in determining the future effectiveness of our citizens and in the long-range prevention of crime, poverty, addiction, malnutrition, neurosis, and violence. Even though research is still in progress and conclusions continue to evolve, we believe enough evidence is in to indicate that the following are clearly warranted now:
>
> 1. The people of the state of California must make a long-range commitment of funds to the proposition that the first eight years of life are the most important period in determining the future effectiveness of all our citizens.
> 2. Implicit in this commitment is the recognition of the desirability of providing educational opportunities for all children. . . .
> 3. School should be a happy place,

*Benjamin S. Bloom, *Stability and Change in Human Characteristics*. New York: John Wiley & Sons, 1964.

a stimulating environment without the traditional artificial barriers, which provides an opportunity for continuous progress to each child, based upon his own unique needs, interests, talents, and capabilities. . . .

4. Because we recognize the importance of the parents in the education of children, we strongly affirm that parent education and involvement must be an integral part of all programs. . . .

5. There must be encouragement of local autonomy and creativity in program development, with provision for maximum flexibility within broad state guidelines. . . .

6. We believe it is essential that California establish at once for primary children a broadly based educational program that extends at least one year below the system now in existence. . . .*

Plan Before Legislature

A bold, creative effort to redesign primary education in California is being made. Under the proposed plan, state financial support of public education is revised to devote a greater proportion of funds to the critical primary years. The pending legislation provides for completely restructuring the kindergarten and the present primary grades 1, 2, and 3 so that the individual needs of children can actually be met by means of an educational program that is appropriate for each child. This will obviously require more and better prepared adults in the classroom, as well as better trained management personnel.

It is important to note that the California plan also provides for the optional inclusion of four-year-olds if their parents want them to have this educational opportunity, just as kindergarten has always been optional in this state. Such learning experiences will be oriented toward the child's development and should not be confused with "for-

mal schooling" in the traditional sense or efforts to begin "academics" earlier. Age six is the legal age for school entrance in California. The new plan does not change that.

The key issue in the California proposal, however, is not the admission of four-year-olds. Rather, it is establishing an improved, more effective program for all primary children. There is, of course, no point in sending a four-year-old into any type of learning environment not geared to his needs, interests, talents, and capacities. The primary school as visualized by the task force is characterized above all by an educational environment which is responsive to the individual differences of all children, slow or fast, disadvantaged or not, of whatever race and color.

Implementation Plans

Planners expect a gradual phase-in over the next six years. Plans call for each local school district to submit a master plan for early childhood education which must focus on the needs of the children to be served. Districts must define their goals and objectives for those children. They must design appropriate learning experiences for them. Evaluation must be provided for. Parents and the community must be included in the planning and evaluation. Coordination of all existing school and community resources which affect the education of primary children is required in order to secure program approval under guidelines to be adopted by the state board of education.

What Results Can We Expect?

What will the California plan do for children? It offers individualization, with parents, volunteers, aides, and older students working under the direction of the teacher to provide help for each child when it is needed, not in a later grade when it is more costly and less effective; to inspire interest and motivation; to allow for continuous progress,

*California State Department of Education, *Report of the Task Force on Early Childhood Education,* Sacramento, December, 10, 1971, pp. 1-2.

44

building upon success and ensuring positive attitudes of self-worth, self-confidence, and self-control. Included, for those who qualify, will be whatever additional services are needed, if not otherwise available. It is recognized that such things as extended day care, health, nutrition, and other social services are all factors which affect a child's well-being and success in school.

These are not new ideas. They just need to be put into action. The heart of the California plan is to stop talking and start doing.

The goal of the early childhood education proposal is that, by the end of the primary level, all our children will be excited about learning and able to proceed successfully with the rest of their school experience, having achieved sufficient command of the skills basic to reading, language, and arithmetic to enable them to do so.

What will it do for families? No longer can we afford the mistakes of the past in telling parents "hands off," that only educators know what is best for their children. This plan will create a parent-school partnership that will strengthen the family by closer home-school ties, make parent education available, and give parents a real voice in the education of their children to an extent we have never before realized.

What will it do for communities? It will create a school-community partnership; provide for coordination of all community services and resources, public and private, with the school; offer an opportunity for older students to work with primary pupils to the great benefit of both. It will coordinate community, state, and federal agency efforts for young children, and will involve the community in assessing the total early childhood education effort.

Summary

I think a fitting close to this brief description is the following quotation from the task force report:

> It is time to do a better job of what we already know should be done for young children in school. Let us incorporate the best of what we have learned from all the various kinds of existing pre-school programs, from kindergarten, and from the primary grades with the most promising results derived from a continual review of new research. Given the time, effort, thought, and public resources necessary, we believe the primary school described in this report would welcome rather than fear the increasing emphasis on accountability.

—Wilson Riles

WILSON RILES (130, Sacramento California Field Chapter) is superintendent of public instruction and director of education, California Department of Education.

THE CALIFORNIA REPORT:
EARLY SCHOOLING FOR ALL?

Raymond S. Moore
Robert D. Moon
Dennis R. Moore

T he United States is currently witnessing one of its most remarkable educational developments — a drive for earlier and earlier schooling for all children which appears to be either overlooking or ignoring many of the most important findings of developmental research. While such oversight is not new to American education, in this instance the evidence and implications are not only clear, but also warn of formidable costs — first, in tax moneys, and second and far more important, in possible damage to young children.

A look at the early schooling (ES) movement reveals many developments, e.g., mounting problems of child behavior, parents chafing at the "shackles" of parenthood, inadequate and unregulated care of children, and federal and state interest in early schooling. Educators are intrigued by research which points up the rapid early development of intelligence. (See Bloom's review, *Stability and Change in Human Characteristics.*[1]) But many of these well-intentioned people overlook scientific findings which point in other directions than that in which early childhood education is now generally going, e.g., studies on early *vs.* later school admission, neurophysiology, cognition, and maternal deprivation. If such findings are not carefully considered, early childhood educators may threaten the very childhood development they design to improve.

In order to develop a fair and somewhat comprehensive viewpoint, the Hewitt Research Center has involved leading educators, legislators, scholars, and researchers at local, state, and national levels from

PHI DELTA KAPPAN, 1972, Vol. 53, pp. 615-621, 677.

coast to coast in a review of early childhood research. A limited cross-section of the resulting analysis is presented here.

We acknowledge, of course, the need of special education for the seriously disadvantaged or handicapped. There is also a need to care for children who have handicapped parents or whose parents are compelled to work. No position is taken here against early intervention where indicated by research. The principal questions we shall treat here are: What is the best kind of intervention or care for young children? What is generally the best — and most financially feasible — environment for early childhood development (ECD)?

We will attempt 1) to analyze typical goals of early schooling proponents, 2) to examine their use of research in support of their conclusions, 3) to see what systematic research actually says about typical ES programs and proposals, and 4) to report some practical solutions growing out of research and experimentation. In order to maintain a sharp focus this will be done primarily with reference to one state — California.

The California Report. The report of the California Task Force on Early Childhood Education[2] is relatively middle-of-the-road as ES proposals go. For example, it proposes to take schooling at first only down to four-year-olds, rather than to children aged three or three and one-half as planned in New York State and Houston. The task force plan may soon be presented to the California legislature. Because California has long been among the pioneers in U.S. education, it will exercise a telling influence among other states. Yet the California proposal, with some variations, appears typical of current ES rationale.

Typical Early Schooling Goals

The California task force offers a philosophy and goals that would build on a substantial body of research:

> The past decade has produced a new body of educational, psychological, and medical research documenting the crucial importance of the first eight years of life. And we are convinced that these early years are critical in determining the future effectiveness of our citizens and in the long-range prevention of

47

crime, poverty, addiction, malnutrition, neurosis, and violence.[3]

The report assumes that "even though research is still in progress and conclusions continue to evolve, enough evidence is in" to justify certain goals, namely, "to bring about the maximum development of every child" down to age four.[4] And it is proposed that this goal will be accomplished by providing for *academic* as well as personal development and requiring "school districts to restructure and expand existing programs."[5]

Typical Use of Research

The California goal of maximum development surely is consistent with the ideals of most Americans. The report cites many examples of ECD research and experimentation which it assumes will provide substance for its implementation plan. Yet in no case does it clearly show how this research supports its plan. In fact certain research quoted in the report actually contradicts the task force's conclusions that *schooling* under carefully selected teachers is desirable for *all* four-year-olds. For example:

1. Harold Skeels's study[6] of orphanage children is quoted as demonstrating how the young child, given a favorable environment, can make marked intellectual growth. But the report does not continue its analysis to show that Skeels's "environment" was an institution in which *retarded teenagers* provided the orphans a *warm, free, one-to-one, continuing* mother or mother-surrogate relationship. Skeels's study had little to do with academic instruction or credentialed teaching.

2. The report quotes findings of the White House Conference of 1970: "We must free ourselves from our antiquated and erroneous beliefs that school is the only environment in which creativity is enhanced and learning takes place, or that the teacher is the sole agent of such achievements."[7]

3. Another task force item cites the June, 1971, report of the Education Commission of the States, which says in part:

> It is not recommended that states establish formal classroom pre-school programs for all three- and four-year-olds because there is no

48

evidence that all children need a structured group experience if they are receiving some kind of systematic training and because there are viable, less expensive alternatives.[8]

4. The report calls for "at least one adult to every ten children"[9] in educating four-year-olds. Yet every experiment quoted in the report in which adult-child ratios were given (six out of eleven examples) the adult-to-child ratio was 1:5 *or less,* or a need for at least four to six times the number of adults required for a standard kindergarten-primary grade ratio of 1:20 to 1:30. Although the California cost proposals are still in the formative stages, Superintendent Wilson Riles is counting on a per-child annual cost of about $500 to $600. Yet one of the documents quoted in the report (*Preschool Breakthrough*[10]) notes that the pre-kindergarten experience of New York State sees an annual $1,800-per-child cost as necessary for "adequate day care" and "much more if the program reaches a desirable standard."

In view of such examples as this, it is difficult to understand how the task force concludes that all four-year-olds should be provided academic schooling. And the discrepancy between research and projected implementation goes much farther. Unfortunately, California's proposal is not an isolated illustration of such disparity, as Earl Schaefer, one of the nation's leading early childhood education specialists, notes:

> ... Although much of this [ECD] research data has been generated during the last decade, earlier studies of intellectual development have motivated the current volume of research. Unfortunately, interpretations of the significance of this data, although they have guided the course of research, have as yet had minimal impact on educational planning. ...[11]

This may be one of the reasons for the findings of William Rohwer (University of California, Berkeley) and others that "the research and development phases of early childhood programs have succeeded but the implementation phases, thus far, have largely failed."[12]

While there is evidence of some desirable effects

of ES programs for disadvantaged children, the assessment of failure of large-scale programs is related primarily to academic or cognitive achievement, a goal strongly stressed in the California report.[13] Referring to a number of large-scale ES programs it studied, the U.S. Commission on Civil Rights concluded that "A principal objective of each was to raise academic achievement of disadvantaged children. Judged by this standard the programs did not show evidence of much success."[14] The Westinghouse/Ohio University study found Head Start to have been "ineffective in producing any [lasting] gains in cognitive and affective development" and stressed the present "limited state of knowledge" about what would constitute effective intervention.[15]

What Systematic Research Says

For the purposes of this report, key factors in three types of studies will be considered among many on which there is substantial research evidence: 1) studies comparing early and later school entrants; 2) neurophysiological research, including brain changes which affect vision, hearing, cognition, etc.; and 3) maternal deprivation studies.

These will be followed by a brief review of research on family attitudes toward children and comparisons between the home and the school as alternatives for early childhood development.

Early and Late School Entry. Most academic schooling, it will be assumed, eventually rests upon an ability to read. In turn, Nila Smith points out, "Dozens of investigations indicate that reading maturation accompanies physical growth, mental growth, emotional and social maturity, experiential background, and language development."[16] Willard Olson found that "children of the same age and the same grade location are regularly found to differ by as much as four or five years in their maturation and their readiness to perform tasks."[17]

The question then is not only, Is the child *ready* for school? but even more important, Does he demonstrate his readiness by sufficient maturity to *sustain* learning? and, Will the early starter be *as well or better motivated and less frustrated and anxiety-ridden* than the one who starts later? A wide variety of studies provides the answers.

50

Inez King[19] reports an Oak Ridge, Tennessee, study of two groups totaling 54 children who were five years and eight months to five years and 11 months old when they started school. They were compared with 50 children who started at six years and three months to six years and eight months of age. Stanford Achievement Tests at the end of grade six showed a distinct difference, strongly in favor of the older group. In this study, of the 11 children who were retained, only one had started after six years of age; 19 boys and 16 girls of the younger group appeared to be maladjusted in some way, while only three boys and three girls from the older group were considered maladjusted.

ECD studies involving retention of learning have been done at virtually all grade and socioeconomic status (SES) levels, with remarkably uniform results. B. U. Keister[20] reported that five-year-olds could often develop enough skills to get through first-grade reading, but the learning was generally not retained through the summer vacation. Other comparisons of reading achievement of early and late starters were made by Marian Carroll[21] in the third grade, Joseph Halliwell and Belle Stein[22] in the fourth and fifth grades, and Richard Hampleman[23] in the sixth. All found generally that later entrants significantly excelled those who started earlier. Similar studies with similar results have also been reported by Elizabeth Bigelow,[24] Inez King,[25] Lowell Carter,[26] Clyde Baer,[27] Donald Green and Sadie Simmons,[28] and Margaret Gott.[29] There are many more.

John Forrester[30] did a vertical study of 500 grade 1-12 children in the Montclair, New Jersey, public schools. The very bright but very young pupils at the time of school entrance did not realize their school success potential. From junior high on, 50% of them earned only C grades. However, the very bright but older group excelled generally throughout their school careers.

While many of these studies were undertaken with a combination of low and middle SES children, higher SES groups perform similarly. Paul Mawhinny[31] reports how children from Detroit's elite Grosse Pointe, Michigan, families were selected by psychologists because they were considered mature enough or of sufficient potential to be admitted to kindergarten before age five. But after 14 years an evaluation was made. More than one-fourth of the

51

selected group were below average or had repeated a grade.

Arnold Gesell and Frances Ilg, after extensive research and clinical analyses, found that school tasks such as reading, writing, and arithmetic "depend upon motor skills which are subject to the same laws of growth which govern creeping, walking, grasping." The resulting awkwardness and immaturity "are often sadly overlooked by teachers and parents":

> When the school child was a baby the adult attitudes tended to be more reasonable. One did not say he should walk at this or that age. Feeling confident that he would walk at the most seasonable time, one was more interested to observe the stage and degree of his preliminary development. If reading readiness and walking readiness are appraised on similar grounds, more justice is done the child.[32]

Neurophysiology and Cognition. The findings of neurophysiologists, psychologists, and medical personnel are remarkably similar in their timing of stages at which children are normally ready to think abstractly, or organize facts, and to sustain and retain learning without undue damage or strain. Many neurophysiological studies demonstrate significant changes in brain patterns which occur between ages seven and eleven. These include impressive experiments which lead one to question if children should be required to participate in regular academic instruction until they are at least eight years old. Some researchers and scholars suggest even until adolescence, e.g., Rohwer[33] and Fisher.[34]

A number of studies of the young child's brain, including Penuel Corbin's, Jean Nicholson's, G. C. Lairy's, W. E. Nelson's, and very recent studies by David Metcalf and Kent Jordan,[35] show that appreciable brain changes take place from birth into adolescence, including the shifting of control from the emotional centers to the reasoning centers. They point to ages seven to eleven or twelve as this important period during which a child eventually develops the ability to sustain high cortical thought.

A. Davis[36] records Paul Yakovlev's findings that the child's brain is not fully insulated or completely developed until after seven years, and sometimes not until age ten or later. H. G. Birch and M. Bortner[37] and M. Bortner and H. G. Birch[38] found that until these ages young children and brain-damaged adults were inaccurate in the perception of shapes and grossly inaccurate in attempts to reproduce them.

The findings of cognitive psychologist Jean Piaget coincide remarkably with those of the neurophysiologists. Willis Overton summarizes Piaget's four major steps in the development of the child:

> ... (a) the sensory motor period – birth to two years; (b) the preoperational period – two years to seven years; (c) the period of concrete operations – seven to eleven years; and (d) the period of formal operations between eleven and fifteen years.[39]

Overton notes that the change from preoperational to concrete operational periods of childhood finds the very young child involved in direct perception relationships with a minimum of reasoning. So this child relates quantity to shape and form of objects, but if the shape or form is changed he is confused. He must also change the quantity. For instance, he cannot understand how a low, wide glass can hold as much water as a tall, narrow one. It is not until he is seven or eight or later that he becomes a fully "reasonable" creature. As he goes through this transition he begins to reason abstractly instead of limiting himself to direct relationships.[40]

Millie Almy's replication of Piaget's work demonstrated "that only 48% of the second-grade children in the middle class school, with a mean chronological age of seven years and four months, were able to conserve in all three of the [Piagetian] tasks"[41] which were designed to measure cognitive maturity in terms of abstract thinking normally required for primary grades. Almy concludes that "failure to begin to conserve [Piaget's term for ability to understand certain problems] at an early age may be associated with a failure to grasp much that goes on in the classroom and elsewhere."[42]

William Rohwer sees schooling as an intrusion on the child's freedom to learn associatively during his preoperational years. He found "little evidence to support the rationale for progressively lowering the age of required school entrance if by evidence one requires data demonstrating a positive effect of early school entrance on later school achievement." He suggested that schooling, as commonly understood, be delayed "several years."[43]

Psychiatrist J. T. Fisher supports this thesis from clinical observation and affirms a need for a primary effort in behalf of the home. Speaking for greater initial freedom for developing a strong affective base for later stability in cognition, and incidentally for nongradedness, he says:

> Psychologists have demonstrated that a normal child commencing his education in adolescence can soon reach the same point of progress he would have achieved by starting to school at five or six years of age. I have often thought that if a child could be assured a wholesome home life and proper physical development, this might be the answer to a growing problem of inadequate classroom space and a shortage of qualified teachers — and the instinctive reluctance of all of us to hand over tax dollars for anything that doesn't fire bullets.[44]

William Rohwer (12) in doing rank correlations on the findings from Torsten Husen's international study(45), found a strong negative correlation between early entry age and attitudes toward school.

D. Elkind[46] found no support for "the claims of lastingness of pre-school instruction, [but] ... evidence in the opposite direction. . . . The longer we delay formal instruction, up to certain limits, the greater the period of plasticity and the higher the ultimate level of achievement." He sees frustrated, anxiety-ridden, "intellectually burned" children who lose motivation for intellectual success which they deserve.

Visual Maturity. Findings on the child's visual system are highly similar to those of his brain: The processing of visual stimuli in the brain traces the same electrical path as do the impulses involved with cognitive activity that occur between the thalamus and the cortex. Therefore, if these connections are not completed in their development, the visual signals will not be interpreted clearly, according to James Chalfant and Margaret Scheffelin. These authors add that

The processing of visual stimuli at the higher cortical levels involves: (a) visual analysis, the separation of the whole into its component parts; (b) visual integration, the coordination of mental processes; and (c) visual synthesis, the incorporation or combination of elements into a recognizable whole. A review of literature reveals a variety of cognitive tasks requiring the analysis, integration, and synthesis of visual information.[47]

Luella Cole[48] observed that some children are unable to fixate on objects at close range until age seven or eight or later. Stanley Krippner[49] notes how hard it is to explain to parents that it is not the child's eye that reads but his brain. Chalfant and Scheffelin[50] confirm that "the retina is an outward extension of the cerebral cortex." Thus the visual system is not ready for reading until the brain is relatively mature.

An interesting longitudinal illustration of this relative maturity is provided by Moselle Boland's report of a paper presented by a Texas ophthamologist at the 1963 meeting of the Texas Medical Association:

Dr. Henry L. Hilgartner said there has been a tremendous increase in nearsightedness in [Texas] school children in the past 30 years. . . . He blames use of their eyes for close school work at an early age. . . . The constant pull of the eye muscles to do close work, he said, causes the eyeball to become larger. This is the basic defect in nearsightedness. . . . Prior to 1930, he said, 7.7 children were farsighted to every one nearsighted. . . . In 1930, Texas compulsory school age was lowered from seven to six years. Today, he added, five children are nearsighted for every one farsighted. . . . "I believe the chief cause is children being required to start school at the early age of six instead of being allowed to grow for another year or two," Dr. Hilgartner commented.[51]

Ruth Strang[52] and Homer Carter and Dorothy McGinnis[53] note that when children cannot adjust to the difficulties and discomforts of tasks requiring close vision, they simply give up trying to read.

Carter and McGinnis explain how the six small muscles of each eye must coordinate precisely to focus on near objects and produce only a single mental image. At six years the "visual mechanism" is still "unstable."[54]

Luella Cole[55] and others report also that not more than 10% of five-year-olds can see any difference between "d" and "b" or "p" and "q." Not until children are eight years old can one "be perfectly certain the eyes are mature enough to avoid such confusions."

Auditory Maturity and Other Factors. As a child matures there is a progressive increase in sound discrimination. According to Carter and McGinnis,[56] this ability to differentiate similar speech sounds is considered by many investigators to be of prime importance in successful reading. If a child is unable to hear the difference in sounds, he will be unable to reproduce the sound correctly in speaking. This would also handicap him in recognizing written words, since improper pronunciation would lead him to expect a different spelling of the word. Luella Cole[57] notes specifically: "If he has normal six-year-old ears he will still be unable to distinguish consistently between the sounds of 'g' and 'k' and 'm' and 'n,' 'p' and 'b' or any other pair of related sounds."

H. G. Birch and A. Lefford[58] did not find intersensory maturity emerging until the children are at least seven or eight years of age. Joseph Wepman[59] found that in some children the combination of auditory discrimination and memory — "ability to retain and recall speech sounds" — is not well developed until the age of nine.

Maternal Deprivation. When a child is taken from home for early schooling or remains at home without loving care from someone he trusts, research says to expect mental and emotional problems which affect his learning, motivation, and behavior. John Bowlby presented evidence, formulated a statement of principle, and defined maternal deprivation in his 1951 report to the World Health Organization:

> . . . the infant and young child should experience a warm, intimate, and continuous relationship with his mother (or permanent mother-substitute) in which both find satisfaction and enjoyment. . . .

A state of affairs in which the child does not have this relationship is termed "maternal deprivation." This is a general term covering a number of different situations. Thus a child is deprived even though living at home if his mother (or permanent mother-substitute) is unable to give him the loving care small children need. Again, a child is deprived if for any reason he is removed from his mother's care.[60]

He reiterated this view nearly 20 years later, reporting that in the Western world much the commonest disturbances of attachment "are the results of too little mothering, or of mothering coming from a succession of different people." And these disturbances "can continue for weeks, months, or years" — or may be permanent.[61]

Many ES proponents believe that the young child needs social contact outside the home. There are a number of reasons to doubt that he does. Research is specific. Marcel Geber's work in Uganda demonstrates, much like Harold Skeels's, that such attention or deprivation reaches beyond the emotional responses of young children.[62] Using tests standardized by Arnold Gesell, Geber tested over 300 Uganda babies during their first year. The babies for the most part were from low-SES, tribal-oriented families in which mothers were child-centered, continually caressing, cuddling, and talking to their little ones. He found these infants to be superior to Western children in physiological maturation and coordination, adaptability and sociability, and language skills. It may be observed that African children often do mature earlier than Westerners. Yet Geber reports that in his sampling those babies from relatively high-SES Uganda families with less maternal contact but more involvement in formal training were much less mature in the above qualities than the babies of the low-SES mothers.

L. J. Yarrow also reports that "besides the retardation of development caused through emotional factors, maturation in adjustment is markedly slowed by deprivation of sensory, social, and affective stimulation when a child cannot be with his mother."[63] Bowlby adds that even partial deprivation "brings in its train acute anxiety, excessive need for love, powerful feelings of revenge, and . . . guilt and depression."[64]

The Mother's Attitude. The mother's acceptance of her role is of greatest importance in the child's development. Mary Ainsworth found

> ... significant differences ... when the mothers were grouped in terms of satisfaction with their role, whether the homemaker or the worker role. Dissatisfied mothers, both working and nonworking, reported undesirable child-rearing practices and attitudes more frequently than mothers who were satisfied with their role.[65]

Education and reassurance of parents thus become a vital concomitant of any ECD program, whether in the home or in school, whether the mother works or not, but particularly with the mother who does not have a wholesome appreciation of her role. Thus, says Bowlby, numerous direct studies

> make it plain that, when deprived of maternal care, the child's development is almost always retarded — physically, intellectually, and socially — and that symptoms of physical and mental illness may appear ... and that some children are gravely damaged for life.[66]

Some educators believe that parents are either too ignorant or obsessed with a desire for freedom to be willing to give their children the care they need for optimum development. A number of studies demonstrate that this is not necessarily so. Louise Daugherty,[67] Robert Hess and Virginia Shipman,[68] Mildred Smith,[69] Hylan Lewis,[70] and Phyllis Levenstein[71] found that parents are concerned, regardless of socioeconomic status. When Mildred Smith took study-help materials to homes and induced parental help, 90% of the homes responded, and of these 99% of the parents asked that the program be continued.

Levenstein[72] not only found generally that if approached rightly, disadvantaged mothers "take seriously the family's responsibility to lay groundwork for school learning," but also noted that their "aspirations for their children are very similar to those of middle-income mothers." The fact that the mother saw the practical teacher as less effective than she, yet sensed her own inadequacies, suggests as the more urgent role of the state the development of home education programs for adequate parenthood.

School vs. *Home*. Then should the young child be taken from home to be trained in a school? There may be cases of acute or extreme deprivation where this is necessary. Yet Bowlby insists, on the basis of many investigations, that "children thrive better in bad homes than in good institutions," and children "apparently unreasonably" are even attached to bad parents. "It must never be forgotten," Bowlby observes,

> ... that even the bad parent who neglects her child is nonetheless providing much for him. ... Except in the worst cases, she is giving him food and shelter, comforting him in distress, teaching him simple skills, and above all is providing him with that continuity of human care on which his sense of security rests.[73]

Burton Blatt and Frank Garfunkel found it necessary to reject the research hypothesis of their own study involving low-SES children who "were at least two years away from entering the first grade." They concluded that (a) the home is more influential than the school, (b) the school can do little without strong home support, (c) disadvantaged parents "are often anxious to cooperate," and (d) school organization and requirements are often "foreign" to these parents who in turn are blamed by the school for not readily accepting them.[74]

Special education would certainly appear to be indicated for many specific cases of disability such as speech, vision, hearing, cerebral palsy, severe mental retardation, and certain neuroses, psychoses and advanced emotional problems. Yet it is difficult to find research support for *generalized* early schooling as described in the California Task Force report. In fact it is difficult to understand, in the face of substantial evidence to the contrary, how educators can justify existing generalized schooling down to ages five and six, or compulsory education below age eight.

On the other hand, certain child-care needs must be met. These are not generalized needs, but are specific problems growing out of parents' inability to care for their young children, e.g., physical or psychological handicaps, ineptness, immaturity, or severe economic stress requiring the mother to work. Any lesser reason which simply accommodates a growing demand for parental "freedom" must, in terms of research findings, be considered parental dereliction. And while research may not yet always be definitive in placing the blame, there is considerable evidence that points toward maternal deprivation and early schooling as primary reasons for childhood maladjustment, motivational loss, poor retention, deterioration of attitudes, visual handicaps, and a wide variety of other physical and behavioral problems, including minimal brain dysfunction.

In summary, research and comparisons of school entry ages clearly point to the need 1) to delay any type of educational program that proposes or permits sustained high cortical effort, or strain on the visual or auditory systems, before the child is seven or eight, and for 2) a warm, continuous mother or mother-surrogate relationship (without a succession of different people) until the child is at least seven or eight.

Investigators (Daugherty, Hess and Shipman, Levenstein, Lewis, Smith, *et al.*) have shown that parents, when clearly shown their children's needs, overwhelmingly respond to them. Likewise, other researchers (Rohwer, Elkind, Husén, *et al.*) make clear that the earlier children go to school the more likely they are to develop negative attitudes toward school.

Some Practical Solutions from Research

So the closer the child's early environment can be kept to his home (or other home with a low adult-to-child ratio) which may provide a continuous warm and free growing place, the more likely his maximum development will be. And this home should neither propose nor permit such learning as violates the child's normal developmental crescendo.

Parent Education. With some of these principles in mind, Susan Gray,[75] Phyllis Levenstein,[76] David Weikart,[77] Ira Gordon,[78] and others have been experimenting with home schooling. While research does *not* indicate the need for schooling as such, there is much to be learned from these researchers toward effective parent education which can lead to appropriate pre-school environments regardless of cultural background or socioeconomic status. And indeed, if as psychiatrist J. T. Fisher infers, the state desires to save money, one of the most effective

60

ways may be to help in the development of "wholesome home life."[79]

Home Schools. Both Susan Gray and Phyllis Levenstein experimented with home schools. Levenstein describes her successful experience with such a program which she calls the "Mother-Child Home Program."[80] Because of the resistance of some mothers, particularly of low-SES families, to *teacher* visitation, she calls the professional visiting personnel "toy demonstrators." Gray notes that "the potential [of the home] is sometimes difficult to tap but it is there."[81]

Such programs may well provide a *modus operandi* for such child care as is really necessary and avoid heavy capital and operating costs which California's present proposal is certain to bring.

There is now a sufficient research base to suggest several procedures in lieu of early schooling as commonly conceived. The state should:

1. Carefully restudy the needs of its children in the light of research. It should realize that research provides no more reason for early schooling for all four-year-olds simply because they have intelligence than it does for early sex for twelve-year-olds simply because they have generated reproductive equipment. They must await the development of balancing factors. Great damage may be avoided.

2. Embark upon a massive parent education program, assisting first those who are in greatest need, but educating all parents, by all media available, concerning the developmental needs of their children. Parents who are neither handicapped nor forced to work should be helped to better understand their privileges and responsibilities as parents, to see that "freedom" sacrificed now will bring larger benefits later.

3. Make such provisions as are necessary for all exceptional children: the severely handicapped or disabled or others requiring special education. Even here research indicates that programs should be kept as close to the home as practicable.

4. Take an interest in providing care for the relatively normal children of handicapped parents or those forced to work, by selecting homes nearby, if possible, as home-schools. Those homes and mothers (or other adults) who are qualified would be selected for their warmth, continuity, aptness for children, and dedication to their welfare. These may

well be operated as enlightened care centers on a small adult-to-child ratio (normally not more than 1:4 or 1:5), and might be subsidized by the state where parents cannot meet the costs. Traveling teachers on state or local payroll could monitor these home-schools to see that they were provided adequate materials and equipment and to coordinate them with existing ADC and other social service programs.

Conclusion

It would be hard to find an area of educational research more definitive than that on child development and school entry age. It is difficult to see how planners can review this evidence and conclude that four- or five-year-olds generally should be in school, much less three-year-olds.

Goals of maximum development of the child are generally sound, but research says that California's proposed way to reach them can only lead to greater trouble. In short, it appears that California's planners, and others with similar plans, have either overlooked or ignored or seriously misinterpreted responsible research. If such evidence is questioned, then further research should be undertaken before legislating in areas so delicate as the young child's mind. Meanwhile, scientific evidence comparing the validity of the home and the school as early childhood environments clearly favors the home.

It is hoped that the California legislature and the State Board of Education will ponder these facts and that other legislators and educators — federal, state, and local — will also consider carefully the dangers of veering from the guidelines which research has supplied.

1. Benjamin S. Bloom, *Stability and Change in Human Characteristics.* New York: John Wiley & Sons, 1964, p. 88.
2. "Report of the Task Force on Early Childhood Education." Sacramento, Calif.: Wilson Riles, State Superintendent of Public Instruction, and the State Board of Education, November 26, 1971, p. 29.
3. *Ibid.,* p. 1.
4. *Ibid.,* p. 1.
5. *Ibid.,* p. 10.
6. Harold M. Skeels, *Adult Status of Children with Contrasting Early Life Experiences: A Follow-Up Study.* Monograph of the Society for Research in Child Development, No. 105. Chicago: University of Chicago Press, 1966, pp. 1-68.
7. White House Conference on Children and Youth, 1970, *Report to the President.* Washington, D.C.: U.S. Government Printing Office, 1970, pp. 97-98.

8. Education Commission of the States, *Early Childhood Development, Alternatives for Program Development in the States.* Denver, Colo.: The Commission, 1971.

9. *Ibid.,* p. 3.

10. *Ibid.,* p. 40.

11. Earl S. Schaefer, "Toward a Revolution in Education: A Perspective from Child Development Research," *The National Elementary Principal,* September, 1971, p. 18.

12. William D. Rohwer, Jr., "On Attaining the Goals of Early Childhood Education." (Paper presented at OEO Conference on Research in Early Childhood Education, Washington, D.C., 1970.)

13. *Ibid.,* pp. 1-5, 17-19.

14. U.S. Commission on Civil Rights, *Racial Isolation in the Public Schools,* Vol. 1. Washington, D.C.: Government Printing Office, 1967, p. 138.

15. Westinghouse and Ohio University, "The Impact of Head Start: An Evaluation of the Effects of Head Start on Children's Cognitive and Affective Development," in *The Disadvantaged Child,* Joe L. Frost and Glenn R. Hawkes, editors. Boston: Houghton Mifflin, 1970, pp. 197-201.

16. Nila B. Smith, "Early Reading: Viewpoints," in *Early Childhood Crucial Years for Learning,* Margaret Rasmussen, editor. Washington, D.C.: Association for Childhood Education International, 1966, pp. 61-62.

17. Willard C. Olson, *NEA Journal,* October, 1947, pp. 502-03.

18. H. M. Davis, "Don't Push Your School Beginners," *Parent's Magazine,* October, 1952, pp. 140-41.

19. Inez B. King, "Effect of Age of Entrance into Grade 1 Upon Achievement in Elementary School," *Elementary School Journal,* February, 1955, pp. 331-36.

20. B. U. Keister, "Reading Skills Acquired by Five-Year Old Children," *Elementary School Journal,* April, 1941, pp. 587-96.

21. Marion Carroll, "Academic Achievement and Adjustment of Underage and Overage Third-Graders," *The Journal of Educational Research,* February, 1964, p. 290.

22. Joseph W. Halliwell and Belle W. Stein, "A Comparison of the Achievement of Early and Late Starters in Reading Related and Non-Reading Related Areas in Fourth and Fifth Grades," *Elementary English,* October, 1964, pp. 631-39, 658.

23. Richard S. Hampleman, "A Study of the Comparative Reading Achievements of Early and Late School Starters," *Elementary English,* May, 1959, pp. 331-34.

24. Elizabeth Bigelow, "School Progress of Underage Children," *Elementary School Journal,* November, 1934, pp. 186-92.

25. King, *op. cit.*

26. Lowell Burney Carter, "The Effect of Early School Entrance on the Scholastic Achievement of Elementary School Children in the Austin Public Schools," *Journal of Educational Research,* October, 1956, pp. 91-103.

27. Clyde J. Baer, "The School Progress and Adjustment of Underage and Overage Students," *Journal of Educational Psychology,* February, 1958, pp. 17-19.

28. Donald Ross Green and Sadie Vee Simmons, "Chronological Age and School Entrance," *Elementary School Journal,* October, 1962, pp. 41-47.

29. Margaret Ellen Gott, *The Effect of Age Differences at Kindergarten Entrance on Achievement and Adjustment in Elementary School.* (Doctoral dissertation, University of Colorado, 1963.)

30. John J. Forrester, "At What Age Should Children Start School?," *The School Executive,* March, 1955, pp. 80-81.

31. Paul E. Mawhinny, "We Gave Up on Early Entrance," *Michigan Education Journal,* May, 1964, p. 25.

32. Arnold Gesell and Frances L. Ilg, *The Child from Five to Ten.* New York: Harper and Brothers, 1946, pp. 388-89.

33. Rohwer, *op. cit.,* p. 37.

34. James T. Fisher and Lowell S. Hawley, *A Few Buttons Missing.* Philadelphia: J.B. Lippincott Company, 1951, pp. 13-14.

35. Penuel H. Corbin (master's thesis in pediatrics, University of Minnesota, 1951. NA Med Library, W4A, 9C791E, 1951, C1); Jean M. Nicholson *et al., EEG and Clinical Neurophysiology,* Vol. 8, 1956, p. 342; G. C. Lairy *et al., EEG and Clinical Neurophysiology,* Vol. 14, 1962, pp. 778-79; W. E. Nelson, *Textbook of Pediatrics.* Chicago: Saunders Co., 1967, p. 1088; David Metcalf and Kent Jordan, "EEG Ontogenesis in Normal Children," in *Drugs, Development, and Cerebral Function,* W. Lynn Smith, editor. Springfield, Ill.: Charles C. Thomas, 1972, pp. 127-28.

36. A. Davis, *Regional Development of the Brain in Early Life.* Cambridge, Mass.: Harvard University Press, 1964.

37. M. Bortner and H. G. Birch, "Perceptual and Perceptual Motor Dissociation in Cerebral Palsied Children," *Journal of Nervous and Mental Diseases,* 1960, pp. 103-8.

38. H. G. Birch and M. Bortner, "Perceptual and Perceptual Motor Dissociation in Brain-damaged Patients," *Journal of Nervous and Mental Diseases,* 1960, p. 49.

39. Willis F. Overton, "Piaget's Theory of Intellectual Development and Progressive Education," in *Yearbook of the Association for Supervision and Curriculum Development, 1972.* Washington, D.C.: The Association, pp. 95-103.

40. *Ibid.,* p. 103.

41. Millie Almy, Edward Chittenden, and Paula Miller, *Young Children's Thinking.* New York: Teachers College Press, Columbia University, 1966.

42. *Ibid.,* p. 99.

43. Rohwer, *op. cit.,* pp. 7-8.

44. Fisher, *loc. cit.*

45. Torsten Husen, *International Study of Achievement in Mathematics,* Vol. II. Uppsala: Almquist and Wiksells, 1967.

46. D. Elkind, "Piagetian and Psychometric Conceptions of Intelligence," *Harvard Educational Review,* 1969, pp. 319-37.

47. James C. Chalfant and Margaret A. Scheffelin, *Central Processing Dysfunctions in Children: A Review of Research* (Ninds Monograph 9). Washington, D.C.: U.S. Department of Health, Education, and Welfare, 1969.

48. Luella Cole, *The Improvement of Reading, with Special Reference to Remedial Instruction.* New York: Farrar and Rinehart, Inc., 1938.

49. Stanley Krippner, "On Research in Visual Training and Reading Disability," *Journal of Learning Disabilities,* February, 1971, p. 16.

50. Chalfant and Scheffelin, *op. cit.,* p. 23.

51. Moselle Boland, "Going to School Too Soon Blamed for Eye Troubles," *Houston Chronicle* (Texas), April 30, 1963.

52. Ruth Strang, *Diagnostic Teaching of Reading.* New York: McGraw Hill, 1964, pp. 164-65.

53. Homer L. J. Carter and Dorothy J. McGinnis, *Diagnosis and Treatment of the Disabled Reader.* London: MacMillan, Collier-MacMillan Ltd., 1970.

54. *Ibid.,* p. 48.

55. Cole, *op. cit.,* p. 284.

56. Carter and McGinnis, *op. cit.,* pp. 51-52.

57. Cole, *op. cit.,* p. 282.

58. H. G. Birch and A. Lefford, "Intersensory Development in Children," *Monographs of the Society for Research in Child Development,* No. 89, 1963.

59. Joseph M. Wepman, "The Modality Concept — Including a Statement of the Perceptual and Conceptual Levels of Learning," in *Perception and Reading,* Proceedings of the Twelfth Annual Convention, International Reading Association, Vol. 12, Part 4, pp. 1-6. Newark, Dela.: The Association, 1968.

60. John Bowlby, *Maternal Care and Mental Health.* Geneva: World Health Organization, 1952.

61. John Bowlby, *Attachment and Loss,* Vol. I. New York: Attachment Basic Books, 1969.

62. Marcel Geber, "The Psycho-Motor Development of African Children in the First Year, and the Influence of Maternal Behavior," *Journal of Social Psychology,* 1958, pp. 185-95.

63. L. J. Yarrow, "Separation from Parents During Early Childhood," in *Child Development Research* I, Martin and Lois Hoffman, editors. New York: Russell Sage Foundation, 1964, p. 127.

64. Bowlby, *op. cit.* p. 12.

65. Mary D. Ainsworth *et al.,* "The Effects of Maternal Deprivation: A Review of Findings and Controversy in the Context of Research Strategy," in *Deprivation of Maternal Care, a Reassessment of Its Effects.* New York: Schocken Books, 1966, p. 117.

66. Bowlby, *op. cit.,* p. 15.

67. Louise G. Daugherty, *NEA Journal,* December, 1963, pp. 18-20.

68. Robert D. Hess and Virginia C. Shipman, "Maternal Attitudes Toward the School and the Role of Pupil: Some Social Class Comparisons," in *Developing Programs for the Educationally Disadvantaged,* A. Harry Passow, editor. New York: Teachers College Press, Columbia University, 1968, pp. 127-28.

69. Mildred Beatty Smith, "School and Home: Focus on Achievement," in *Developing Programs for the Educationally Disadvantaged,* A. Harry Passow, editor. New York: Teachers College Press, Columbia University, 1968, pp. 106-7.

70. Hylan Lewis, "Culture, Class, Poverty, and Urban Schooling," in *Reaching the Disadvantaged Learner,* A. Harry Passow, editor. New York: Teachers College Press, Columbia University, 1970, p. 24.

71. Phyllis Levenstein, "Learning Through (and From) Mothers," *Childhood Education,* December, 1971, pp. 130-34.

72. *Ibid.,* p. 132.

73. Bowlby, *op. cit.* (fn. 60), pp. 67-68.

74. Burton Blatt and Frank Garfunkel, *The Education of Intelligence.* Washington, D.C.: The Council for Exceptional Children, 1969.

75. Susan W. Gray, "The Child's First Teacher," *Childhood Education,* December, 1971, pp. 127-29.

76. Levenstein, *op. cit.*

77. David P. Weikart, "Learning Through Parents: Lessons for Teachers," *Childhood Education,* December, 1971, pp. 135-37.

78. Ira J. Gordon, "The Beginnings of the Self: The Problem of the Nurturing Environment," *Phi Delta Kappan,* March, 1969, pp. 375-78.

79. Fisher, *op. cit.,* pp. 13-14.

80. Levenstein, *op. cit.,* p. 134.

81. *Ibid.,* p. 127.

KINDERGARTEN IS TOO LATE

By ESTHER P. EDWARDS, *associate professor, The Eliot-Pearson Department of Child Study, Tufts University.*

EDUCATION of the young child has come with a rush and a swirl out of the quiet backwater where it sat so long in its own reflection and has swept into the mainstream of American concern and controversy. At last we are hit hard with the fact that young children's experiences in their first years are of crucial creative importance for their total future lives. The heredity-environment dilemma having been laid to rest with the recognition that both are significant in continual interaction, we are ready to accept the thesis that intelligence is not fixed once and for all at birth but can be shaped by experience. We are just beginning to look seriously at the kinds of stimuli we provide for children. What should these be? When should they occur? How should they be presented? By whom? In what setting?

But what is the basis for this growing awareness that the early years are of incalculable significance? Any attempt to give a capsule explanation will be an oversimplification; yet the attempt must be made.

The word "cognition"—knowing—became respectable in American psychology in the Fifties. Piaget in Switzerland and Vygotsky in Russia had shown as long ago as the Twenties and Thirties that human intellectual functioning could not be sufficiently explained in any purely mechanical fashion. American psychology of the ruling behaviorist school came more reluctantly to recognize that thinking, learning, and behaving as we know them cannot be reduced wholly to a direct stimulus-response hookup.

What gives an intelligent adult the ability to focus his attention on *this* rather than on *that*? What allows him some degree of choice, of voluntary control? What gets him out from under the domination of his environment—not always, not entirely, but in part, and part of the time? Why can the absorbed reader fail even to hear the clock tick in the corner, the rain on the roof, the hiss of the fire, yet leap to instant attention when his child cries out softly in its sleep? Why, and how, have we human beings attained waking consciousness, that demanding burden and endless de-

SATURDAY REVIEW, June 15, 1968, pp. 68-70 ff.

light? What gives us alone of all life on this planet symbolic language—created, shared, used to build and sustain our cloud-palace cultures that float from generation to generation on the mind of man?

D. O. Hebb of McGill University has shown that there is a relation between the level of complexity of a species, the slowness and difficulty of early learning in its members, and the ease and speed with which they can deal at maturity with complex ideas. Whatever an ant learns—if it learns anything at all, functioning as it does chiefly through instinct—may be learned in the first moments of its life, learned once and for all. Thereafter it functions well as an ant, but with no possibility of varying its set pattern. "Go to the ant, thou sluggard"—but not for help with calculus. A rat reared in darkness, Hebb tells us, is capable of a selective visual discrimination, definitely learned, after a total visual experience of less than fifteen minutes; within an hour or so it has learned to function as well as its peer reared normally. A rat is an ingenious and canny beast, but calculus is not its meat either.

The young human creature spends months and years completing the intellectual structures which at his birth are present only as possibilities. Slowly he develops, with little visible change from hour to hour or day to day. His early learning is more laborious than that of neurologically simpler creatures. It is not only that the baby's period of development is longer than the ant's or the rat's, but that the human child is involved in a more difficult task. So difficult, indeed, that his first learning is less efficient, less fluent than any other creature's. It has been said: "The longest journey in the world is the journey from the back of the head to the front of the head." The infant is building the pathways that will make this journey at first possible, then easy, then lightning swift and marvelously effective. What pathways these, through what trackless jungle? Connected and interconnected systems of neurons, branching and coiling back, going off in new directions and returning, making patterned ave-nues through the forest of nine billion nerve cells that lies between the incoming sensory areas of the brain and the outgoing motor centers. Without this development, conceptual thought is forever impossible.

So at maturity the intelligent adult, whose potential has thus been translated into reality, perceives with understanding, speaks and thinks symbolically, solves problems, categorizes, appreciates, and does all this with an instantaneous flash of insight that is alone of its kind in nature. He deals conceptually with the universe—a universe he first had to construct for himself. How does he do this? As each of us must, he has built it during his earliest years out of the myriad perceptual cues coming into the nervous system from "out there"— cues impinging continually on nerve endings, but meaningless until his system has built the structures that allow a reading of the signals and a response to them.

THIS is what the infant in his cradle is doing. We adults, rushing about harassed and busy, look at the baby and think: "How restful—to be fed, kept warm and clean, to have nothing to do but play with a toe, eat, cry a little, sleep. . . ." But the infant lying there is building his universe, and building himself. He must do both of these things, do them *then*, do them *at once* (for one is the converse of the other), or never do them at all. Never to do them is never to develop, to be cut off, to be a thing and not a man.

How construct a universe? The newborn baby possesses a nervous system which already receives and responds reflexively to signals from the outer world —to light, sound, temperature, pressure, and other stimuli. But though he responds through reflex action, the baby does not yet understand the signals: he cannot *read* them. He must learn to interconnect sets of cues—to see what he hears, for instance, and to learn that a light and a sound may describe one and the same object. So he begins to define reality. He must develop ability to deal with more and more signals at once. In time, perceptual cues gain meaning: the baby has begun to know what they signify. Memory, judgment, intention all stem from this moment in his intellectual life. First he acts as a purely physical being and learns how to solve problems by means of bodily acts. Then he learns to represent physical action by mental symbol, and thought has begun.

His first symbols are images, pictures which allow him to hang on to fleeting reality ("I remember my mother's face though she is out of the room"). Then the child learns a word, and another, and another, and begins to put words together. At eight months, or a year, he has begun to grasp the shorthand which allows him to hold in his head the whole of reality and to manipulate it, to solve the problems it sets him, through mental operations. Until he is five or six or older, the chief intellectual task of his life will be the creation of a symbolic vocabulary, or several of them (words, numbers images, musical notes), which become the medium of his life as a human being.

How vital this is to human development is implied by the linguists' suggestion that the supremely difficult feat of building language recognition and response which takes place during the first years of life can occur because there is a built-in neurological mechanism for language learning present in every normal human organism. But like the image on the sensitized negative, this potential will not appear as reality unless the proper circumstances develop it. Experience—the right experience—is essential.

Heredity and environment interact. Hereditary possibilities are shaped by the influences that only human culture can provide; they are potentialities that must be developed while the young neurological organism is still rapidly growing, malleable, open to stimulus. If the "critical periods in learning" hypothesis applies to human beings (as we know it does to other creatures—dogs, for instance—and as evidence increasingly indicates it does to us), then the right experience must come at the right time, or the potential must remain forever unrealized.

Benjamin Bloom of the University of Chicago implies this when he says that the early environment, during the first five to seven years of life, is the significant one for intellectual development. This is why we are finally realizing that the young child's experience is of indelible importance, not only for his emotional life, but also in the formation of that aspect of man which is perhaps most crucially his own—his sapience.

If all this can be accepted as in some degree reflecting truth, where are we? We are at a point where we can see why education for the young child can matter enormously. It matters not as much as the family. The family is basic. But the good family is good precisely because it provides so much of the young child's education. Still, other appropriate experiences can add to what even the best family can do.

For the child born into a family which cannot give him what he needs in emotional security or intellectual stimulus, such experiences may act as a lifeline to essential development. What early education is offered to what children becomes, therefore, of first importance. Perhaps the right choices here can make a difference comparable to the release of nuclear energy—a release of human potential energizing our whole society.

This sense that the choices matter tremendously is why the present debate as to what constitutes good education for young children is more a battle than a scholarly discussion: Montessori—or not; "Teach your child to read at two"—or don't; imaginative play as the focus of the preschool experience vs. structured cognitive stimulation. Every aspect of the preschool is up for reconsideration, defended with zeal, attacked with fury. Partisanship is prevalent, the grounds for decision-making uncertain.

Part of this malaise stems from the attempt of psychologists and teachers to create activities appropriate for the thousands of urban — and rural — slum children who have come into preschool classes through such programs as Head Start. Once these children would never have seen the inside of a nursery school classroom. Now they are here. Teachers are responsible for them. And teachers

67

have found that their tried and true techniques don't work with these children. How do you make contact with a nonverbal, uncooperative, frightened, dirty, doleful, thumb-sucking four-year-old dragged to school by a slightly older sister who can't tell you anything about him except that his name is Buzzer?

So it is perfectly true that many Head Start programs are not making a significant difference in the intellectual capacities or the academic readiness of children thrust into them for a brief six to eight weeks the summer before they go to "real" school. Head Start has been oversold in an effort to enlist citizen support: "It will bring the slum child up to the level of his middle-class age mates in one quick and easy exposure." That was a line that salved the taxpayer's conscience with a minimum of damage to his bank account. But it was a lie. No one with the faintest understanding of the realities of mental, social, and emotional growth ever thought it could do any such thing. Head Start may be better than nothing (in some cases even this is questionable), but it is vastly less good—and *less* than is needed.

The solution, however, is not to damn previous educational goals and means across the board. New circumstances and children with new needs do not prove that the established ways of going at the education of young children are valueless—only that we now are dealing with a wider range of children and must supplement the older ways with different aims, content, and techniques. We need a more varied repertoire. We need to know when to do what, and why. That's all. But that's a tall order.

THE situation, then, calls for a plea to the embattled camps in preschool education to beat a few swords into plowshares, to leave their respective strongholds, to stop maintaining that each holds all the truth, and to begin to share questions and insights. A vast amount of hostility can be dissipated if we can accept two basic truths:

1) There is no one method of teaching young children which is ideal for all

of them. Like the rest of us, they differ in temperament, in background, in needs, in readiness for this or that experience. As children vary, so must educational approaches.

2) Human beings are totalities: they have bodies, and they have minds; they exist in social contexts within which they act and feel. Small children are people, and their life in school needs to be a whole life in which physical, emotional, intellectual, and social aspects of the self are all given adequate nourishment. It is wrong to leave out any major segment, though emphasis can and should vary with the particular set of circumstances.

Perhaps the first step is acceptance of the individual differences among children. Some of these are genetic in origin; others are caused by environmental accidents. Within groups of children from similar cultural and social strata are wide ranges in health, energy, temperament, aptitudes, and innate potential. Even among children in the same family this is so. Dozens of factors can affect the quality of early experience. One child's mother was sick when he was at a vulnerable stage; another child had an illness that required hospitalization; for a third, everything went along smoothly and success bred success. The gap between one socioeconomic group and another magnifies the differences. The early life histories of children living within a few blocks of each other in an American city may be as remote from one another as is the Arabia Desert from Manhattan. How foolish then to think that any one approach can be the best, much less the only one for such diverse bits of mortality, so variously shaped by their three or four years of life.

Proponents of cognitive preschool experience have recently leveled severe criticism at the less-structured types of nursery school curricula. "Only play," they say, "only messing around with finger paints . . ." The Montessori schools point to their abundance of graded materials which can be used by the individual child to move step by step from growing mastery of sensory-motor skills to a knowledge of letters, of numbers, of ordering and labeling. The child's attention span increases. He learns to work independently, systematically, following a coherent pattern established by materials and setting. For children from the often chaotic homes of poverty this may mean a significant gain.

O. K. Moore, of the University of Pittsburgh, uses his "talking typewriter" (actually a total language environment, rather than a typewriter in an ordinary sense) as a tool whereby children as young as three years have learned to read and write in the natural way in which they learn to talk—inductively—with personal choice of activity and pace. Carl Bereiter and Siegfried Engelmann, formerly of the University of Illinois and now of the Ontario Institute for Studies in Education, have created what is perhaps at the moment the most controversial program in preschool education. It has been called a "pressure-cooker approach." In this setting, under direct academic force-feeding, groups of four- and five-year-olds from lower-class families are taught verbal and number patterns:

This is a ball.
This is a piece of clay.
Is this a ball?
Yes, this is a ball./No, this is not a ball.
This is a what? This is a ball. . . .

The aim of this exercise is to develop the ability not merely to label "ball" and "clay," but to know the use and significance of such essential carriers of meaning as the simple word "not." Verbal skills, numbers, and reading are taught. Drill is the medium. The adults unashamedly pressure children to learn. Hopefully their own desire to achieve competence will be fired by the sense that they are doing something tough and important, but praise, exhortation, and tangible rewards and punishment are freely used. The atmopshere is intense. These children have no time to lose. They must move into the world created by adult society. The whole thrust of the program is to make this possible for them.

These and other preschool programs focused on cognitive development add a dimension that was underplayed if not lacking in the older nursery schools, organized as these were around the child's social and emotional growth, his creative activity in the graphic arts and in music, and (with varying degrees of effectiveness) around introductory experiences in those areas recognized at a higher level as the basic disciplines (literature, mathematics, sciences, social sciences). Such a curriculum assumed that the young child entering preschool brought with him a fund of organized sensory and motor learnings. His language development was already well under way, chiefly through many months of interaction with an intelligent, loving, verbal, and attentive mother. Often what he needed most was to be a child among children in an environment which allowed him to explore and to play. He had already been molded and stimulated by the adult world, represented by his vitally concerned parents, and every day he went home to continue this part of his education.

But the Head Start children come from homes which have failed to nourish them in health, in emotional stability, in intellect. They need desperately to develop language, to learn to think. For these children such a program as Bereiter and Engelmann's can perhaps give the all-essential forward thrust without which nothing else can have meaning. They come to school late in the day to establish basic learnings. Their tendency is not to listen, not to focus. They know in their bones that no one is paying attention to them. They have to undo false beginnings. From a mile behind the starting line they have to start the race their more fortunate peers are already running. Under such circumstances, if pressured instruction will get them ready for school, blessings on it and let them have it.

But young children are being made ready for more than the first grade, and there is more to them than a brain, however vital that may be. William C. Rhodes of the National Institute of Mental Health writes in *Behavioral Science Frontiers in Education*:

The imposition of culture upon the child, without relating the culture to his inner substance, is forcing a foreign body into his being . . . He will only mobilize defenses against the culture in an attempt to neutralize its harsh, abrasive denials of what he is.

This we must not make children do by being too demanding in our concern for cognitive growth. There are other values also of major importance.

Maya Pines, in her October 15, 1967, *New York Times Magazine* article "Slum Children Must Make Up for Lost Time," quotes disparagingly from the Head Start *Guide to a Daily Program,* which advocates that children:

> . . . learn to work and play independently, at ease about being away from home, and able to accept help and direction from adults . . . . learn to live effectively with other children, and to value one's own rights and the rights of others . . . . develop self-identity and a view of themselves as having competence and worth.

This is not mere cant. It is not necessarily accomplished, but these are worthy goals. Anyone who has worked with young children, whether they be culturally deprived or not, knows it to be the most sober of cold facts that such children do need to develop independence, social competence, and a sense of self. Until they do, their growth toward other sorts of learning is enfeebled. The child who lacks adequate ego development neither cares nor dares to learn.

Hopefully children can learn both to use their minds and to become more fully human. Social and intellectual growth are not mutually exclusive. The valid criticism of the Bereiter and Engelmann program is not made on the ground that it gives drill in cognitive patterns, but that it gives little else except such drill, in a setting where teacher imposes and child conforms. This is too narrow a segment of experience. It ignores vital components of the totality that is a child. What the end result for these children after some years will be, no one knows. But one must wonder whether so intense a focus on

the growth of knowledge and the means of its verification will not diminish other aspects of personality.

Preschool educators criticize the Bereiter and Engelmann program because of its frank admission of dependence on rewards (cookies, praise) and its use of punishment (physical coercion, isolation in unpleasant surroundings). These are gross inducements toward learning. If they are used only to prime the pump, as is recommended, then one may consider them symptomatic not of the program so much as of the damage already done to the child by his stultifying early experience, a damage demanding heroic measures to overcome. But if they must remain in the teacher's repertoire, if they are not left behind in favor of satisfaction from the achievement itself, then they form an indictment of the meaningfulness of this approach to children. A learning that takes place only when the teacher doles out candy or brandishes a switch (hypothetical or not) is a learning without intrinsic satisfaction. Performance can be evoked temporarily through pressure, but will not last. This is one touchstone of valid education.

Bᴜᴛ why must we wait so long, and then resort to pressure? Already there are several experimental programs which are attempting significant intervention before the age of two in the lives of "high risk" children (the younger brothers and sisters of academically retarded children from deprived homes, or children from markedly nonverbal backgrounds). Appropriate education must be made available to every child as soon as he can benefit from it. We know that as early as eighteen months disadvantaged children start trailing their middle-class age mates in tests of general intelligence and language development. Already the subtle undermining brought about by inadequate experience has begun. It is simply not true that all lower-class children are lacking in potential compared with their middle-class peers. Some, no doubt, are. But for many, if not most, the deficit that so early becomes visible is more likely caused after conception by various environmental lacks (poor nutri-

70

tion, the mother's ill health during the baby's intrauterine life, and inadequate sensory-motor stimulation after birth). Such lacks can be reversed, and they ought to be.

We are going to have to make educational stimulation available from babyhood on for the children whose families cannot provide it for them. Whether tutors should go into the homes, whether children should be brought into carefully planned, well staffed *educational* (as distinct from baby-sitting day-care) programs, we do not now know. Experiments going on in several places in the country should help us decide. But however we do it, intervention by the age of eighteen months should be the rule for the children of deprived inner-city or poor rural families. As it is now, few children reach Head Start before the age of four. We are not making use of the golden period when we can most easily and effectively work with children without using pressure, without having to force on them a culture already so foreign that it cannot be learned unless, as William Rhodes says, we make the child "give up completely the content of the self." We are not coming to children when there is still time to help them build effective roadways through the neurological labyrinth, to help them create a universe rich, diverse, satisfying. We can, if we will. And we must.

We must build programs designed to amplify the child's world as the middle-class child's parents do, when he is still an infant in the crib. We must do this not to cut the lower-class child off from his home and his family, but to assist his overburdened mother, to help make the family milieu better for the child. We must create kinds of stimulation that become a constant part of his life, involving him daily in meaningful interactions, just as the child from a more fortunate home interacts with his mother every day for years, until the time that the thousands of exchanges, each modifying and adding to his understanding, give him mastery of thought and speech. We know that this is the most deeply meaningful education for the one-, two-, or three-year-old child. We must try to approach it for every child.

Such special interventions are not yet widely available. Large numbers of deprived children remain, in a sense, accident victims in need of first aid. Perhaps the Bereiter and Engelmann type of program is that first aid. Perhaps it is the best solution to an unfortunate situation. Perhaps it can build in children who have missed out on the normal growth toward competence some of the abilities they would have developed more gradually had their backgrounds been more intellectually stimulating. Perhaps it cannot. We do not know, but surely it is worth trying, with the sobering thought that force-feeding programs, though they rescue the starving, do not make up for deficits already incurred.

But because people who have been hurt need first aid is no reason to prescribe first aid as the all-important component of everyone's experience. Because deprived children may benefit from intensive work in the cognitive areas where they lack development does not mean that a broader, more inclusive type of program which meets the equally real needs of the intellectually advanced child deserves ridicule. What we really want is to bring into our repertoire a much wider range of experience from which we may select intelligently those aspects which are most useful and appropriate for each group of children—indeed for each child.

Here we take issue with Miss Pines's description of the "established" nursery school, quoted from her *New York Times Magazine* article but similar in tone to what she writes in her new book, *Revolution in Learning: The Years from Birth to Six*. Miss Pines states:

> Middle-class nursery schools operate on the theory that they can directly influence only the child's emotional and social development—not his mental growth. They assume that if they build up a shy child's confidence, or redirect an angry one's aggression, the child's intellectual development will take care of itself, following a sort of built-in timetable. Therefore they concentrate on teaching children to "get along with

others" and "adjust to the group."

Undoubtedly this neglect of the cognitive dimension is true of many preschools, but it is not true of the good ones, and certainly it is false to the philosophy behind early education. It overlooks a range of experience which is very present when young children are well taught by intelligent teachers who are themselves cultivated and concerned people. Children do not get over being shy; they do not learn to redirect their anger or interact with others in a vacuum. They are able to develop as people, in the social and emotional sense, most effectively when their minds are occupied with challenging ideas. "Why does the ice cube melt? What is *melting*? Why does the wind blow, and what is air, and what are the words that let me talk about it? How can I draw a picture of what I felt like when I was in the hospital? What is a dream? Why am I afraid? How many nickels do we need to buy fresh food for our guppies if a box of fish food costs a quarter? What makes my baby brother cry at night and wake me up? How can a rocket go around the world so fast? When is tomorrow? How far is far?" These, and the millions of other questions small children ask every day, are *intellectual* challenges. The preschool exists to help children formulate them, examine them, and, in some degree, answer them. It can only do this by giving children some of the multiplicity of interlocking experiences through which they can move slowly toward mature answers. As nursery-school children they will not arrive, but they make progress.

BECAUSE in the past the intellectual component of the preschool has been implicit rather than explicit, this does not mean that it has been lacking. It means that the skilled preschool teacher has done a good job only when she has turned every experience to the benefit of intellectual growth as much as to social or emotional growth. It has given her the task of picking up the children's leads and building her program about these, on the presumption that children are readiest to learn in areas where they already show interest.

Let us not be so foolish as to say that the established nursery school curriculum—if it is taught well—lacks intellectual content, or that it ignores children's growth toward cognitive ability, for it does not. It has been subtle in its approach to these. Perhaps it has been too subtle to allow the critics to recognize the presence of these strands of experience, but not too subtle for children to learn from them—provided the children were ready to do so.

But let us also admit that children who have lacked the requisite preparatory growth are *not* ready for such a program and need something else, something with a more explicit structure, something which is geared specifically to their level of attainment and their deficits. If these children are not always to be accident victims, they need educational intervention years sooner than we are giving it to most of them now. But in trying to do this, we must also bear in mind that to teach is not to bulldoze. Nonverbal, immature, dirty Buzzer is still a person, not a thing to be obtusely shoved into any mold we choose. This is why we need teachers to create programs that as yet do not exist, programs which can combine structured cognitive stimulation with full respect for the inalienable right of each human being to be himself.

LET us admit, also, that when we create these new approaches to cognitive growth, they may also be able to add something vital to the multiple stimuli offered by the middle-class nursery school. To object to an exclusive focus on structured intellectual learning for the middle-class child is not to say that he cannot gain from some of it. No one is talking in terms of taking the bloom off frail butterfly wings. Children who have learned how to learn are eager and resilient, and gobble up new information, skills, and insights in every conceivable way. If they are given some leeway to choose those aspects of a program on which they will spend most of their time, they can only benefit from encountering a wider range of possibilities. Teachers should know all the materials—the fullest spectrum of approaches—and should not be afraid to use them.

We are wasting time and energy, good humor and understanding, in opposing each other. No school of thought has all the light. There is no one ideal approach to learning for all young children. Instead, there are many possible variations of emphasis which can make the preschool experience maximally valuable for a wide range of children from differing family backgrounds, social strata, and levels of development. Let's stop this fruitless squabbling and instead fight ignorance (our own as well as that of others) and the limitations to children's potential growth, however these may occur. Let's be grateful for every addition to the armament of techniques and tools which we can use to help children. Let us try to find out how best to employ each approach: when, with whom, for what reasons, under what circumstances. And for heaven's sake, let's get going.

For Better Results —
a Full-Day Kindergarten

Harry B. Gorton
District Superintendent
Penn-Trafford School District
Harrison City, Pennsylvania
Richard L. Robinson
Assistant Superintendent
Penn-Trafford School District

E DUCATORS are slow to change, or even to examine too closely new ideas which might alter the traditional patterns in which they have worked for generations. The impact of Federal Funds has helped to break some resistance to change by requiring the application of innovative methods to qualify for funding. However, local districts need to take a critical look at their obligation to research and to bring about change in the public schools with the express goal of improving educational patterns in the United States.

The Traditional Pattern

Kindergarten has always been considered as a transitional period to help the child adjust from the relaxed atmosphere of the home to the structured discipline of the first-grade classroom. This theory has resulted in a program of "play" time which is almost completely activity oriented. The over-protective parent has helped to perpetuate this pattern and to keep the time element limited to a half-day of school. Educators have abetted the parental thinking by mouthing such theories as: "The five-year-old is not ready for formal learning." "We don't want to interfere with first-grade work." "The child will be too tired to spend more than a half-day in school." "He needs his nap."

Little research has been done in the United States to test the validity of these arguments for the half-day kindergarten. However, the Head Start programs of recent years and the European policy of starting formal education at four or five years of age point up the fact that learning can take place at an earlier age and that a small child can adapt to the change in time. The ever-increasing scope of human knowledge, and the core of detail that a child must acquire at an earlier age, require that educators consider exposing the child to the basic elements of reading and mathematics at an earlier age.

A New Concept

In recent years, there has been an acceptance of the idea that some academic training could be started before first grade and so the readiness programs have gradually been worked into many kindergarten curriculums. This program however is very inadequate in meeting the real needs; this is where the full-day kindergarten could fit. An adjustment period to the regimen of the classroom is needed; therefore, the present activity-centered program will be continued, but

EDUCATION, 1968, Vol. 89, No. 3, pp. 217-221.

it would be changed to meet different goals than some of the activities carried on in the present kindergarten program.

Creative Activity

Equipment used for individual or group exercise would require creative rather than the merely physical, reaction of the child. Swings, slides, and seesaws would have little space in this new program. Mr. Asher B. Etkes, president of the Playground Corporation of America, said to the staff of the Lacey, Washington School District:

> "Five basic characteristics are exhibited in child play: (1) uninhibitedness, (2) imagination, (3) energy, (4) very short spans of interest, and (5) ego building.
> ". . . our children lose interest in physical activity early in life because they are over-challenged and there is too much emphasis today on the good athlete . . . if they are successful (in creating equipment to meet the needs of the child) our children will become adults with a continued physical interest and a concept of confidence."

The new kindergarten would have equipment which would create stages for play acting with trees, rocks, shelters, and webs in various combinations. These playscapes would give every child an opportunity for success, either alone or as part of a group.

The Lunch Program

The child in a full-day kindergarten would have a new experience through participation in the school lunch program. The act of eating together, sharing tidbits, learning table manners, and conversing with his peers is a learning experience that the small child rarely gets. His dining patterns at home place him as the youngest child in an adult-dominated atmosphere where the indulgent parent often contributes to poor nutritional habits which last for life. The cafeteria experience, in addition to its training in the social graces, provides a hot lunch for the child who otherwise would have a cold, nutritively deficient lunch, and also helps to establish good eating habits at an early age.

The Academic Program

The academic program in the full-day kindergarten would include formal activities in language development, science, mathematics, social sciences, and music. Many of these areas are a part of the present half-day programs, but limitations of time make them very ineffective. The full-day program would permit regularly scheduled time segments with a well-defined pattern for developing activities to meet objectives in each subject area.

The lengthened days would permit the teacher to develop in greater depth the story-telling, role-playing activities which have been a part of her language arts program. More time could be devoted to science and understanding, and appreciation of the machines, plants, and animals which make up the world in which the child lives. There would be time to lead the child into the elements of fractions, addition, substraction, simple graphs, and basic geometric designs. In the social sciences the child's world would be expanded to define his relationship, both historically and economically, to his home and community; the five-year-old also should be introduced in broad terms to the idea of citizenship responsibilities in his nation and the whole world.

The staff of the Fort Myers School in Arlington, Virginia, developed a set of "Long-range Goals for Full-day Kindergarten" which are worthy of note. These goals were defined as part of an application for Federal monies to implement a study of the effectiveness of full-day versus half-day kindergarten:

1. Help the child explore the world of people and things.
2. Help the child toward self-development in: human relationships, independence, self-control, and cooperation.
3. To develop conceptualization (to think and reason, classify and categorize, learn cause and effect relationships).
4. To challenge the child intellectually in areas of language, science and math and the social sciences.
5. To develop creativity in the child through a variety of experiences.
6. To give attention to the physical development and well being of the child.
7. To provide opportunity to study the child, identify his strengths and weaknesses, and work to enrich the child's program and build from his weaknesses.

Structuring the Daily Schedule

Flexibility in scheduling the time segments of a kindergarten program is essential to maintaining the interest level of the child. Certain routines must take place at about the same time each day to meet physical needs, but other activities have greater potential for educating if they are freed from the restrictions of a tight schedule.

The present kindergarten program, with its narrow brackets of time, requires the teacher to schedule activities rigidly spaced in short time slots. If a concept is being developed, little deviation can be made from this rigid schedule to take care of individual physical problems; if something interrupts the development of an idea, the teacher has to start all over again at some later date to teach her concept because the child will have almost completely forgotten what he was learning. The greater freedom of the full-day program would permit leaving a learning activity when it is interrupted by boredom or physical needs, but returning to the same activity one or more times later in the same day to reinforce the seeds of learning that were begun earlier.

If a particular activity held the interest of the group, it would not have to be cut short because of a fear of losing time in some other activity. The teacher will have much more freedom of changing her daily program to meet immediate needs and not endanger her over-all goals.

One important phase of the daily program should be directed to outdoor activity. The aggravating strain of dressing and undressing during the cold weather months makes outdoor experiences a rarity during most of the school term. With more time available, there is no reason why the class should not go outdoors every day except in the most inclement weather. The child needs to develop his large muscle skills in activities which cannot be undertaken in the confines of a room. Exploratory hikes in the school neighborhood should be mapped out by the teacher to expand the awareness of nature.

One aspect of the present half-day program that merits close study is the required rest period. Some children have little or no need for extended naps or rests that are imposed on the group. Provision should be made for some quiet activities so that those who do not have this need can be developing their creative abilities.

The program of the full-day kindergarten would tax the ability and ingenuity of the best of teachers. She would not have the endurance to meet its physical demands. The assistance of a paraprofessional would be essential to a well-planned full-day kindergarten. This aide could help in the dressing and undressing for outdoor excursions. She could supervise rest periods while the teacher took care of those who did not need rest. Large group activities, both indoor and outdoor, could be handled by this person, freeing the teacher for a few minutes of planning or preparing materials and equipment for the next activity. This teacher-aide would assume full responsibility for the cafeteria-lunch routine of the daily schedules, thus relieving the teacher.

Increased Costs

The expansion of any program is expensive since capital outlay is involved. If a district has been operating half-day kindergartens, going to a full-day schedule would involve provision for additional classroom space. Theoretically one would need half again as many rooms as are currently in use. If empty rooms are available in the district this item is minor, but if new rooms must be built or space rented, the cost could be high. Minimum equipment to furnish one kindergarten is estimated at $2,000.00. Continuing yearly costs are teachers' salaries at an average $6,000.00 and transportation costs (one additional bus, $6,300.-00). Miscellaneous supplies are estimated at $1,700.00.

In the state of Pennsylvania, these additional costs would be offset by additional state reimbursements in the year after the program is put into effect. State aid is based on the average daily membership so that the kindergarten portion of ADM should be more than double. This is based on the theory that more children will attend full-day programs if transportation is provided.

Conclusion

Investigation reveals few programs of full-day kindergartens in effect in public school systems. The state of Hawaii established some full-day kindergartens in 1945 and since 1955 full-day kindergartens have been an integral part of all elementary schools in the state, according to Mary Musgrove, Program Specialist in Kindergarten-Primary Education, Department of Education, State of Hawaii. In 1965, the state of New York had 24,482 full-day pupils out of a total of 282,462 kindergarten enrollments.

Arlington, Virginia, began a pilot study of the program in 1967 using federal funds. Two school districts in the state of Pennsylvania have some full-day kindergartens in operation primarily because of transportation difficulties with half-day sessions.

Although no research has been done at this date on the advantages of a full-day kindergarten, most educators contacted in a survey indicated a feeling that educational benefits would result. Providing free transportation should increase participation. At present 15 percent to 20 percent of eligible children in the local district do not attend kindergarten primarily because of transportation difficulties.

The increased time element, combined with some help from para-professionals, should provide more individualized attention, less time lost in "getting out" and "putting-away" activities, better preparation for the all-day program of grade one, and greater teacher influence in development of good work habits.

Disadvantages which could result deserve recognition also: Some persons feel that the young child needs contact with the mother as long as possible. The added costs of any innovative program always raises a question of whether the ends justify the expense. Several corres- pondents expressed the belief that two half-day sessions with twenty to a group would be preferable to an all-day session with thirty pupils.

CREDITS

The United States Office of Education: Minnie P. Berson.

The Departments of Education of Illinois, New York, Pennsylvania, New Jersey, Hawaii, and California.

Several public and private schools and universities who responded to our questions.

Mr. C. Gordon Higgins, principal of Fort Myers School, Arlington, Virginia, for sharing his materials.

THE "DOMINO EFFECT" OF EARLY CHILDHOOD EDUCATION ON THE ELEMENTARY SCHOOL

HAROLD G. SHANE

WHEN properly conceived, early childhood education (ECE) is appreciably more than a mere downward extension of current elementary school programs. It is a significant source of input, of important learning experiences, which will soon begin to feed a new type of client into the primary years.[1] This new client may have memory banks encoded with behaviors that differ, both in extent and in depth, from those of children who enter school for the first time at age 5 or 6.[2]

Judging by the absence of comment in current educational literature, there is virtually no planning of curriculum change under way at the elementary school level, which anticipates the needs of children who will bring to the primary school two, three, and even four years of carefully designed experience. To use a simile, these children, like the first piece in a low row of falling dominos, should have a far-ranging influence on practice throughout the elementary school and, subsequently, throughout the entire spread of the educational community.

Early Childhood Education as a Source of New Encoding

The extent to which ECE will implant new behaviors in children before they enter the primary school will depend heavily on the nature and the quality of the programs provided. Most current programs fall into one of four categories:[3]

1. *Custodial* types, which provide care, it is hoped, in safe, healthy surroundings
2. *Academic* programs, which stress the early acquisition of skills in reading, number concepts, and so forth
3. *Cognitive* approaches, which emphasize rich inputs designed to increase whatever it is that we measure and label "intelligence" but which avoid structured academic content
4. *Developmental* types, which seek cognitive and affective input as "balance" in the curriculum and which endeavor to stimulate maximum, personalized human development.

Assuming that developmental programs become widespread and that they will largely replace custodial or day care types, we can anticipate at least 10 developmental and behavioral changes in the children they educate.

One cluster of changes in children who have experienced ECE for two or more years presumably will be found in the improved quality of their nutrition.

NATIONAL ELEMENTARY PRINCIPAL, 1971, Vol. 51, pp. 31-35.

Second, their general physical and mental health should be improved through early dental-medical examinations and through correction—when possible—of latent or early psychophysical problems that could later become more serious or even irremediable.

A third attribute of the new elementary school client should be his appreciably improved level of socialization. This will be reflected in the child's better adjustment to school routines and organization and to the roles of teachers and other personnel.

Fourth, research [4,5] suggests that child-rearing practices associated with social class may have considerable influence on subsequent behavior and performance.

Many children should acquire the fifth attribute of being less adversely influenced by disadvantaging socioeconomic environments than would otherwise be the case, especially if they have had as many as three years of ECE.

Sixth, there should be an increased range of ages in the ranks of youngsters moving from ECE programs into the primary sequence. This speculation is based on the probability that a "good" pre-primary program would provide a kind of "ready room" experience for the primary school. Some children as young as 4 might be deemed ready to move into the primary years; others could be as old as 7—or even 8 if they are physically or culturally hampered. Patently, this breaks sharply with the "fixed-admission-at-age-6-if-born-before-midnight-on-November-30" policy that is widely substituted for professional judgment.

Our "young dominos" by age 6 also should be thoroughly exposed to the idea of an educational continuum, rather than to the traditional graded school structure. This, in turn, suggests that they will have a seventh characteristic: familiarity with diversified staffing policies involving both teachers and paraprofessionals which will help many younger children, by 1975 or 1980, feel at home in "open" type schools.

An eighth possible characteristic of the elementary school's potential new client is cognitive or academic in nature. While early formal instruction (say, in reading) seems difficult to defend, sound ECE programs will undoubtedly serve to stimulate general intellectual development. This might well influence mental ability scores, since such scores apparently can be increased by rich input.[6]

Ninth, it seems inevitable that any well-designed ECE program will distinctly increase language skill [7]—the ability to encode "expressive" language and to decode the "receptive" communications transmitted (both verbally and nonverbally) by others.

Finally, by age 5 or 6, children should have been exposed to the inquiry approach to varied science, mathematics, and social studies learnings—a rich but informal body of experience on which teachers can build as children move from 6 to 8 years of age.

The Domino Effect and Elementary School Practices

To avoid hasty action, as the domino effect crests first in the primary school and then in middle schools of the late 1970's, what kinds of changes in practices might we contemplate and explore *now* while there is ample time for carefully reasoned changes in policies and in practices? Here are eight suggestions:

1. We should decrease and then drop our long-standing fixation on routines, bells, and schedules. This implies moving toward the so-called open school, a term that is losing its sharply milled meaning but which is used here to refer to schools that are "open" with respect to space, their low pressure psychological climate of instruction, and new ideas that promise to foster humane, personalized learning.

2. We should begin to "match" teachers and children, recognizing that certain personality mixes are better than others.

3. We might start to find more mean-

ingful ways for children to learn from children as, say, 11's or 12's tutor 6's or 7's.

4. We should move beyond the continuous progress approach to the broader concept of a seamless curriculum: a life-long, unbroken learning sequence through which one moves as his readiness, his motivation, and his maturity mandate.[8]

5. We should be flexible in our thinking and first modify and then abandon the 150-year-old structure of the graded school. Even now, children cannot be assigned effectively to graded groups. The children coming from ECE programs will increase the heterogeneity of the primary school population.

6. As a concomitant of greater flexibility in the elementary school, we would do well to encourage more cooperative teaching, teaming, flexible teaching partnerships, and the multiage groupings they facilitate.

7. We should anticipate a somewhat higher initial level of academic performance (although these often will not lend themselves to conventional standardized evaluations) and an appreciably greater "progress potential" as a result of ECE experiences. This performance cannot be maximized, however, if children of 5, 6, and 7 are subsequently exposed to retrogressive drill and memoriter learning in a graded primary.

8. The school environment itself might be made a more nutrient medium—a massive teaching aid—which serves to promote learning. Thus construed, the school milieu becomes a microcosm of society in which child-teacher participation and inquiry create maturing insights.[9]

Improved Teacher Education: A Critical Imperative

When discussing changes in elementary education that may be brought about by educating 2- and 3-year-olds, it is important to comment on the role of teacher education. As of the school year 1971-72, a number of changes have been made in the preparation of teachers. For instance, methods courses have been modified to accommodate the mathematics, science, and linguistics input of the 1960's; new models for preparation have been devised and student teaching has become a bit more flexible; more relevant academic majors have been encouraged; work in special areas or fields (such as urban education) has been added.

But most recent innovations were made to meet present needs or to remedy errors of the past. Very few changes have been made in anticipation of future demands that are likely to be made on the schools.

While adequate time remains, we need to concentrate on a radical regeneration of teacher preparation. Major changes are in order at all levels in the teacher preparation institutions. This is particularly true of those seeking an advanced degree in teacher education. Without being strident or alarmist, we might ask ourselves: What do our future teachers really need to experience in order to work effectively in the climate being created by the freshening winds of change? Let us consider this question, for example, with respect to preparing teachers for ECE programs.

When, at about age 18, a future teacher enters the collegiate sector of a seamless lifetime educational continuum, why not "pair" him with a 2-year-old during the first phases of his preparation? (This would be one feature among many modifications in the academic components of his "formal" education.) He could thus be methodically implanted with knowledge of the early years of a child's life through extensive personal contacts. These could include an understanding of social environment analysis, the contributions of dentistry, medicine, early age psychometry, and parental contacts—all carried out in connection with "his" 2-year-old. At 19, when "his" child is 3, the tyro teacher could be introduced to the responsibilities and duties of paraprofessionals as a member of a differentiated team and per-

81

haps serve half-time for a year in this capacity.

If he did not decide at this point to continue as a paraprofessional, he might, at 20 and 21, work with 4- and 5-year-olds, if possible still "paired" with a child for whom he had special personal study and guidance responsibilities. In this way, clinical experience, direct contact with actual programs, cross-disciplinary learnings, and a variety of equally important input could be brought to bear on teacher education.

Teacher educators, too, like principals and classroom teachers, should contemplate substantial changes in the environments they create for learners.

New Content for the "Domino Kids" and for All Learners

Necessary changes in the educational experiences of *all* learners in our schools pose important challenges. In this special early childhood issue of *The National Elementary Principal*, the "domino kids" from ECE programs simply serve to focus attention on pressing problems that confront us as we work with children, youth, and adults of virtually all ages. So far, we have discussed possible modified entry behavior or characteristics of the "new product" from ECE programs and broad program changes that may be in order in primary and middle schools; we have commented on needed changes in teacher education. However, we need to consider what might be desirable input for today's domino youngster as he begins the years of schooling that lie before him.

Conjecture suggests, before the river of human reason becomes further muddied by dilemmas of technology and social change and by the value conflicts they create, that United States citizens need to decide the kind of world for which our children and youth are to be educated. Also, if we are to work to improve the content of learning, what image of an educated man or woman do we hope to hold up to our children?

Certainly, the world we must work toward will have to be a simpler one—one in which people are more self-disciplined and compassionate, more respectful and more accepting of others, less materialistic, and more inclined to recognize, and to assume responsibility for, the general welfare than has been true in the past. Attitudes and behaviors such as these are now survival behaviors. This suggests that without downgrading our present respect for content in mathematics, the language arts, and so on, we need to transcend such subject matter in our planning and more closely link the individual to purposes he recognizes as relevant to his present self-concept and to his emerging image of his place in the world of the future.

Although the scope of such responsibility may make some educators uneasy, we probably should begin to concentrate as much on modifying behavior as we do on academic skills. We have become aware, especially in the last decade, that more enlightened ways of behaving are important if we are to protect living things by protecting their planet. A growing body of survival insights should, and probably will, provide much of the new content of the curriculum in the 1970's.[10]

Specifically, much of what children and youth learn in the near future is likely to be permeated with more realistic treatments of the promise and threat of biogenetics, problems related to overbreeding and its bearing on poverty, naive contemporary interpretations of democracy, mass media as forces for both good and evil, the danger in advanced nuclear weaponry, dilemmas related to technology and pollution, and the individual learner's development of a future-focused role image. "Future-focused role image" refers to the child's vision of a meaningful place for himself in tomorrow's world; a realistic future role in which he finds self-respect, satisfaction, and the motivation to ready himself to live in an improved environment during a new century in which he will spend the best part of his lifetime.

To summarize, we need to begin to do more thinking now as to the ways in which our schools can best accommodate themselves to an expanding program of education for the youngest. This implies making substantial changes in the organization of the schools, as well as in the psychological climate of schooling. It also involves reinterpretation of the content of instruction, as well as a remaking of teacher education.

One of the most significant aspects of early childhood education may, in the long run, prove to be the chain reaction of innovations it could trigger in education as a whole. Early childhood education has few dusty traditions, and it is relatively free of rigid organizational structure and fixed curriculum patterns. Perhaps we will find the wisdom to use these early years as a model for desirable changes, for greater flexibility in practice in the educational community. Conversely, it will be a pity if we throw away our opportunity and let the promising domino effect create only confusion a few years hence.

FOOTNOTES

1. Anderson, Robert H., and Shane, Harold G. *As The Twig Is Bent.* Boston: Houghton Mifflin Co., 1971. Also cf. Anderson and Shane, "Implications of Early Childhood Education for the Primary and Middle School Years." In Gordon, Ira J., editor, *Early Childhood Education.* Seventy-First Yearbook, National Society for the Study of Education. Chicago: University of Chicago Press, 1972. (In press)

2. Strickland, Stephen F. "Can Slum Children Learn?" *American Education* 7: 3-7; July 1971. Reviews promising gains made in early childhood by disadvantaged children in the Milwaukee Project.

3. Bernard Spodek, Department of Early Childhood Education, University of Illinois, suggested these four categories.

4. Deutsch, Martin, editor. *The Disadvantaged Child.* New York: Basic Books, 1967. pp. 31-38, 59-75.

5. Kagan, Jerome. "Motivational and Attitudinal Factors in Receptivity to Learning." In Bruner, Jerome, editor, *Learning About Learning: A Conference Report.* Education Cooperative Research Monograph No. 15, U.S. Department of Health, Education, and Welfare, Office of Education, Washington, D.C., 1966. pp. 34-39.

6. See footnote 2, pp. 6-7.

7. Smith, Frank. *Understanding Reading.* New York: Holt, Rinehart and Winston, 1971. Contains an excellent and deftly written presentation of language development.

8. Shane, June Grant, and others. *Guiding Human Development.* Worthington, Ohio: Charles A. Jones Publishing Co., 1971. Cf. Chapters 5 and 6 for a treatment of the curriculum continuum concept.

9. Some of the most interesting approaches to making the school itself serve as an educational medium were begun decades ago. Cf. Logan, S. R., "Adventuring with Little Corporations." *Clearing House* 20:2; October 1945; and "More Adventures with Little Corporations." *Clearing House* 21:4; December 1946.

10. Wallia, C. S. editor. *Toward Century 21.* New York: Basic Books, 1970. Presents a readable and frequently disturbing synthesis of technology, social change, and human values, with a bearing on decisions regarding a "good" world for tomorrow. Distinguished authorship.

DAY CARE:

A TIMID GIANT GROWS BOLDER

BETTYE M. CALDWELL

IN recent months, "day care"—an awkward and somewhat insulting term that few people used in either professional or personal voçabularies as recently as five years ago—has become a household term. Widely heralded by its advocates as a near panacea for many public ills, demanded by women as a civil right, offered as an employment lure by companies hiring large numbers of women, requested by city planners and boards of anti-poverty organizations, and recommended as an essential first step in reducing the large numbers of persons receiving welfare—how could the field have more status? But this pleasurable situation is very new.

Until recently, day care was but a poor relation of both social service and education. Neither field seemed disposed to embrace it fully or to recognize its legitimacy. But, historically speaking, day care has been much closer to the field of social welfare than to education. In fact, it is from the field of social service (child welfare, in particular) that day care received its definition as *care and protection* for children from *families with some type of social pathology.*

Early literature on day care generally took special pains to differentiate day care from education. For example, in the 1960 edition of the Child Welfare League

of America's *Standards for Day Care Service* (which sets the standards for all agencies in the field), one finds day care delimited as follows:

Day-care service has to be differentiated from the nursery school or kindergarten, and from extended school services and other programs for school-age children offered as part of elementary school systems. These have education of young children as their main purpose. The primary purpose of a day-care service is the care and protection of children. This purpose, the reasons for which a child and family may need it, and the responsibility shared with parents distinguish a day-care service from education programs.

At the time the day care movement gained adherents and momentum in America, we wanted to protect young children from such hazards as inadequate supervision, insufficient food, lack of shelter, and physical abuse. As today's knowledge about the importance of early experience for child development was only faintly limned in our consciousness at that time, it is not surprising that the prevailing concept of quality day care failed to recognize education as an integral part of "care and protection."

A second factor that undoubtedly kept the day care field slightly outside the bounds of general respectability was the designation of the family with problems as the primary group for whom the service

NATIONAL ELEMENTARY PRINCIPAL, 1971, Vol. 51, pp. 74-78.

was appropriate. To quote once again from the Child Welfare League's influential *Standards*:

Day care, as a child welfare service, is an expression of the community's concern for the welfare and protection of *children whose parents need help* in providing the care, protection, and experiences essential for their healthy development [emphasis added].

The pamphlet goes on to identify such children as those whose mothers work, whose fathers might not be in the home, who are ill or have emotional problems, or who live in poor housing conditions. Certainly, if families must see themselves as exemplifying social pathology in order to use day care services, the field is not likely to be embraced by those who could give it status in the larger society.

Suddenly, however, day care is "in," and the groups that once neglected it now claim it as their own. Money that cannot be obtained for "early childhood education" may possibly be found for day care. Fundamental child welfare programs that cannot be launched independently can possibly be made available as riders on day care appropriations. How do we explain the sudden popularity?

One reason that the number of day care centers did not increase substantially for many years was the implicit fear that if more such facilities were available, more mothers would be tempted to work outside the home. Yet more mothers *have* gone to work outside the home, including mothers with children younger than 6. And these are generally conscientious mothers who want good child care during their working hours. Although relatives and neighbors still constitute by far the most frequently used child care resources, more and more women have learned about day care, especially educational day care, and have come to request or demand such facilities for their own children. Furthermore, whereas national social policy formerly endorsed financial subsidies to keep mothers with young children at home (the Aid to Families

with Dependent Children Program), this policy is currently being reexamined. Training and employment of mothers are being urged, and quality day care is recognized as essential to this policy.

Employers also are turning to day care programs as a way of attracting female workers and reducing absenteeism from the job. The best-known modern program exemplifying this is the day care program operated in conjunction with the KLH factory in Cambridge, Massachusetts. Similar programs were funded under the Lanham Act during World War II, only to be discontinued at the end of the war when returning veterans dramatically changed the employment picture and displaced large numbers of women from their jobs.

Today, that pattern is being reversed by advocates of civil and personal rights for women. It has taken this group to strip day care of its social-pathology orientation. Stressing that personal fulfillment is a right to be shared by men and women alike and that child care is not the only valid avenue through which women may gain fulfillment, proponents of the Women's Liberation movement have demanded quality day care as a means to that personal fulfillment. At the 1970 White House Conference on Children last December, delegates representing various women's groups were among the most vocal in their demands that child care be made available around the clock throughout the year for all who want it, not just for indigent or minority groups. Such delegates also vehemently urged that federally supported day care be completely divorced from public assistance—thus officially removing the taint of social pathology from day care services.

Despite the importance of these developments, however, the most fundamental influence has been the steady flow of information about the importance of the early childhood years. Evidence has gradually accumulated that certain kinds of experiences during the early years greatly influence how a child grows up in this society. Although the data are based on only about five years of research, the results have filtered out from scientific laboratories to popular magazines and thence to parents of all social classes, and the result is that parents are clamoring for more such programs for their children. As many of these same parents need child care, the request is generally for day care rather than "early education" per se.

The professionals who give semantic shape to social trends have not been indifferent to the new demands and conceptual changes. In 1969, the Child Welfare League's *Standards* was revised:

At present, a wide range of resources and facilities, including informal arrangements and organized programs under various auspices, is used for the care of children outside of their homes during some part of the day. These resources and facilities have been established to serve many different purposes. They place differing emphases, reflected in their programs and the children whom they serve, on the responsibility for *care, protection, child development, education, or treatment.*

This new statement recognized that care and protection involve an inherent developmental and educational component. Day care can no more be separated from education than it can from welfare or health. In breaking away from the earlier narrow concept that artificially tried to separate the two patterns of service, the day care movement in this current definition has now given itself a new charter.

In a second radical departure from the earlier concept, the new *Standards* suggests that day care services may be offered more as a service to the mother than to the child. The pamphlet states:

Day-care programs are promoted and used for purposes in which the interests of the child may be a secondary consideration. Day care is provided to allow mothers, particularly those who are unmarried, to complete their schooling or to train for new careers; to help financially dependent mothers attain self-support and to reduce public assistance expenditures; and to recruit women for, and retain them in, the labor force.

The League is not an organization that can lightly take the subordination of the needs of children, however, and the report goes on to caution:

Under these circumstances, it is necessary to ensure that day care is in the best interests of the individual children, and that the daily experiences are of benefit to them, or at least not detrimental.

In a subsequent section of the new *Standards,* a third subtle but major conceptual shift is encountered. While the old *Standards* declared, "The primary purpose of a day care services is the care and protection of children," the new version states, "The primary purpose of a day care service is to *supplement* the care and protection that the child receives *from his parents* [emphasis added]." It seems as if the field were more willing to share the responsibility at this time or else were more aware that care and protection for the young child attempted *in loco parentis* has little chance of providing much of either. The implication is that the family carries the major burden and the day care service only supplements the family's endeavors.

The varied purposes of day care are reflected in a healthy diversity of programs. They include care provided by family members or baby-sitters, day care centers operated as demonstration and research agencies, centers controlled by parents or offered as a public service by a church or secular organization or provided as a lure by industry, and centers run for profit by a private operator or as a franchise unit of a national corporation. Still relatively scarce are programs that involve a complete blending of day care with education.

The subtle changes in the day care concept reflect a shift in orientation that is at once both honest and refreshing, and yet just a little alarming. The new

Standards has the audacity to suggest that day care is more than a noble service to the next generation, being, in addition, an important service and convenience for the present generation. The League is to be credited with recognizing the validity of that orientation. Day care people *do* tend to get just a bit sugarcoated in talking about what the experience will do for the children—all the social, affective, and cognitive gains that will accrue as a result—that we tend to forget about the families of the children. And often, when we remember them, it has been in terms of concern with modifying their behavior in order to facilitate *our* goals for *their* children.

One of the reasons many persons have resisted day care on a large scale has been the fear that, no matter which generation it focused on, it would weaken the bond between children and their families. This fear has been more presumptive than factual and has been built upon an irrational equation of day care with institutional care. Day care—daily separation followed by nightly reunion in the context of social relationships that permit a sense of identity to be formed—appears to have none of the socially toxic effects of prolonged institutional care or even of temporary separations (such as hospitalization) during which family contacts might be terminated for a given time. My colleagues and I in Syracuse recently published data that demonstrated rather persuasively that 2½-year-olds who had been in day care since around 1 year of age were as attached to their mothers as were comparable control children who had never had such a day care experience.

Whatever the source of the fear, it appears to be a strong one. And some of the parent groups advocating more day care facilities are also reminding the professionals that they, the parents, have a right to share in the planning and decision making. During the summer of 1970, a workshop was held in Airlie House, Virginia, to prepare a number of pamphlets that could be used as guides by inexperienced groups wishing to initiate and operate day care programs. A set of principles was prepared that went considerably beyond the League's position in recognizing that day care could sometimes be structured to meet the needs of the parents. Although the document is not now in its final version, the early draft proposed that the primary focus of any day care program should be the individual child and his family—not the child alone or the parents alone. Furthermore, day care was described as a program that could either bring parents and children together or else drive a wedge between them. The statement of principles supported the former goal and stressed that quality day care should never do anything to reduce the family's commitment and responsibility. One suggestion was to supply parents with the information needed to make informed judgments and then to have them participate fully in decisions about what would be desirable for their children in day care, as well as in the home.

Thus, day care, formerly an advocate for the child, then for the parent (especially the mother), seems now to speak for the family. The policy implications of these different orientations are profound and far-reaching.

Because of its importance in the lives of children, one can imagine day care becoming a bold instrument of social policy. In fact, day care has not made policy; it has followed along when policy has been made. It has grown somewhat haphazardly, changing its own definition every 10 years or so. At present, it does not know whether it should serve the child, the parent, or the family. It cannot make up its mind whether it is a service for families with social pathology or for all families, whether it should be limited to children from underprivileged families or be offered to all children, whether it wants to change children or preserve cultural styles from one generation to the next. It does not know where to obtain its official identity. This confusion can be seen in state licensing patterns. The welfare department handles licensing in 36 states, the health department in five, and some different agency or combination of agencies in, the remainder. The department of education is the licensing body in only one state, although it shares the task with welfare in one other and makes recommendations in many.

Thus, it is precisely in this area of planning for our children, except in the grossest sense, that we are most timid in this country. With our tradition of valuing rugged individualism, we have been reluctant to say much about the kinds of children we want. Do we want obedient children? Happy children? Adaptive children? Children who remain faithful to the values of their families? Militant children? Bright children? Group-oriented children? Woodstock and Maypole youth or Peace Corps youth? Eventual adults who can slip from one type to another? Professor Urie Bronfenbrenner has commented on the extent to which child rearing in the U.S.S.R. has a clear objective to train children as responsible citizens of the Soviet state, in contrast to the lack of objectives and belief in autonomy in the United States. In our concern for individuality, we occasionally find license for evasion of the responsibility for guidance.

What the day care field needs in order to be a powerful instrument of social policy is a forum from which to advertise its potential and a willingness to proclaim its importance. To this author, that forum ought to be public education—albeit education defined more flexibly and comprehensively than it is today. Actually, there is little justification for a conceptual separation between public education and public day care, for most schools are "day schools" and represent "day education" with or without the supportive family services generally offered under the rubric of day care. The significant difference,

however, is that day care generally enters the lives of children at an earlier age, and as infant day care becomes more respectable, the age of entry will become even lower. Any experience that enters the lives of children at a time when they are impressionable, when basic patterns of expressing, thinking, feeling, and problem solving are being developed and value systems are being assimilated has no need to feel apologetic.

The suggestion that day care find a forum in education may sound like a partisan recommendation. But I am talking more about a conceptual model for program design than about professional auspices for program operation. This orientation need not close out any of the diverse models now being tried. Essentially the same suggestion has been made by others, including Florence Ruderman in her book *Child Care and Working Mothers:*

Day care, regardless of the auspices under which it is offered, should be developed as a child-care program: a program directed to optimum social and psychological health of the young child whose mother cannot care for him for some part of the day. . . . But a given family's need for social casework or other forms of help should no more define day care, nor determine eligibility for it, than the existence of social service departments in schools and hospitals now defines these facilities as social work services. For organized child-care service in this country to develop and meet adequately a growing social need, it must be recognized as a positive social institution and enabled to stand in its own right as an essential child-care program.

The challenge becomes one of having comprehensive child care embraced as a legitimate endeavor of that behemoth of public policy, public education, without having it consumed in the fire of an encrusted bureaucracy and without any loss of concern for "care and protection." Public education would do well to stop and reflect occasionally that one of its concerns should be with the care and protection of the children and youth who come within its sphere of influence.

At this moment in history, when we are on the threshold of embarking on a nationwide program of social intervention offered through comprehensive child care, we let ourselves prattle about such things as cost per child, physical facilities, or even community control. And when we begin to think big about what kinds of children we want to have in the next generation, about which human characteristics will stand them in good stead in a world changing so rapidly, we fall back on generalities such as care and protection. Yet, any social institution that can shape behavior and help instill values and competencies and lifestyles should also shape policy. Early child care is a powerful instrument for influencing patterns of development and the quality of life for children and adults. Because of its power, those who give it direction must not think or act with timidity.

DAY CARE:
EDUCATION OR CUSTODY?

WALTER F. MONDALE

ERIK Erikson once said, "The most deadly of all possible sins is the mutilation of a child's spirit." He could well have added that it is also the most costly and the most irreparable sin. Yet we permit it to be committed every day to hundreds of thousands of innocent children. And we let it happen, perhaps most tragically, to children in the earliest years of life.

Jonathan Kozol called it "death at an early age." He saw how Boston's ghetto schools were helping to destroy—spiritually and educationally—the very children they are designed to educate. He understood the impact of verbal and physical brutality, of self-fulfilling expectations of failure, of depressing and dilapidated facilities.

Charles Silberman called it "crisis in the classroom." He forced us to remember that this mutilation is not restricted to the ghetto. He made us admit that too many of our schools have been basic training camps in discipline, rather than places where children find the way to become humane and sensitive adults; that

Walter F. Mondale is United States Senator (D) from Minnesota.

in many instances we are damaging, rather than encouraging, the creative impulses of even our most privileged children.

The terrible irony is that Kozol's and Silberman's revelations, for all their insight, are only part of the tragedy. Millions of children are destroyed before they ever enter those classrooms. The "death" and the "crisis" these authors document often come, in fact, at a much earlier age.

They come, first, in the shamefully high infant mortality rates, which actually climbed last year in Washington, D.C., despite a slight downward trend nationally. They come to those children who survive birth but have been permanently damaged during pregnancy or delivery or who have had their minds irreparably stunted by malnutrition in the early years of life. They come when ghetto youngsters lose on the average of 17 IQ points between 15 months and 3 years of age if they receive no preschool education or tutoring, as they did in a District of Columbia study.

We *know* why and how much of this happens. Research tells us of the critical

NATIONAL ELEMENTARY PRINCIPAL, 1971, Vol. 51, pp. 79-83.

effect of the first few years of life when a child needs the most nourishment for his feelings of self-worth, his sense of self-respect, his motivation, initiative, ability to learn and achieve. Research has shown how a child's intelligence is shaped by his experiences, how his mental development is heavily determined by the conditions and environment he encounters in the first few years of life. And these are more than academic concepts. Children who are vulnerable to the disasters of early childhood and open to its opportunities are all around us:

• There are 3.2 million children under age 6 living in poverty, with a like number living in near poverty, who could benefit from nutritional, health, educational, and social services.
• There are 6 million preschool children whose mothers are working.
• A study several years ago indicated that 8 percent of all children with working mothers, including 18,000 preschoolers, were left alone to take care of themselves during the day.

We have never adequately provided for these early childhood years. We have left things to chance. We have neglected, in particular, those children with the greatest educational and economic need.

Licensed day care centers can accommodate less than 700,000 children. What little quality preschool work that is being done, including some limited but encouraging efforts under Head Start, barely scratches the surface of need. And much of what is being done is downright tragic.

Consider this account of a day care center in Washington, D.C., visited recently by a reporter from *The Washington Post*. This center, as she characterized it, was "not the best and not the worst" of the centers we have in the nation's capital.

In one corner of the large, neat, and very bare room, 21 children, 3 to 6 years old, and two adults sit, watching Captain Kangaroo on a small-screen black-and-white television set perched far above their heads on a room divider.

About half the children seem attentive, a handful are squinting or glassy-eyed, and five have their heads down on the table either resting or sleeping. . . .

There is no talk, either during the commercials or after the program ends. The images flitting across the small screen are the only movement, their mechanically jolly banter, the only sound.

According to the reporter, there are few books in the center, no educational toys, little if anything to stimulate creative play. The children spend up to 11 hours in the sparsely equipped room, with a schedule that includes an hour of television, three hours of naptime, morning and afternoon devotions, an hour and 15 minutes "getting ready to go home," and an hour and a half for "going home." Only one hour is set aside for "class."

We all know the cruel and costly results of this neglect. Reginald Lourie, Director of the Joint Commission on the Mental Health of Children, pointed to one shameful product in his testimony to the recently created Subcommittee on Children and Youth, which I chair. Dr. Lourie reported that the President's Panel on Mental Retardation found that the United States "had a higher percentage of retardation than almost any other country in the civilized part of the world—3 to 4 percent. In every other country where there are programs for early child care," he testified, "maybe 1/10th of 1 percent of the population is retarded."

This doesn't have to happen. Why can't we benefit from the experience of our neighbors? Their particular approaches or techniques may not be directly relevant in the American experience, but their goals and commitment can be.

Consider the strong commitment Israel makes to her children. Over 50 percent of Israeli children are from Oriental backgrounds. Because they often have experienced severe social and economic disadvantage, these Oriental children are entitled by law to participate in preschool programs beginning at age 3.

Virtually all of the disadvantaged 5-year-olds and about one-half of the disadvantaged 3-year-olds now attend preschool in Israel, and Israel's goal is to provide preschool for all disadvantaged youngsters by 1972.

By contrast, Head Start serves less than 10 percent of America's disadvantaged preschool children. The Israeli preschool efforts may have some problems, but their commitment to children is an example to follow.

Even the Russians, with whom we like to compete in gadgets, have made major commitments to child care. Dr. Lourie testified that:

"Every (Russian) mother who is pregnant has to have prenatal examinations . . . and if she doesn't turn up for them, the police go out to get her. Special additions to her diet are made available. If she is working, she gets the last six to eight weeks off from work with full pay. In other words, there is in action in Russia a basic concern for the child."

And there are exciting, but isolated, examples of quality preschool efforts in this country.

The same reporter mentioned earlier visited one of these child development centers in Washington, D.C. She found that the center has qualified teachers, "equipment ranging from gerbils and rabbits to paints and clay to books and educational toys. Each classroom is equipped with a one-way glass booth, wired for sound, so that teachers can observe and evaluate—and so parents can watch their offspring in action." The children there were really learning. Unfortunately, it costs $750 to $800 a child for only 2½ hours a day, five days a week, nine months a year. This tuition puts it out of the reach of the poor and, she reported, "the $10,000 a year family" as

well. By offering quality services only at the socioeconomic extremes, we neglect the majority of our children. Even more ominous, we seem to assign poor children to a track system even before they enter public school. We are ignoring the very promising opportunity for children to learn from one another.

As Edward Zigler, now Director of HEW's Office of Child Development, testified:

"Another important reason for . . . socioeconomic mix in Head Start centers is the growing body of evidence that children learn a great deal from one another. The middle-class child does have a number of attributes that the poor child could profitably model. By the same token, we often find in poor children particular strengths and characteristics worthy of emulation by the middle-class child. We must see to it that Head Start centers are institutions where our Nation's children, regardless of economic status, can enrich one another."

Yet we have simply failed to translate these insights into practice. We are losing more children than we save. Existing programs tend to be uncoordinated, underfunded, and largely custodial. The big question is: Where do we go from here?

There are some hopeful signs. For a variety of reasons, including a steadily increasing number of working mothers, women's lib, welfare reform, and a growing realization of the significance of the first few years of life, the prospects have improved for expanded government support of early childhood efforts. We will have some kind of legislation shortly and, along with it, more money. But what we do with this opportunity is much less clear. We have a chance to build a truly creative program of early childhood development for all children. But we could also squander this opportunity and institutionalize, by default, an elaborate system of baby-sitting for the poor.

Our choice depends on whether this

new legislation puts the developmental need of children first or whether it treats those needs as an afterthought. I see a real danger of making the wrong choice.

The reporter I referred to earlier concluded that "the focal point of government interest seems to be shifting . . . from the 'develop the child' emphasis of the Great Society days to the 'free the mother to work' emphasis of the Nixon Administration's proposed welfare reform bill." The day care provisions in that legislation and in the Federal Child Care Corporation Bill reflect this emphasis. Their explicit purpose—and it is spelled out precisely in each bill—is to permit mothers to work. They scarcely mention the needs of children. They ignore almost completely considerations of parental involvement, socioeconomic diversity, and bilingual-bicultural needs. We need a comprehensive, child-oriented developmental proposal to serve the needs of *both* children and parents—and in that order.

A bill I introduced recently—with Senator Javits and 30 other Senators from both parties—and whose major provisions are included in S2007 that was just approved by the Labor and Public Welfare Committee and will be voted on by the Senate in early September is designed to do just that. The bill was developed in conjunction with a large coalition of organizations interested in child development.* A similar version of this bill was

---

* The Coalition included: Americans for Democratic Action; Americans for Indian Opportunity Action Council; AFL-CIO; Amalgamated Clothing Workers; Committee for Community Affairs; Common Cause; Day Care and Child Development Council of America, Inc.; Friends Committee on National Legislation; Interstate Research Associates; International Ladies Garment Workers Union; League of Women Voters; Leadership Conference on Civil Rights; National Council of Churches; National Council of Negro Women; National Education Association; National League of Cities—U. S. Conference of Mayors; President and Vice-President for Legislation of the National Organization of Women; UAW; U. S. Catholic Conference, Family Life Division; and the Washington Research Project Action Council.

introduced in the House by a bi-partisan group of congressmen led by Representatives Brademas and Reid and has been reported by the Select Subcommittee on Education.

The bill places priority on the needs of the child; on comprehensive services, including education and health; on parental involvement; socioeconomic diversity; accountability; and respect for a child's heritage, language, and culture. Specifically, it contains the following elements:

• Comprehensive services are required, including whatever educational, nutritional, social, and health services are necessary to help participating children reach their full potential.

• Prenatal care is covered to help prevent the developmental problems that arise out of inadequate medical attention during pregnancy and delivery.

• Parental and family involvement is assured by requiring parental participation in the development and implementation of the programs.

• Local levels of government—counties, cities, Indian reservations—will have preferences over the state in administering these programs, to assure maximum opportunities for local control and parent involvement.

• Priority is placed on preschool and infant care efforts, and services are also authorized for children through age 14.

• Adequate funding is encouraged by authorizing $100 million in planning, training, and technical assistance in fiscal year 1972 and $2 billion in operating funds for fiscal year 1973. The first year of the bill is deliberately designed to provide leadtime for these programs and to provide six months' or nine months' training and retraining programs for professional and paraprofessional personnel, including the estimated 35,000 skilled, yet unemployed, education majors who graduate each year but who are unable to find jobs in their chosen profession.

Socioeconomic diversity is assured by providing free services to children from families with incomes below the Bureau of Labor Statistics minimum living standard ($6,900 for an urban family of four, with adjustments for regional and urban-rural differences). Also, the bill authorizes up to 35 percent of the funds to help pay the cost, on a sliding scale fee basis, of children from families with incomes above $6,900. Each program will include, to the extent possible, children from a broad range of socioeconomic backgrounds.

• Bilingual-bicultural efforts, as well as special reservations of funds for *Indians* and *migrants,* are required.

• The bill authorizes construction grants, programs for training child development personnel, and a strengthened research and evaluation program in child development.

The point about making service available through age 14 should be stressed. There is no question that research demonstrates the critical nature of the early childhood years. That is why the bill places priority on early childhood. But let us make sure we understand exactly what this early childhood research and emphasis means.

It means that neglect, hunger, inadequate health care, and lack of stimulation during this period can cripple a child's intellect for life, or at least make it exceedingly difficult and expensive to recover what has been lost. But it does not mean—and this fact cannot be overemphasized—that quality preschool programs alone will guarantee that children reach their full potential.

Early childhood services are not an innoculation that lasts for life. We know that there are no neatly bracketed magic periods of learning in childhood. Child development is continuous, and the risk of damage is constant. We must provide adequate support and services throughout these critical years.

We have placed a priority on the preschool years, not because those alone are "magic years," but because we can be sure that they are just as magic as any other, and they are the years that are most neglected in our existing pattern of services for children.

We have drawn heavily in this bill on the experiences of public education and the talents of educators. Our concept of free services for families with incomes up to $6,900, rather than up only to the poverty line—with one-third of the funds reserved to help children from higher incomes participate—is based on our desire to make this program reflect the philosophy of free public education. It is also based on the knowledge of educators that socioeconomic diversity within a program makes good educational sense.

Our solution to the apparently inadequate supply of trained child development personnel is, in large measure, to tap the growing number of talented education graduates who are unable to find teaching jobs in our public schools.

Our major goal is to assure that these programs are truly educational, not simply custodial.

The one non-negotiable criterion is that these programs—especially the early childhood programs—enhance the child's education and development, rather than simply enabling the mother to work.

There is growing pressure to provide five days a week, 10 hours a day child care for preschool children whose mothers work, or who would work if these services were available. In some cases, this would be an improvement. There are thousands of young children—latchkey children—who are left at home to care for themselves or who are looked after by brothers or sisters barely older than they are. Unquestionably, a program with adult supervision and hot meals would be an improvement for them. But merely creating institutions with warm rooms, several adults, and breakfast, lunch, and dinner does not add up to child development.

There are numerous cases in which developmental programs can be offered in a day care setting, but there are also times when the needs of child development and day care conflict. I wonder, for example, whether many preschoolers, especially the very young, would not be served better by programs lasting several hours, rather than all day. Perhaps a program should make it possible to send tutors into their homes to work with them and their mothers.

I had an opportunity to visit the Infant Research Project in the District of Columbia. It sent tutors to the homes of ghetto youngsters of 1½ to 3 years for several hours a week and was extremely successful in preventing IQ declines of 15 to 20 points that other ghetto youngsters were experiencing.

That was not a day care program. It did not make it possible for the mothers to work, but it was a tremendously impressive child development program. And that is what the primary goal should be.

The bill we are working on in the Senate is hardly the final answer. It will not solve the tremendous educational problems we face. It does not mean we can relax our efforts during the school years or reduce funding for other education programs, but it is a long overdue and promising approach. It can mean that more of our children will be prepared to take advantage of our public education system when they arrive at school.

III. THE LEARNING ENVIRONMENT

SCREENING KINDERGARTEN CHILDREN: A REVIEW AND RECOMMENDATIONS

MARYROSE M. ROGOLSKY[1]

Kindergarten children display a variety of handicaps which directly affect their capacity to learn. Emotional disorders, intellectual deficits, learning disabilities, visual motor defects, and sensory deficits can markedly influence the child's academic, emotional and social development. About 40% of all children have problems which can seriously interfere with their learning or adjustment in the primary school years. Cowen, Zax, Izzo, & Trost (1966) reported that about 30% of first grade children are emotionally disturbed, with moderate to severe pathology. Estimates of intellectual deficit vary with the social class of the population. Cronbach (1960) noted that about 8% of the original Terman standardization group had IQs below 80. Roswell & Natchez (1964) reported that 10 to 30% of school age children have severe reading problems. (These estimates probably overlap to some extent and should not be taken as cumulative.) The incidence of children with visual motor disabilities, sensory defects, cerebral dysfunction, or other sources of learning disability is not known.

Early identification is needed if these large numbers of children are to be helped effectively. Comprehensive screening to detect a wide variety of handicaps is needed so that all children who might benefit from an individualized or special program will be recognized.

"Screening" refers to measures which can be used with groups of children, as contrasted with individually administered procedures. This paper reviews screening techniques mentioned in recent psychological literature, focussing on emotional disturbance, intellectual abilities, and learning disorders.

EMOTIONALLY DISTURBED CHILDREN

Most methods of screening for emotional disturbance in children rely upon teacher ratings of behavior, although a few investigators have attempted other measures. White & Harris (1961) reviewed the early literature on screening for emotional disturbance since Wickman's initial study (1928) which used teacher ratings.

The emotionally handicapped child was defined by Bower (1960) in terms of visibility to the teacher. Although Bower relied on many sources for information about the child, this discussion will be limited to teacher ratings as they are most applicable at the kindergarten level. The subjects of Bower's study were 5,000 children in grades

[1]The author is indebted to Raphael Minsky, Director of Psychological Services, Montgomery County Public School System, who suggested that there was a need for this study. Saul Rogolsky and Margaret Beyersdorfer provided valuable editorial assistance.

JOURNAL OF SCHOOL PSYCHOLOGY, 1968/1969, Vol. 7, No. 2, pp. 18-27.

four, five and six. His criterion group of moderately to severely emotionally handicapped children were 207 youngsters who had previously been designated by the clinician in the school system as emotionally handicapped rather than situationally maladjusted. The teacher ratings of the known disturbed group were compared to the ratings of the rest of the children in the classrooms: 87% of the clinically known children were rated by their teachers as among the most poorly adjusted children in the classroom, which indicates that teacher ratings are a highly valid technique.

Schaefer et al. (1964, 1966) developed a teacher rating check list of 12 behavioral traits which is detailed and useful at the pre-school primary level. It includes verbal expressiveness, hyperactivity, kindness, social withdrawal, perseverance, irritability, gregariousness, distractibility, considerateness, self consciousness, concentration, and resentfulness. Schaefer also used a global rating of pupil behavior, ranking it on a four-point scale ranging from well adjusted to clinically disturbed, which resembles that of Gildea (1959). Schaefer's scales can be used as a basis for well differentiated class grouping in a school system which has the time and professional sophistication to devote to such groupings; its overall assessment of adjustment could prove useful in all school systems.

Spivack & Swift (1968) described other teacher rating scales suitable for kindergarten children. Their scale has been used to ascertain academically related problem behavior with over 1400 children from kindergarten to twelfth grade rated by 147 teachers. This measure would be particularly useful in longitudinal studies of emotional disturbance. Each of these scales has its virtues: Bower's is recommended on the basis of many years of use, Schaefer's is particularly suited to behavioral research, and Spivack & Swift's scale is designed for longitudinal studies.

Landsman & Dillard (1967) recently reported a study of figure drawing as a screening device for kindergarten children. Their method of scoring the drawings, called the Evanston Early Identification scale, can be used by the kindergarten teacher and distinguishes reliably between high and low risk children. However, it is not a diagnostic instrument as it does not differentiate among children with emotional, perceptual and other problems.

In screening for emotional disturbance, various factors in the child's environment should be noted, as they may have affected adjustment. Certain demographic material should be collected. Although Bower did not indicate a correlation between social class and emotional disturbance, his sample might have been preselected to avoid this. Other major studies (Hollingshead & Redlich, 1958) demonstrated the strong association between social class and mental disorders in adults. Parents' occupation and education are probably the indices of social class most readily available in the schools. Available ethnic and racial information ought to be tabulated so that the predictive value of the material can be ascertained. Family size and position of the child in the family might also prove relevant.

Within the school scene, absences during the kindergarten year, referrals to the nurse, tardiness (as a possible index of school phobia), age and sex are also important variables. The child's family residence and changes of residence might be noted. The length of experience of the teacher within the school, within the school system, and her total experience might be found to affect the adjustment of the children in her classroom.

Intellectual Functioning

Early assessment of intellectual capacity is a justifiable goal of a comprehensive screening program. Intellectual capacity may be viewed in terms of the underlying "innate" ability, present level of functioning, and future potential for development. Recent research has abandoned the belief that innate ability can be measured. With greater awareness of the interaction of social class and race with intelligence (Lesser, 1965; Deutsch, 1963; & John, 1963), the determination of current functioning is now emphasized, although the clinician is often asked to predict intellectual potential. Deutsch (1963) indicated that the lower class child enters school so poorly prepared that initial failures are almost inevitable, and that various forms of stimulus deprivation affect both formal and contentual aspects of cognition.

To "screen" such children and compare them with middle class children may be very misleading. Lesser (1965) used psychologists from the same ethnic background as the subject to assure good communication and rapport. Anastasi (1958) stressed the importance of matching the cultural backgrounds of tester and testee. Ideally, this precaution should be followed in every screening program.

The simplest instrument for measuring intellectual development is the Harris-Goodenough Draw a Person Test. Harris (1963) reported moderate correlations between Harris-scored drawings and other measures of intelligence at the kindergarten age level. Harris believes that the drawing test at this age measures the child's ability to form abstract concepts; his drawing score is more highly correlated with the handling of spatial and quantitative concepts than with perceptual speed or verbal meaning abilities. Although the drawing test generally overlooks verbal abilities, Harris indicates that it is a sufficiently valid measure of intelligence to be included in a screening program.

Ahr (1967) recently reported on a group pre-school screening instrument (Screening Test of Academic Readiness, or STAR) used in an upper middle-class community, and, subsequently, with Head Start programs. Correlations with individual and group intelligence and achievement tests compare very favorably with the predictive coefficients of other group intelligence tests at this age level. The test can be administered in less than one hour, and to large groups of children simultaneously. Its eight subtests are: Human Figure Drawing, Picture Vocabulary, Letters (recognition and printing), Picture Completion, Copying geometric designs, Picture Description, Relationships (size, space, direction, and position of mutilated pictures), and Numbers. Five items involve copying, drawing, or printing; three involve multiple choice where the subject chooses one drawing by outlining with a pencil. Ahr's instrument, still in an experimental stage, may prove to be more useful than other well established intelligence measures: it systematically taps a variety of numerical, receptive verbal, visual motor, and relational abilities.

Well established measures such as the Kuhlmann-Anderson or Lorge-Thorndike, which yield only verbal and non-verbal scores, might be used when the school psychologist's time and research possibilities are very limited. Buros (1965) criticized other standard group intelligence measures (Otis Group Intelligence Scale, California Short Form Test of Mental Maturity, SRA Tests of General Ability) which the reader is advised to consider.

Besides testing for intellectual development, Kirk (1966) recommended that kindergarten teachers be trained to assess bright and slow learning children in nine areas: reasoning, speed of learning, ability to deal with abstract ideas, perceptual discrimination, psychomotor abilities, verbal comprehension, verbal expression, number and space relations, and creativity. Guidelines indicated which classroom situations were relevant to each area. The Binet IQ was used as the criterion for the teacher's judgments. Teachers tended to identify young children as slow and older ones as rapid learners, but when age adjustments were made the composite scores culled from the nine areas of prediction correlated moderately with the Binet in the various classrooms (N-112 children).

LEARNING DISORDERS

Bateman (1966) defined a "learning disorder" as a deviation in the learning process associated with an educationally significant discrepancy between apparent capacity for and actual level of language or cognitive behavior. This definition might be sharpened by limiting learning disorders to those discrepancies which are not due to primary emotional disturbance or poor hearing or vision. Perceptual-motor deficits, however, are included in this definition.

To predict which children will become learning problems, psychologists generally use individually administered instruments (de Hirsch et al., 1966a; Gallagher, 1957), but some instruments can be used efficiently with young children in a group.

Pate & Webb (1966) developed a group measure called the First Grade Screening Test (FGST) which can be administered at the end of the kindergarten year. This test is reported to identify young children with potential learning problems, and extensive validity and reliability information is given by the authors. FGST takes about 45 minutes to be administered to a kindergarten class by their teacher. The 27 items of the test are not categorized by the authors but can be grouped as follows: picture vocabulary (10 items), drawings and visual motor functioning (5), social and practical perception and information (4), memory for pictures (2), following directions (2), and pictures which call on the child to identify with the well adjusted (4). No tests of number con-

cepts are included. Many of the items in FGST are similar to those in Ahr's STAR, which can be administered earlier in the kindergarten year. STAR's organization into sub-tests gives the examiner more detailed information than FGST's unitary score. However, FGST is an attractive, easy to administer screening technique, and its standardization on a variety of populations (described in terms of class and rural-urban distinctions but not by race) is a notable achievement.

The standard reading readiness tests were reviewed by Buros (1959), who found the Lee-Clark (1962) test satisfactory. Mitchell (1962) and Robinson (1966) reported that the Metropolitan Reading Readiness Test (Hildreth, Griffiths, & McGauvran, 1964) is a valid and reliable instrument, although Robinson noted that its administration is complex and time-consuming. Ahr's measure (1967) overlaps to some extent with the more established readiness tests, but is more comprehensive than either of those tests and is reportedly very efficient to administer.

The work of Silberberg et al. (1968 a,b), Wolff & Stein (1967), and Landsman & Dillard (1967) raises some doubt as to the efficacy of reading readiness tests in predicting later reading achievement. Silberberg administered the Gates Reading Test (1942) to kindergarten children and compared these scores with reading test scores achieved at the end of first grade. The resultant equations based on stepwise linear regression procedures raised some questions concerning the validity of readiness testing. Silberberg et al. (1968a,b) found that the Letters and Numbers subtest of the Gates Reading Readiness Test, administered in kindergarten, predicts end of first grade reading achievement as well or better than the complete Gates test or IQ tests. Landsman & Dillard (1967) also reported that the Metropolitan Reading Readiness Test did not predict serious learning problems.

The Bender Gestalt test, scored according to Koppitz (1964), discriminates (up to age eight) both those who are above and below average in achievement test performance. For children seven and younger, the Bender Test is useful for the identification of both immature and bright youngsters. Koppitz suggested that good school achievement can be predicted with some assurance if a child does well on the Bender Gestalt Test at the beginning of first grade. If a child does poorly, he should be retested after a few months to assess his rate of maturation; if the rate of progress on the Bender is in keeping with the child's age, he will probably do satisfactory work in school. This retest concept is useful in that it ascertains not only level of development but rate of developmental change. Keough & Smith (1961) demonstrated that the Bender can be administered to groups of school beginners with the use of large cards, and that correlations with school achievement are higher for group than for individual administration. Keough & Smith reported that children who performed well on the Bender in kindergarten tended to be good school performers but that poor Bender performance was non-predictive.

Frostig, Maslow, Lefever, & Whittlesey (1963) developed the Developmental Test of Visual Perception, suitable for teacher administration at ages three to nine. This test breaks down visual perception into five areas: eye-motor coordination, figure-ground, constancy of shape, position in space, and spatial relations. Frostig et al. (1963) wrote that "each of these five abilities developed relatively independently of the other, and that there should be specific relationships between them and a child's ability to learn and adjust [p. 464]." A few validity studies on the relationship between Frostig Visual Test scores and predicting reading suggested that the scores do have some predictive value. However, Frostig's reports often confound the use of her methods as pre-

dictive tests and as training devices (Rosen, 1966).

Culbertson & Gunn (1966) compared children's functioning on the Bender-Gestalt, Frostig, and an intelligence measure. Their work indicated that level of intellectual functioning was an important factor in visual perceptual performance and that the Bender and Frostig were closely related and probably tapped the same variables. Since the Bender is less time-consuming than the Frostig, it would seem preferable for group screening.

Haring & Ridgway (1967), who screened kindergarten children for potential learning difficulties, found that teacher ratings of learning problems were more effective than their group testing battery, and that learning ability was not associated with motor coordination. A principal component factor analysis of the 31 variables revealed general language ability to be the most powerful factor associated with learning ability, but the principal factor accounted for only 20% of the variance; an array of factors contributed weakly to learning ability.

De Hirsch, Jansky, & Langford (1966b) used individual tests. Their discussion of predicting reading failure at the kindergarten level emphasized reading, writing, and spelling. Fifty-three children were seen individually for two and one-half years. The following tests failed to be predictive: gross motor skills (hopping , etc.), figure ground discrimination, and ill-defined lateralization. Their best predictor was the number of words used in a story. Whether this richness of language is related to environmental stimulation or to inherent linguistic endowment is not known, but this individual test could be used if there is enough time for individual testing. Word reproduction and recognition tests, such as those found in Gates (1942) and de Hirsch et al. (1966) might be valuable additions to a screening battery.

PROBLEMS IN THE PREDICTION OF LEARNING DISABILITIES

Many basic questions regarding learning remain unsolved. For instance, what is the predictive value of meaningful verbal material? De Hirsch reported that her best predictor of reading ability was the number of words used to tell a simple story. Bateman (1966), commenting on research done with the ITPA, stated that "psycholinguistic factors which correlated with reading ability occur at the *non-meaningful* (rote or automatic-sequential) level of language usage and not with comprehension or representational functions [p. 16]." In a short period of individual screening, both meaningful and non-meaningful verbal-expressive instruments might be used to discover which instrument better predicted later reading achievement.

Another problem is the relative importance of visual and language abilities. Haring & Ridgway (1967) indicated that language factors are the major indices of learning abilities. Koppitz's work with the Bender suggested that the visual-motor abilities are strong predictors of school success. De Hirsch used both methods but did not use a statistical analysis that would clarify the relationship of visual motor or language abilities to reading prediction. In a group screening procedure, the testing of visual motor functioning is possible but should be supplemented with classroom-administered meaningful and non-meaningful verbal measures.

Most investigators believe that learning disability arises from a poor environment, emotional disturbances, manifest brain damage, less manifest suspected cerebral dysfunction, or a combination of these factors. The orientation of the specialist will determine his estimate of the importance of each of these factors. The description of cerebral dysfunction can range from the spontaneously reversible maturational lag described by Koppitz (1964) to the deficiencies in neurological organization and motor functioning described by Delacato (1966). Motor disabilities are also important in Frostig's theory. Doll (1966a), one of the original discussants of the relationship of specific learning disability and motor disabilities, cautioned that "what we need to know is how specific or general motor awarenesses affect the 'higher' learning processes . . . In short, are perceptual-motor training hypotheses really supported by controlled experience and analysis of related variables? . . . There is a strong hint that through some occult process transfer of training will occur with generalized educational improvement in non-motor, especially visual perceptual areas [p. 220]." De Hirsch, Haring and Ridgway indicated that gross motor disabilities are not predictive of learning problems.

Perceptual handicaps are frequently cited as an index of minimal brain dysfunction. Eisenberg (1966) noted that "the confusion about the proportion of dyslexics with perceptual deficits takes on some pattern when it is realized that perceptual handicaps are more often found in younger than in older dyslexics . . . the older child may no longer exhibit the handicap which may have been prominent at a critical stage in the learning process and contributed to his failure to learn to read [p. 15]." This suggests that the underlying disorder is reversible and more akin to a maturational lag than to brain damage, or that compensatory functions can disguise the disorder. Money (1966) associated this functional maturational lag with most reading disabilities, and wrote that "two possible neuropsychological deficits that may tie in with reading disability are disability for conceptualizing space-form relationships and disability for right-left orientation in space [p. 40]."

This disability in laterality and directionality has frequently been cited as either contributory to or associated with reading disability. Laterality refers to hand use, and hand, eye, leg consistency; directionality refers to awareness of sidedness in self and others. Confusion about these terms may contribute to the confused state of the literature. Birch & Belmont (1964) found that consistent eye use and hand-eye consistency continue to be undetermined even at older age levels, and that disabled readers are no more ambilateral than normal readers. However, in another study Belmont & Birch (1965) found that although laterality did not differentiate 150 poor reading nine year olds from 50 normal peers, the sense of right-left direction and identification of own body parts did significantly differentiate the poor readers from the normals. It is doubtful if questions about directionality would be applicable to kindergarten or first grade children, but Birch & Belmont suggested that tests of laterality at any age in childhood may be pointless. Tests of reversals in writing, which tap both directional sense and space form relationships, predict reading achievement at the kindergarten level (de Hirsch, 1966a).

The Geneva Medico-Educational group (1968) extensively reviewed American and European literature on dyslexia. They considered various causative factors, such as central nervous system injury, speech problems, perceptive disorders, spatiotemporal disorganization, and affective (personality) disorders, and concluded that "none of the factors we have studied here explain the combination of problems found in the reading learning process and each of these disorganizations can be found in disorders other than dyslexia [p. 165]." Since the etiology of learning problems is so unclear, a screening program should use a variety of measures which tap visual perceptive, spatial and verbal fields.

To predict learning problems in a screening program, the Bender-Gestalt Test, administered in a group and scored according to Koppitz, is strongly indicated. Graphomotor ability should be noted. The word recognition and reproduction tests of de Hirsch might be used.

Language tests at the kindergarten level require individual administration, but time might be allotted to a word count in a story reproduction measure and a short measure of non-meaningful verbal ability—perhaps the ITPA Digits.

APPLICATIONS OF GROUP SCREENING

Ideally a screening program should first be used experimentally to test its predictive value: a large number of children should be screened and the results should be examined after a year or two. The initial measures can then be scrutinized to see how well they predicted intellectual, emotional, and academic functioning in the end of first or second grade in a particular school system. Rosenthal & Jacobson (1968) showed the effects of teacher expectation upon children's performance in the classroom. To know the effectiveness of the screening device, the initial results should be withheld so as not to influence the teacher's response to the children. After the effectiveness of the screening procedure is demonstrated, it should be used as a basis for planning in the primary school years.

Results of screening should always be viewed with skepticism: low scorers should be reappraised by one of two methods. If the child's performance suggests serious disorder, individual testing is indicated. If the results are questionably spotty and inconsistent, reassessment with the group measure should be done in about six months. No child should be expected to perform routinely at a certain level, but gross developmental inconsistencies may be noted. Rate of developmental change, especially in the visual motor areas, may be estimated by retesting.

Screening results should be studied both for individual weaknesses and strengths. Lesser (1965) stressed differential patterns of cognitive development; this pattern concept might be applied to individual assessment and in the planning of classroom composition and activities. If a teacher knows that a child has poor visual motor coordination, good memory, and excellent social potential, she can plan a remedial program for the visual motor area, exploit his good memory in other learning situations thereby enhancing self esteem that might be deflated by his visual motor weaknesses, and consider his good socialization when grouping the class for activities.

Kindergarten screening may also facilitate placement of children. It offers the teacher an objective aid when she considers the child's advancement or retention, or the grouping of children within the classroom. Screening will allow the school to forego rigid adherence to chronological age as a basis of grade placement.

If a child needs to repeat a grade, the retention should generally occur at the earliest time, so that there is less failure in the acquisition of basic skills, and less of a negative social-emotional experience for the child. Screening in kindergarten should reveal which children are to repeat kindergarten, or, if the school has a transition class between kindergarten and first grade, which children belong in it. Screening at the end of transition should help indicate which children are to go to first and which to second grade.

Screening programs should be supervised by a psychologist, who can interpret results to the teaching staff and alert the teacher to children who need specific attention. Screening, including teacher observations, will help the psychologist decide which children need early individual appraisal.

Screening results can help the teacher deal with parents as well as children. Parents should be informed of the goals, potentialities and weaknesses of the screening program. The psychologist should consult with the teachers on interviewing parents about their children and using the information gained from the screening program. Teachers often need support and insight in their dealings with parents. Parents are often open to suggestion and reorientation at the start of their child's school career. A screening program can broaden both teacher's and parent's perception of and participation in the child's learning experience.

REFERENCES

AHR, A.E. The development of a group preschool screening test of early school entrance potential. *Psychology in the Schools,* 1967, *4*(1), 59-63.

ANASTASI, A. *Differential psychology.* New York: MacMillan, 1958.

BATEMAN, B. Learning disorders. *Review of Educational Research,* 1966, *36*(1), 93-119.

BELMONT, L., & BIRCH, H. G. Lateral dominance, lateral awareness and reading disability. *Child Development,* 1965, *36*(1), 57-72.

BIRCH, H. G., & BELMONT, L. Auditory-visual integration in normal and retarded readers. *American Journal of Orthopsychiatry,* 1964, *34,* 852-61.

BOWER, E. M. *Early identification of emotionally handicapped children in school.* Springfield, Ill.: Charles C. Thomas, 1960.

BOWER, E. M. & LAMBERT, N. M. *A process for in-school screening of children with emotional handicaps.* Princeton: Educational Testing Service, 1962.

BUROS, O. K. *The fifth mental measurements yearbook.* Highland Park, N. J.: Gryphon Press, 1959.

BUROS, O. K. *The sixth mental measurements yearbook.* Highland Park, N.J.: Gryphon Press, 1965.

COWEN, E. L., ZAX, M., IZZO, L., & TROST, M. A. Prevention of emotional disorders in the school setting: A further investigation. *Journal of Consulting Psychology,* 1966, *30*(5), 381-387.

CRONBACH, L. J. *Essentials of psychological testing.* New York: Harper, 1960.

CULBERTSON, F. M., & GUNN, R. C. Comparison of the Bender Gestalt Test and Frostig Test in several clinical groups of children. *Journal of Clinical Psychology,* 1966, *22*(4), 439.

DE HIRSCH, K., JANSKY, J. J., & LANGFORD, W. L. *Predicting reading failure.* New York: Harper & Row, 1966a.

DE HIRSCH, K., JANSKY, J., & LANGFORD, W. L. Comparisons between prematurely and maturely born children at three age levels. *American Journal of Orthopsychiatry,* 1966b, *36*(4), 616-628.

DELACATO, C. H. *Neurological organization and reading.* Springfield, Ill.: Charles C. Thomas, 1966.

DEUTSCH, M. Some social psychological and developmental considerations in education in depressed areas. In H. Passow (Ed.), *The disadvantaged child and the learning process.* New York: Teachers College Press, 1963.

DILLARD, H. K., & LANDSMAN, M. The Evanston Early Identification Scale: Prediction of school problems from the human figure drawings of kindergarten children. *Journal of Clinical Psychology,* 1968, *24*(2), 227-228.

DOLL, E. A. SLD and motor training. *Perceptual and Motor Skills,* 1966a, *23*(1), 220.

EISENBERG, L. Epidemiology of reading retardation. In J. Money (Ed.), *The disabled reader.* Baltimore: John Hopkins, 1966. Pp. 3-20.

FROSTIG, M., MASLOW, P., LEFEVER, D. W., & WHITTLESEY, J. R. B. *Developmental test of visual perception.* Palo Alto, Calif.: Consulting Psychologists Press, 1963.

GALLAGHER, J. J. A comparison of brain-injured and non-brain-injured mentally retarded children on several psychological variables. *Child Development Monographs,* 1957, *22* (No. 65).

GATES, A. *Manual of directions for Gates Reading Readiness Tests.* New York: N. Y. Teachers College, 1942.

GENEVA MEDICO-EDUCATIONAL SERVICE. Problems posed by dyslexia. *Journal of Learning Disabilities,* 1968, *1*(3), 158-171.

GILDEA, M. C. L. *Community mental health: A school centered program and a group discussion program.* Springfield, Ill.: Charles C. Thomas, 1959.

HARING, N. G., & RIDGWAY, R. W. Early identification of children with learning disabilities. *Exceptional Children,* 1967, *33*(6), 387-395.

HARRIS, D. B. *Children's drawings as measures of intellectual maturity.* New York: Harcourt, Brace, & World, 1963.

HILDRETH, G. H., GRIFFITHS, N. L., & McGAUVRAN, M. E. *Metropolitan readiness tests.* New York: Harcourt, Brace, & World, 1964.

HOLLINGSHEAD, A. B., & REDLICH, F. C. *Social class and mental illness.* New York: Wiley, 1958.

JOHN, V. P. The intellectual development of slum children—some preliminary findings. *American Journal of Orthopsychiatry,* 1963, *33*(5), 813-822.

KEOUGH B., & SMITH, C. Group techniques and proposed scoring system for the Bender Gestalt Test with children. *Journal of Clinical Psychology,* 1961, *17,* 172-175.

KIRK, W. D. A tentative screening procedure for selecting bright and slow children in kindergarten. *Exceptional Children,* 1966, *33*(4), 235-241.

KOPPITZ, E. M. *The Bender Gestalt Test for young children.* New York: Grune and Stratton, 1964.

LANDSMAN, M., & DILLARD, H. *Evanston Early Identification Scale.* Chicago: Follett, 1967.

LEE, J. M., & CLARK, W. W. *Lee-Clark Reading Readiness Test.* Monterey, Calif.: California Test Bureau, 1962.

LESSER, G. S. Mental abilities of children from different social class and cultural groups. *Monographs of the Society for Research in Child Development,* 1965, *34*(102), 115.

MITCHELL, B. C. The Metropolitan Readiness Tests as prediction of first grade achievement. *Educational and Psychological Measurement,* 1962, *22,* 765-772.

MONEY, J. On learning and not learning to read. In *The disabled reader.* Baltimore: Johns Hopkins, 1966. Pp. 21-40.

PATE, J. E., & WEBB, W. W. *First Grade Screening Test.* Circle Pines, Minn.: American Guidance Service, Inc., 1966.

ROBINSON, H. A. Reliability of measures related to reading success of average disadvantaged and advantaged kindergarten children. *Reading Teacher,* 1966, *20*(3), 203-209.

ROSEN, C. L. An experimental study of visual perceptual training and reading achievement in first grade. *Perceptual and Motor Skills,* 1966, *22*(3), 979-986.

ROSENTHAL, R., & JACOBSON, L. F. Teacher expectations for the disadvantaged. *Scientific American,* 1968, *218*(4), 19-23.

ROSWELL, F. G., & NATCHEZ, G. *Reading disability, diagnosis, and treatment.* New York: Basic Books, 1964.

SCHAEFER, E. S., DROPPLEMAN, L. F., & KALVERBOER, A. F. Development of a classroom behavior check list, and factor analyses of children's school behavior in the United States and the Netherlands. Mimeo of paper delivered to Society for Research in Child Development, 1964.

SCHAEFER, E. S., & AARONSON, M. *Classroom Behavior Inventory.* Form for preschool to early primary. National Institutes of Mental Health, 1966.

SILBERBERG, N. E., & IVERSEN, I. A. The effects of kindergarten instruction in alphabet and numbers on first grade reading. Mimeo, Kenny Rehabilitation Institute, Minneapolis, Minn., 1968a.

SILBERBERG, N., IVERSEN, I., & SILBERBERG, M. The predictive efficiency of the Gates Reading Readiness Tests. *The Elementary School Journal,* 1968b, *68*(4), 213-218.

SPIVACK, G., & SWIFT, M. *Patterns of disturbed classroom behavior—the nature and measurement of academically related problem behavior.* Devon, Penna.: Devereux Foundation, ERIC ED 012, 545, 1968.

WHITE, M., & HARRIS, M. *The school psychologist.* New York: Harpers, 1961.

WICKMAN, E. K. *Children's behavior and teachers' attitudes.* New York: Commonwealth Fund, 1928.

WOLFF, M., & STEIN, A. Six months later: A comparison of children who had headstart with their classmates in kindergarten. Mimeo, New York: Ferkauf Graduate School of Education, Yeshiva University, 1967.

FACILITATING DEVELOPMENT IN
THE PRE-SCHOOL CHILD: SOCIAL AND
PSYCHOLOGICAL PERSPECTIVES

MARTIN DEUTSCH

A large portion of the following discussion will be the examination of some of the psycho-social highways that criss-cross the early life of the child, and how socio-educational engineering might provide the most facilitating architecture for maximizing human achievement.

Massive evidence makes it clear that a child's social experience is a very influential factor in his development; yet it is also obvious that the relationship between experience and development is an extremely complex one. A basic assumption of the approach to be presented in this paper is that there is a continual and influential interpenetration of environmental experience and psychological development along a broad front, and that therefore simple cause-effect models can be accurate on only the grossest level.

In a sense, our current social dilemma has the usual contradictions that every period feels are unique to its particular time. Historically, the present era may or may not have more contradictions that other periods. But the rapid development of automated, highly skilled, labor-reducing techniques does have revolutionary consequences for man's relationship to the social order, to work and leisure, and to intellectual activity. Further, the level of our technology, particularly in the field of communication, creates conditions in which these new techniques are rapidly disseminated. Thus, the time within which institutional and structural adjustments can take place is greatly reduced. This necessitates the deliberate and planned manipulation of social conditions in order to avoid, or at least attenuate, the sometimes invidious consequences of rapid change.

In a society of abundance, there is an amazingly large segment of our population living in a subsociety of social, economic, and educational impoverishment. The estimates range from 20 to 40 per cent of our population, depending on criteria. (For example see Harrington, 1963.) The problems associated with marginal employment and crowded, dehumanizing living conditions are, of course, characteristic of the lives of most of the peoples of the world. But here in this country we have the facilities, the

MERRILL–PALMER QUARTERLY, July 10, 1964, pp. 249–263.

productive capacity, and at least some of the knowledge required consciously to reorient social development. A necessary focus for such orientation should be the child, so that he can develop the requisite basic skills for the new technology and changing social institutions.

A thesis presented in this paper is that the behavioral scientist and the educator can facilitate the evolution of the educational institution so that it will be capable of preparing all children for optimal social participation, as the racial, social class, and sex gatekeepers become inoperative. The contemporary problems of education are to some extent a reflection of current technological, racial and urban conflicts inherent in accelerated social change. At the same time, the human sciences (though beset by similar problems) could become major instrumentalities for the resolution of social conflict, since they are among the few systems oriented toward change. For example, the intervention concepts in social psychology and psychiatry are relatively quite new. These disciplines can thus be seen as possible agents for the construction of blueprints to harmonize human needs with cultural transformations.

In general, the human sciences are moving from social and individual diagnosis to remedial therapies. Those sciences are now, in some of the more advanced thinking, concerned with primary prevention, ranging from mental illness and juvenile delinquency to disabilities in learning and socialization. To speculate on a possible avenue of future development, it might be that from this stage an orientation will develop toward assisting the individual to potentiate his intrinsic capacities for productive living and full individual realization.

This is by no means meant to minimize the importance of activities in other disciplines; rather, it is an attempt to specify the potential role and contribution of the human sciences. It must also be remarked that the knowledge available in the combined human sciences is still quite limited, and that too frequently formulas have been presented which are insufficiently related to scientific knowledge.

While to a major degree the behavioral sciences and education have run parallel courses, they have insufficiently interacted with and enriched each other. What better place is there to investigate meaningfully the development of learning processes—or of attitudes or of mental health—than in longitudinal studies in the context of the school, from the nursery school through college? It is always surprising to us how many educators are not aware of the exciting investigations of socialization, learning, and cognitive processes in the field of child development. On the other hand, too many social scientists look upon education and work in the educational field as "applied," "atheoretical," and somehow unrelated to the growth of a child into an adult. Just as medicine is the application of physiology, biochemistry, and similar sciences to human problems, so too could education be the application of the human sciences. As medicine discovers principles and laws that are continually being circulated back to its basic sciences, so could education not only evaluate and validate the principles which it derives from the human sciences, but also could lead toward the genesis of methods of influencing and accelerating individual growth.

In order to achieve such integration, a crucial historical difference between education and psychiatry, sociology, and psychology must be recognized. While the latter have the impetus coming from both their newness and their response to challenge, education has the disadvantage of a long and encumbering history. In a sense, the institution of education—the school—*is* the status quo. Often it must operate through politically oriented bureaucracies that continually inhibit its potential for change and for developing strategies to meet social crises such as those inherent in the new urban America. These bureaucracies are often so large that introduction of meaningful change, even when agreed on by the higher echelons, is limited by the clogging of communication channels with paper, red tape, and assorted other artifacts, and by the constraints under which the average classroom teacher operates.

Somehow, this great gap in the educational hierarchy, separating the educator and his concept from the classroom teacher with her idea, creates a discontinuity that results in much wasted energy and distortion of effort. A clear educational philosophy can come best from educators who are free enough from bureaucracy to communicate with the classroom teacher as a full professional, and to attenuate the burden of the past while setting up new relationships with the human sciences. Inherent in this approach is the necessity for effective cooperation between educators and behavioral scientists, so as to incorporate the growing knowledge of the socio-psychological development of the child into educational procedures in the interests of facilitating realization of his greatest intellectual and social potential.

The children most in need of help are from the economically and socially marginal and quasi-marginal segments of the community. These groups are the ones most caught in the technological and social changes; in many of our metropolitan areas they are becoming the majority of the center city population. It is in these groups that we find the highest proportion of unemployment, welfare support, and broken families. And it is in their children that we see the highest proportion of learning disabilities and school dropouts. While in the past it was possible to absorb most of such youth in unskilled, low-paying jobs, now the current adult generation is increasingly being replaced in such jobs by machines. With the number of unskilled and semi-skilled jobs decreasing, in order to find any place in the job market youth must now learn more complex functions, for which a successful educational experience is a prerequisite. This is a central problem for the total community, and a challenge for education. How it is met has wide ramifications for other underdeveloped areas outside our large cities and national boundaries.

There are various avenues of approach to the problem of both pre-venting learning disabilities and facilitating intellectual growth.

In recent years, there have been major curriculum renovations, enrichment programs, new systems for teaching mathematics and the sciences, programmed courses and teaching machines, as well as a multiplicity of new methods for teaching reading. However, in the disadvantaged underdeveloped areas of our communities, where there is the large proportion of underachievers, these new methods are probably least applicable, being most often based on an assumption that the child has reached a particular level in skills which underlie them. As will be pointed out later, for the disadvantaged child this is an unwarranted assumption. For the most part, it is a correct assumption for the middle-class child; but here there are other problems. Too often, new methods are seen mainly as more effective techniques to help the child get into college and achieve occupation status goals, and the aim of education along with its innovations becomes narrowly pragmatic. This is not to say that new methods should not be devised and attempted, but rather, that they might be seen neither as solutions to underachievement nor as substitutions for the development and encouragement of intrinsic motivation toward intellectual mastery and scholastic achievement.

An approach that combines the preventive with the facilitating—and which would establish a basis for the absorption of new methods—is that of planned intervention at the earlier periods of development of the various components of the intellectual spectrum. Evidence which is accumulating points more and more to the influence of background variables on the patterns of language and cognitive development of the child, and a subsequent diffusion of the effects of such patterns into all areas of the child's academic and psychological performance. Deprived backgrounds thus lead to the inadequacy of such patterns. What is proposed is that experiential inadequacies in the social background can be compensated for by a planned enrichment, channeled through improved schools.

Reference has been made to the constellation of factors in lower-class life which are associated with a limited range of experiential variability available to the child. Of course, there are probably differing clusters of economic, social, and family factors associated with greater or lesser retardation. But the fact remains that lower social class status apparently predisposes to scholastic retardation, even though not all children are equally affected. Therefore, before discussing learning processes in the school it might be helpful to delineate some of the major features of urban slum life.

Geographically, there are crowded and dilapidated tenements quite at variance with the TV image of how people live. If the people are Negro, Puerto Rican, or Mexican-American, or poor mountain white, life is in a more-or-less segregated community. There are likely to be extremely crowded apartments, high rates of unemployment, chronic economic insecurity, a disproportionate number of broken families, and (particularly in the case of the Negro) continual exposure to denigration and social ostracism of varying degrees. The educational level of the adults tends to be quite limited. In the homes, there is likely to be a nearly complete absence of books, relatively few toys, and, in many instances, nothing except a few normal home-objects which may be adapted as playthings. In addition—particularly but not exclusively where relatively new in-migrants are concerned—there is a great deal of horizonal mobility. The result is a pattern of life that exposes a child to a minimum of direct contacts with the central channels of our culture. The conditions of social inequality, the absence of an accessible opportunity structure, and the frequent non-availability of successful adult male models create an atmosphere that is just not facilitating to individual development. Moreover, the everyday problems of living, particularly those of economic insecurity and a multiplicity of children, leave minimum time for the adults who may be present to assist the child in exploring the world, to reward him for successful completion of tasks, or to help him in the development of a differentiated self-concept. Even in homes which are not broken, the practical manifestations of economic marginality result in the father sometimes holding two jobs and having little time for interaction with the child. We have found in various studies that children from these circumstances have relatively few shared or planned family activities, again resulting in a narrowing of experience.

The implications of these environmental conditions for the development of the child can be appreciated in terms of Hunt's (1961) discussion of Piaget's developmental theories. He points out that, according to Piaget, ". . . the rate of development is in substantial part, but certainly not wholly, a function of environmental circumstances. Change in circumstances is required to force the accommodative modifications of schemata that constitute development. Thus, the greater the variety of situations to which the child must accommodate his behavioral structures, the more differentiated and mobile they become. Thus, the more new things a child has seen and the more he has heard, the more things he is interested in seeing and hearing. Moreover, the more variation in reality with which he has coped, the greater is his capacity for coping" (pp. 258-259). In essence, it is this richness and variety which a compensatory enrichment program must provide.

Previously, I have said that emphasis on the importance of variety in the environment implies the detrimental effects of lack of variety (Deutsch, 1963). I then postulated that a child from any circumstance, who has been deprived of a substantial portion of the variety of stimuli to which he is maturationally capable of responding, is likely to be deficient in the equipment required for school learning. This does not necessarily imply restriction in the quantity of stimulation; rather, it refers to a restriction in variety—i.e., restriction to only a segment of the spectrum of stimulation potentially available. In addition to such restriction in variety, from the description of the slum environment, it might be postulated that the segments made available to children from that background tend to have poorer and less systematic ordering of stimulation sequences, thereby being less useful to the growth and activation of cognitive potential.

The most promising agency for providing environmental compensations is the school. It is through this institution, which reaches every child, that the requisite stimulation for facilitating learning, psychological maturation, and acculturation can be most efficiently organized and programed. Yet it is now estimated that up to 60 per cent of lower-class children are retarded two years or more in reading, by the time they leave the elementary school.

Before we place the entire responsibility on the school, however, an important fact must be noted. The overwhelming finding of studies on the relationship between social class and learning, school performance, and the like is that children from backgrounds of social marginality enter the first grade already behind their middle-class counterparts in a number of skills highly related to scholastic achievement. They are simply less prepared to meet the demands of the school and the classroom situation. Conversely, though, the school has failed to prepare to meet their needs. The failure of the educational institution to overcome the children's environmentally determined handicaps too often results in early failure, increasing alienation, and an increasingly greater gap between the lower-class and middle-class youngsters as they progress through school. In other words, intellectual and achievement differences between lower-class and middle-class children are smallest at the first grade level, and tend to increase through the elementary school years. It is here where the interaction between school and early environment, instead of having a facilitating influence, has a negative effect. While the school does not contribute to the initial problem (except through its effects on the previous generation), neither does it contribute to the overcoming of the initial handicaps.

It would seem quite reasonable, in the light of this discussion and its supporting evidence, to better prepare the child to meet the school's demands before he enters the first grade, and before there has been an accumulation of failure experiences and maladaptive behavior. It would also seem eminently reasonable that the school should accept this responsibility. At the same time, it does not seem reasonable that an institution which so far has generally failed to meet its responsibility to this group should simply be given a mandate, without the incorporation of new and appropriate knowledge and techniques. Here is where the knowledge from the behavioral sciences can be put to its most effective use.

For example, all peoples have difficulties in spanning cultural discontinuities, and the entrance of the child into school for the first time places him in an environment which, in many respects, is discontinuous with his home. This discontinuity is minimal for the middle-class child, who is likely to have had the importance of school imprinted in his consciousness from the earliest possible age. For him, therefore, the school is very central and is continuous with the totality of his life experiences. As a result there are few incongruities between his school experiences and any others he is likely to have had, and there are intrinsic motivating and molding properties in the school situation to which he has been highly sensitized. Further, there is more likely to be contiguity in the school-faculty orientation with his home-family orientation. Failure can be interpreted to him in appropriate and familiar terms, and methods of coping with it can be incorporated, increasing the motivation or offering the necessary rewards, goals, or punishments to effect the desired change in performance.

For the lower-class child there is not the same contiguity or continuity. He does not have the same coping mechanisms for internalizing success or psychologically surviving failure in the formal learning setting. If the lower-class child starts to fail, he does not have the same kinds of operationally significant and functionally relevant support from his family or community—or from the school. Further, because of the differences in preparation, he is more likely to experience failure.

In this context, let us consider White's concept of competence motivation as a primary drive. The middle-class child comes to school prepared, for the most part, to meet the demands made on him. The expectations of his teachers are that he will succeed. As he confronts material that is congruent with his underlying skills, he is able to succeed; and thus he achieves the feeling of efficacy which White (1959) points out is so necessary to the "effectance motivation" which promotes continuing positive interaction with the environment. The lower-class child, on the other hand, experiences the middle-class-oriented school as discontinuous with his home environment, and further, comes to it unprepared in the basic skills on which the curriculum is founded. The school becomes a place which makes puzzling demands, and where failure is frequent and feelings of competence are subsequently not generated. Motivation decreases, and the school loses its effectiveness.

It is in the transitional years from the pre-school period through the elementary school years that the child is first subject to the influence and the requirements of the broader culture. It is then that two environments are always present for him: the home environment and the school environment. But it is also in these transitional (and especially in the pre-transitional) years that the young organism is most malleable. Thus, that is the point at which efforts might best be initiated to provide a third—an intervention—environment to aid in the reconciliation of the first two. Such reconciliation is required because, especially for the child from a disadvantaged background, there are wide discrepancies between the home and school milieus. In the intervention environment, preventive and remedial measures can be applied to eliminate or overcome the negative effects of the discontinuities.

The importance of early intervention is underlined in the summary by Fowler (1962) of findings on cognitive learning in infancy and early childhood. He points out that seemingly minimal cognitive stimulation in the pre-school years, when organized appropriately to the capabilities of the child, can be highly effective in accelerating the development of intellectual functions.

Critical and optimal time periods for many aspects of development and learning in both humans and animals have long been studied. These concepts are always related to stimulation or interaction between the organism and the environment, and thus represent an important additional dimension when we discuss influences on development and behavior. Apparently, it is not sufficient merely to provide particular stimulation for the growing individual; it must be supplied at a special time, or within particular time limits, if it is to have the most desired effect. Thus, a program intended to compensate for environmental deprivation would be most effective if supplied at a particular stage in the life of the child.

Scott's (1962) summary of the relevant research information on critical stages in development indicates that the period of greatest plasticity is during the time of initial socialization. Since the bulk of the literature in this area is on animals, generalizations must be carefully confined. But seemingly, as one ascends the phylogenetic scale, there are greater ranges of time during which the organism has high levels of plasticity and receptivity. There is an insufficient body of data to hypothesize a most critical period for learning in the human child, and there are probably different critical or optimal periods for different functions. However, at about three or four years of age there is a period which would roughly coincide with the early part of what Piaget calls the "preoperational stage." It is then that the child is going through the later stages of early socialization; that he is required to focus his attention and monitor auditory and visual stimuli; and that he learn through language to handle simple symbolic representations. It is at this three- to four-year-old level that organized and systematic stimulation, through a structured and articulated learning program, might most successfully prepare the child for the more formal and demanding structure of the school. It is here, at this early age, that we can postulate that compensation for prior deprivation can most meaningfully be introduced. And, most important, there is considerably less that has to be compensated for at this age than exists when, as a far more complex and at least somewhat less plastic organism, the child gets to the first grade.

This position and its implications for specially organized early stimulation of the child find support in a recent article by Bruner (1961) on cognitive consequences of sensory deprivation. He says: "Not only does early deprivation rob the organism of the opportunity of constructing models of the environment, it also prevents the development of efficient strategies for evaluating information—for digging out what leads to what and with what likelihood. Robbed of development in this sphere, it becomes the more difficult to utilize probable rather than certain cues, the former requiring a more efficient strategy than the latter" (pp. 202-203). Bruner goes on to a discussion of nonspecific transfer of training in which, I think, he provides the most incontrovertible foundation for a structured, systematic pre-school enrichment and retraining program which would compensate, or attempt to compensate, for the deficiencies in the slum environment. His discussion is not of slums or compensation, but in his pointing up the importance of the "normally rich" environment, the serious cognitive consequences of the deprived environment are thrown into relief. Bruner says, ". . . nonspecific or generic transfer involves the learning of general rules and strategies for coping with highly common features of the environment" (p. 203). After pointing out that Piaget ". . . remarks upon the fact that cognitive growth consists of learning how to handle the great informational transformations like reversibility, class identity, and the like" and that Piaget speaks of these as "strategies for dealing with or, better for creating usable information," Bruner proposes: ". . . that exposure to normally rich environments makes the development of such strategies possible by providing intervening opportunity for strategic trial and error" (p. 203).

What Bruner talks about under "trial and error" requires a certain level of motivation and exploratory efforts. I have previously discussed the possible role of early failure experiences in influencing the motivational and goal orientations, and the self-expectancies, of the lower-class child. When the lower-class child gets into first grade, too frequently his cognitive, sensory, and language skills are insufficiently developed to cope with what for him are the complex and confusing stimuli offered by the school. It is the interaction of these motivational and maturational dynamics that makes it extremely important for society, through institutions such as the school, to offer the lower-class child an organized and reasonably orderly program of stimulation, at as early an age as possible, to compensate for possible cognitive deficit.

The focus has been on deficit because of the general hypothesis that the experiential deprivations associated with poverty are disintegrative and subtractive from normative growth expectancies. The extent of academic failure and reading retardation associated with lower-class status—and especially with minority group membership within the lower class—makes it imperative that we study the operational relationship between social conditions and these deficits, and the subsequent failure of the school to reverse the tendency toward cumulative retardation in the primary grades.

Our work has been directed particularly toward delineating the effects of conditions of life on cognitive structures. For an understanding of these relationships and the scientific development of enrichment programs, we have emphasized the role of specific social attributes and experiences in the development of language and verbal behavior, of concept formation and organization, of visual and auditory discrimination, of general environmental orientation, and of self-concepts and motivation; and of all of this to school performance. It is the areas mentioned which apparently are essential to the acquisition of scholastic skills, and around which a basic curriculum for early childhood should be developed. Pragmatically, this must be a program which successfully teaches disadvantaged children.

Examination of the literature yields no explanation or justification for any child with an intact brain, and who is not severely disturbed, not to learn all the basic scholastic skills. The failure of such children to learn is the failure of the schools to develop curricula consistent with the environmental experiences of the children and their subsequent initial abilities and disabilities.

As has been emphasized previously in this paper, a compensatory program for children, starting at three or four years of age, might provide the maximum opportunity for prevention of future disabilities and for remediation of current skill deficiencies. In addition, such a program might serve to minimize the effect of the discontinuity between the home and school environments, thereby enhancing the child's functional adjustment to school requirements.

For an early enrichment program, one model available is that developed by Maria Montessori (1959) in the slums of Italy. Though her theoretical system need not be critically evaluated here, there is much in her technology that could productively be re-examined and incorporated in compensatory programs. Basically, this includes the organization of perceptual stimuli in the classroom, so that singular properties become more observable, one at a time, without the distraction of competing, overly complex elements. For example, materials used to convey and illustrate the concept of size and size differential are all the same color and shape. This maximizes the attentional properties of size, and minimizes competing elements. Use of such materials should make it possible for size discriminations to be learned more easily. This method is, of course, carried over to many fields, and the availability of such stimuli under the Montessori system gives the child an opportunity to select materials consistent with his own developmental capabilities. This makes possible success experience, positive reinforcement, and subsequent enhancement of involvement and motivation. The attention to the minutiae of learning, and the systematic exposure to new learning elements based on prior experience, could allow for the development of individualized learning profiles. This would be particularly appropriate for a compensatory program, where there is a great deal of variation in individual needs.

There is, however, a major variable which is apparently inadequately handled by this method, and that is language.

115

Language can be thought of as a crucial ingredient in concept formation, problem-solving, and in the relating to and interpretation of the environment. Current data available to the author and his co-workers tend to indicate that class differences in perceptual abilities and general environmental orientation decrease with chronological age, while language differences tend to increase.

In a social-class-related language analysis, Bernstein (1960), an English sociologist, has pointed out that the lower class tends to use informal language and mainly to convey concrete needs and immediate consequences, while the middle-class usage tends to be more formal and to emphasize the relating of concepts.[1] This difference between these two milieus, then, might explain the finding in some of our recent research that the middle-class fifth grade child has an advantage over the lower-class fifth grader in tasks where precise and somewhat abstract language is required for solution. Further, Bernstein's reasoning would again emphasize the communication gap which can exist between the middle-class teacher and the lower-class child.

One can postulate that the absence of well-structured routine and activity in the home is reflected in the difficulty that the lower-class child has in structuring language. The implication of this for curriculum in the kindergarten and nursery school would be that these children should be offered a great deal of verbalized routine and regulation, so that positive expectations can be built up in the child and then met. It can also be postulated that differences in verbal usage are directly attributable to the level of interaction of the child with the adult, and at this age to a lesser extent, with peers.

In observations of lower-class homes, it appears that speech sequences seem to be temporally very limited and poorly structured syntactically. It is thus not suprising to find that a major focus of deficit in the children's language development is syntactical organization and subject continuity. But in analysis of expressive and receptive language data on samples of middle- and lower-class children at the first and fifth grade levels, there are indications that the lower-class child has more expressive language ability than is generally recognized or than emerges in the classroom. The main differences between the social classes seem to lie in the level of syntactical organization. If, as is indicated in this research, with proper stimulation a surprisingly high level of expressive language functioning is available to the same children who show syntactical deficits, then we might conclude that the language variables we are dealing with here are by-products of social experience rather than indices of basic ability or intellectual level. This

---

[1] In a recent discussion, Bernstein indicated that he was replacing the terms "public" and "formal" with the terms "elaborated" and "restricted." He feels that the latter offer better analytic distinctions and operate at a higher level of abstraction.

again suggests a vital area to be included in any pre-school enrichment program: training in the use of word sequences to relate and unify cognitions.

A language training program would require the creation of a rich, individualized language environment, where words are repeatedly placed in a meaningful context, and where the child is allowed multiple opportunities for expressive language demonstrations as well as for receiving language stimuli under optimal conditions and being encouraged to make appropriate responses. More specifically, stress could be placed on the following areas: orienting feedback, so that if the child says "give me the ——" or "where is ——," the teacher consciously instructs him in a complete sentence as to direction, location, placement, context, etc.; the systematic attempt to increase vocabulary; allowing the child to sort symbols, pictures, and artifacts with letters and words; verbal labelling practice; relating objects and experiences verbally, for example, constructing stories using specified objects and events; every child completing differently incomplete stories suggested by the teacher; reinforcing and encouraging the simultaneous articulation of motor behavior. Through the verbal area it is also possible to train memory, to some extent to train auditory discrimination, and to improve environmental orientation. However, it is not the purpose of this paper to go into a detailed description of potential enrichment procedures.

Working out compensatory programs is based on the assumption that retardation in achievement results from the interaction of inadequately prepared children with inadequate schools and insufficient curricula. This in turn is based on the contention that this large proportion of children is not failing because of inferior innate resources. Also implied is the assumption that one does not sit by and wait for children to "unfold," either on the intellectual or behavioral levels. Rather, it is asserted that growth requires guidance of stimulation, and that this is particularly valid with regard to the child who does not receive the functional prerequisites for school learning in the home. Hunt (1961) points out that ". . . the counsel from experts on child-rearing during the third and much of the fourth decades of the twentieth century to let children be while they grow and to avoid excessive stimulation was highly unfortunate" (p. 362). This is particularly true with regard to lower-class children. We have found that, controlling for socioeconomic status, children with some pre-school experience have significantly higher intelligence test scores at the fifth grade than do children with no pre-school experience (Deutsch and Brown, 1964).

But it is not necessary to consider special education programs only on the pre-school level, even though that is what has been emphasized here. Rather, to assure stability of progress, it would be desirable to continue special programs for several more years. The construction of a pre-school program does not absolve a community or a school system from the responsibility to construct an effective strategy for teaching the marginal youngster from kindergarten on. In fact, if there is to be a reversal of some of the sequelae associated with poverty discussed in this paper, programs must have continuity, at least through the period of the establishment of the basic scholastic learning skills. This means that it is necessary for the community to support kindergartens with reasonable enrollments and adequate equipment, as well as specialized training of staff. As far as the primary grades are concerned, the continuation of special programming through establishment of basic skills would involve probably the time through the third grade year. This level is used, because there is empirical reason to believe that levels of achievement for different social classes start their greatest divergence here. This is probably so because here the work begins to become less concrete and more abstract, more dependent on language symbolization, and, probably most important, more related to good reading skills. For these reasons, it would seem that the child from the preschool and enriched kindergarten classes might best remain in a special ungraded sequence through the third grade level, a period in which he could be saturated with basic skill training, and not be allowed to move on until he has attained basic competence in the skills required by the higher grades. Such an ungraded school would also be of considerable interest theoretically, inasmuch as the child would be in its program through the preoperational stage delineated by Piaget. This should make it possible to devise a systematic curriculum that is consistent with the actual developmental levels of the child during the early childhood period.

Fowler (1962) points out that—

> Few systematic methods have been devised for educating young children, especially in complicated subject matter. We have in mind methods for simplifying and organizing the presentation of cognitive stimuli. Equally important, methods must be sufficiently flexible and play oriented to be adaptable to the primary learning levels and personality organization characteristic of the infant and young child.
>
> The advantages of utilizing the now relatively untapped "preschool" years for cognitive education are, of course, manifest. Most obvious, is the availability of more years of childhood to absorb the increasingly complex technology of modern society, a technology already requiring many of the more productive years of development to acquire. A second is the less evident but more crucial possibility that conceptual learning sets, habit patterns, and interest areas, may well be more favorably established at early than at later stages of the developmental cycle (pp. 145-146).

There are those people who seem to fear the word "cognitive," sometimes correctly, because they are reacting to the over-stringent mechanical models of the past. These models are not what is meant. The potentiation of human resources through the stimulation of cognitive growth could represent a primary therapeutic method for developing positive self-attitudes and a meaningful self-realization. For the lower-class child especially, I would postulate that time is extremely valuable if the deficits are not to be cumulative and to permeate the entire functioning of the child.

The overgeneralized influence on some sections of early childhood education of the emphasis in the child guidance movement upon protecting the child from stress, creating a supportive environment, and resolving emotional conflicts has done more to misdirect and retard the fields of child care, guidance, and development than any other single influence. The effect has especially operated to make these fields ineffective in responding to the problems of integrating and educating the non-white urban child. These orientations have conceived of the child as being always on the verge of some disease process, and have assigned to themselves the role of protecting the child in the same manner that a zoo-keeper arranges for the survival of his charges. Too frequently a philosophy of protectiveness that asks only about possible dangers has prevailed over any question of potential stimulation of development. The attitude that perhaps helped to create this policy of protectionism can also be seen in the suburban "mom-ism" that so many sociologists and psychoanalysts have commented on. The child is a far healthier and stronger little organism, with more intrinsic motivation for variegated experience and learning, than the over-protectionists have traditionally given him credit for.

As Fowler (1961) states further—

Much if not most of the energy in child psychology and development in late years has been concentrated on the child's personality, perceptual motor, and socioemotional functioning and development. Originating primarily as a reaction to historically inadequate and stringent methods, fears have generalized to encompass early cognitive learning per se as intrinsically hazardous to development. As legitimate areas of study, the contributions of studies on perceptual-motor and socioemotional problems are obvious. But in the field of child guidance, interest in these areas has come to permeate and dominate work in child development almost to the exclusion of work on cognitive learning. In harking constantly to the dangers of premature cognitive training, the image of the "happy", socially adjusted child has tended to expunge the image of the thoughtful and intellectually educated child. Inevitably, in this atmosphere, research (and education) in cognition has lagged badly, especially since the 1930's, not only for the early years of childhood but for all ages (p. 145).

And as Hunt (1961) says: "The problem for the management of child development is to find out how to govern the encounters that children have with their environments to foster both an optimally rapid rate of intellectual development and a satisfying life" (pp. 362-363).

A curriculum as discussed here should serve both for the primary prevention of the social deviancies associated with deprivation and for the stimulation of healthy growth and utilization of individual resources. This orientation would represent one effective method of offering opportunities to all peoples to overcome and break the chains of social and historical limitations that have been externally imposed on them. This of course has immediate significance to the current critical questions in both race relations and education in America.

REFERENCES

BERNSTEIN, B. Language and social class. *Brit. J. Sociol.,* 1960, 11, 271-276.

BRUNER, J. S. The cognitive consequences of early sensory deprivation. In P. Solomon (Ed.), *Sensory deprivation.* Cambridge: Harvard Univer. Press, 1961. Pp. 195-207.

DEUTSCH, M. The disadvantaged child and the learning process. In A. H. Passow (Ed.), *Education in depressed areas.* New York: Bur. Pub., Teach. Coll., Columbia Univer., 1963. Pp. 163-179.

DEUTSCH, M. Minority group and class status as related to social and personality factors in scholastic achievement. *Monogr. Society for Applied Anthropology,* 1960, No. 2.

DEUTSCH, M. & BROWN, B. Social influences in Negro-White intelligence differences. *J. soc. Issues,* April, 1964, 24-35.

FOWLER, W. Cognitive learning in infancy and early childhood. *Psychol. Bull.,* 1962, 59, 116-152.

HARRINGTON, M. *The other America* New York: Macmillan Company, 1962.

HUNT, J. McV. *Intelligence and experience.* New York: Ronald Press, 1961.

MONTESSORI, MARIA. *Education for a new world.* Wheaton, Ill.: Theosophical Press, 1959.

SCOTT, J. P. Critical periods in behavioral development. *Science,* 1962, 138, 949-955.

WHITE, R. Motivation reconsidered: The concept of competence. *Psychol. Rev.,* 1959, 66, 297-333.

120

THELMA HARMS

Evaluating Settings for Learning

It is very helpful during an evaluation to look at the environment from a child's point of view. To a child, everything that is present in a setting is a stimulus. He responds to what is really there, not only to what we as adults are aware is there. The way people treat him is as real a part of his environment as the materials on the shelves or the space provided for block building. The teacher's tone of voice, the way she walks and her facial expression contribute to the overall atmosphere. Similarly, the child's interaction with other children is an important component of the school setting. Everything present in the environment, even the spacial arrangement, communicates to the child how to live in that setting. Materials that are in good condition and placed far apart on open shelves tell a child that the materials are valued, that they are meant to be considered, and that a child may take them off the shelf by himself. When they are taken off the shelf, they leave a big, empty space so it is easy to put them back where they belong. What kind of a message does a child get from open shelves crowded with an odd assortment of materials, few with all the pieces put together? What kind of a message does he get from a closed cupboard?

Physical environment is a powerful means of communication. To sensitize yourself to physical environment, set yourself the task, every time you walk into a new setting, of reading the messages contained in the room arrangement. The room with a speaker's stand in front of rows of chairs tells us something about the predicted relationship of teacher to student, and student to student in the class. Chairs in a

YOUNG CHILDREN, 1970, Vol. 26, pp. 304-308.

circle imply another kind of learning interaction.

Children respond to the messages given to them by the physical environment, the activities and the time schedule, so we must become increasingly aware of the total environment we are creating for them. Often problems occur because contradictory messages are being simultaneously sent out by the different components making up the environment. The teacher may be trying to prevent running and sliding while the large, slick expanse of floor in the center of the room is inviting the children to run and slide. Improvement in the children's use of materials in that situation might require a reorganization of the physical environment rather than improvement in interpersonal skills or changes in activities or time schedule. In another school, however, the physical environment may be well defined, the interpersonal atmosphere warm and accepting, but the children may need the challenge of more complex activities, or they may need longer periods of unbroken time to become involved in the activities offered. Each setting for learning needs to be looked at individually because it is a unique combination of children.

Suggestions for Using the Check List

The following list of questions is organized into four categories. Each category contributes in a major way to the environment as experienced by the child. The questions are meant to help

Thelma Harms, M.A., is currently Head Teacher at the Harold E. Jones Child Study Center of the University of California at Berkeley. She is also an Instructor through the University of California Extension Division and is pursuing a doctorate in Early Childhood Education.

you identify both strengths and problems in your own setting. Many schools have found it helpful to give each staff member a checklist to think about for several days before the evaluation meeting. Then, when the entire staff meets, each person is prepared to share his observations and suggestions.

Evaluation Checklist
The Physical Environment

1. Can quiet and noisy activities go on without disturbing one another? Is there an appropriate place for each?
2. Is a variety of materials available on open shelves for the children to use when they are interested? Are materials on shelves well spaced for clarity?
3. Are materials stored in individual units so that children can use them alone without being forced to share with a group?
4. Are activity centers defined so that children know where to use the materials?
5. Are tables or rug areas provided for convenient use of materials in each activity center?
6. Is self-help encouraged by having materials in good condition and always stored in the same place?
7. Are cushioning materials used to cut down extraneous noise—rug under blocks, pads under knock-out bench?
8. Are setup and cleanup simple? Are these expected parts of the child's activity?
9. Have learning opportunities been carefully planned in the outdoor area? Painting, crafts, block building, carpentry, gardening, pets, sand and water all lend themselves

to learning experiences outdoors.

10. Is the children's work displayed attractively at the child's eye level?

11. Do the children feel in control of and responsible for the physical environment?

The Interpersonal Environment

1. Is there a feeling of mutual respect between adults and children, children and children?

2. Is the physical environment enough under control so that the major part of the adults' time is spent in observing or participating with children?

3. Can children engage in activities without being disturbed or distracted by others?

4. Do adults observe children's activity and intervene only when it is beneficial to the child?

5. Do adults have "growth goals" for each child based on the needs they have observed in each child? Is individualized curriculum used to reach these goals?

6. Do children feel safe with one another?

7. Is competition avoided by arranging materials in individual units, limiting the number of children participating in an activity at one time, insuring the fairness of turns by starting a waiting list on which the child can see his name keeping his place in line?

8. Do the adults show children how to help themselves? Are children encouraged to learn from one another?

9. Are there opportunities for children to play alone, participate in a small group, and participate in a large group?

10. When limits are placed, do adults use reasoning and consistently follow through? Are limits enforced?

11. Are the adults models of constructive behavior and healthy attitudes?

12. Is there an overall warm interpersonal environment?

Activities to Stimulate Development

1. Are there many opportunities for dramatic play: large housekeeping corner, small dollhouse, dress-up clothes for boys as well as girls?

2. Is there a variety of basic visual art media: painting, drawing, clay, salt-flour dough, wood-glue sculpture, fingerpaint, collage?

3. Is music a vital part of the program: records, group singing, instruments, dancing?

4. Is language stimulation varied: reading books, games with feel boxes, flannel boards, stories, questions and answers, conversation, lotto games, classification games? Are limits enforced through verbal control and reasoning?

5. Are there small manipulative toys to build eye-hand coordination and finger dexterity?

6. Are there some opportunities to follow patterns or achieve a predetermined goal: puzzles, design blocks, dominos, matching games?

7. Do children do things like cooking, planting seeds, caring for animals?

8. Are field trips planned to give experience with the world around us? Is there adequate preparation and follow-up after trips?

9. Are there repeated opportunities for children to use similar materials? Are materials available in a graded sequence so that children develop skills gradually?

10. Are children involved in suggesting and planning activities? How is free choice built into the program?

11. Are new activities developed by teachers as they are suggested by the interests of individual children?

12. Is the range of activities varied enough to present a truly divergent curriculum? Are there opportunities for learning through exploration, guided discovery, problem solving, repetition, intuition, imitation, etc.? Is there provision for children to learn through their senses as well as verbally?

Schedule

1. Is the time sequence of the school day clear to both teachers and children?

2. Has the schedule been designed to suit the physical plant and particular group of children in the school?

3. Are long periods of time scheduled to permit free choice of activities and companions?

4. Are other groupings provided for in the schedule, e.g., small group activities, one to one adult-child contacts, larger group meetings, etc.?

5. Is the schedule periodically re-evaluated and modified? Are changes in schedule and the reasons for these changes made clear to both staff and children?

Extending Your Experience

Visiting other schools and using the checklist as an observation guide is a good way to extend your experience. There are also some helpful films and books you might want to use as resource materials. A selected list of films, books and pamphlets to extend your experience with environment follows:

Films

"My Art is Me." Univ. of California Film Media Center, Berkeley, Calif.

"Organizing for Free Play." Project Head Start, Office of Economic Opportunity, Washington, D.C.

Books

Almy, Millie C. *Ways of Studying Children.* New York: Teachers College Press, Columbia University, 1959.

Ashton-Warner, Sylvia. *Teacher.* New York: Simon & Schuster, 1963.

Pitcher, E. G., Lasher, N. G., et al. *Helping Young Children Learn.* Columbus, Ohio: Charles E. Merrill Books, 1966.

Read, Katherine. *The Nursery School: A Human Relations Laboratory.* Philadelphia: W. B. Saunders Co., 1960.

Pamphlets

"Space, Arrangement, Beauty in School." #101, Association for Childhood Education International, 3615 Wisconsin Ave., N.W., Washington, D.C. 20066.

"Let's Play Outdoors." #101, National Association for the Education of Young Children, 1834 Connecticut Ave., N.W., Washington, D.C. 20009.

"Nursery School Settings—Invitation to What?" #102, NAEYC.

"Space for Play: The Youngest Children." #111, NAEYC.

MISUNDERSTANDINGS ABOUT
HOW CHILDREN LEARN

DAVID ELKIND

Recently, a young mother of my acquaintance said with some pride: "I insist that my four-year-old daughter watch *Sesame Street*—even when she prefers doing something else." Concerned about the intellectual development of her child, this mother believes that *making* the girl watch the program will eventually help her do better in school.

Many mothers today are pressuring their preschool children to learn numbers, letters, shapes, and so on. Unfortunately, this parental concern for children's intellectual development often seems greater than their concern for children's feelings, interests, and attitudes. What many parents fail to understand is that attempting to force young children to learn specific content may produce an aversive attitude toward academic learning in general. This attitude of distaste may have such serious long-range effects on young children's academic achievement that it completely outweighs the advantages of being familiar with letters, forms, and numbers today or next week.

The foregoing example illustrates one of several common misunderstandings about the thinking and learning of young children that seem to be current today. In this article, I briefly describe five such common misunderstandings that hold particularly true for young children—and a few for older ones as well.

One of the pernicious misunderstandings about young children is that they are most like adults in their thinking and least like us in their feelings. It is just this misconception that prompted the mother mentioned earlier to command her daughter to watch *Sesame Street*. The same woman would not think of

TODAY'S EDUCATION, 1972, Vol. 61,
No. 3, pp. 18-20.

insisting that her husband watch a program she thought might "do him some good." Rather, she would realize that this kind of approach would be a sure way to turn him against the program. And yet, because she believes that children's feelings are different from those of adults, she uses a technique with her child she knows would never work with a grown-up.

Parents and teachers are equally prone to regard a child's thinking process as similar to their own. When, for example, a child asks, "Why is the sun hot?" his father is likely to explain that the sun gives off light and that it takes heat to produce the light. The relation between heat and light is not obvious, however, and the young child would hardly understand. Indeed the real intent of the child's question has to do with the *purpose* of the sun's heat. An appropriate reply would be "to keep us warm" or "to give us a suntan." These answers are not entirely incorrect and they correspond to the young child's underlying belief that everything has a purpose.

Because young children are often so capable linguistically, adults often overestimate their capacity to think.

A second misunderstanding about young children is that they learn best while sitting still and listening. This misconception arises because parents tend to generalize from their experiences as adults. It is true that we adults often learn by listening attentively to a lecture or reading a book.

The young child is, however, not capable of mental activity or thinking in the same way as an adult. He learns through engaging in real actions involving tangible objects, such as blocks or dolls.

Thanks to the work of the famed Swiss psychologist, Jean Piaget, we now know that the child's actions upon things are what facilitate his mental activity or thinking. The young child's actions are progressively miniaturized and interiorized until he is able to do in his head what before he had to do with his hands. This internalization of action comes about gradually during early childhood and is completed at age six or seven.

To illustrate this internalization, observe a four-year-old and a six-year-old performing a simple pencil maze. The younger immediately puts pencil to paper and tries to find the right path. The older, in contrast, studies the maze and only after he has mentally decided on the right path does he put pencil to paper.

Accordingly, when we say young children are "active" learners, we must take this in a literal sense. Montessori said: "Play is the child's work." In play, the child is practicing the various actions that he will eventually internalize as thought.

Therefore, however convenient it may be for grown-ups to think that children learn while sitting still, what they learn in this way is likely to have little lasting value. In contrast, *what children acquire through active manipulation of their environment is the ability to think.*

A third common misunderstanding about young children is the belief that they can learn and operate according to rules. Many parents have had the experience of telling a young child over and over again not to hit his little brother or not to take toys apart or to say thank you when he receives something. Because a young child has not yet internalized thought, he cannot internalize rules either. Consequently, while the child understands the prohibition against hitting his brother and against breaking toys in particular instances, he is unable to generalize to new instances. This is true for learning to say thanks.

The young child's inability to learn rules has special implications for the educational programs prepared for him. We have already noted that the young child learns best through playing with and manipulating materials in his environment. His inability to learn general verbal rules supports this observation and argues against his formal education (involving verbal instruction, a curriculum, and educational objectives). Formal education, whether we speak of reading, arithmetic, or spelling, presupposes the inculcation of rules and thus is inappropriate for the majority of preschool children.

On the other hand, many activities are appropriate educational enterprises for preschoolers. Writing and printing letters is a case in point. Both Montessori and Fernald have pointed out the importance of these for later reading.

Writing as preparation for reading makes good theoretical as well as pedagogical sense in light of the ideas offered earlier. Thinking is an internalization of action, so reading can be regarded, in part at least, as deriving from the internalization of writing actions. Obviously, reading involves much more than the ability to reproduce letters but such reproduction is an appropriate prereading activity for children not yet ready for formal instruction in that skill.

127

Another widespread misunderstanding about young children is that *acceleration* is preferable to *elaboration*. Many parents, for example, spend a great deal of time trying to teach their young children to read or do mathematics. These parents seem to believe that if children have a head start in these special skills they will have a head start generally. The opposite is more likely to be true.

A child who elaborates the skills he does have, such as the ability to arrange materials according to size on a wide range of materials (blocks, sticks, dolls, dogs, and so on), is likely to be better prepared for future learning than a child who has learned a great deal in a short time but who has not had the chance to assimilate and practice what he has learned.

The situation is not unlike that in which one student crams for a test and another studies regularly throughout a semester. While the two may not perform too differently on an exam, the one who has been studying regularly is likely to be better prepared for future courses than the one who makes cramming a regular practice. Parents who try to teach their young children special skills and content are, in effect, teaching a cram course, and the results may be as short-lived for the preschooler as for the college student who crams.

A last common misunderstanding about the learning of young children should be mentioned—one involving the belief that parents and teachers can raise children's IQ. To be sure, IQ is affected by environment, but most middle-class children have probably grown intellectually about as rapidly as their endowment permits. Further enrichment is not likely to have marked effects upon their intellectual ability, although it may affect how they make use of this ability.

Children who have been intellectually deprived can, however, make significant gains in intellectual performance as a consequence of intellectual enrichment. Just as a child who has grown up with an adequate diet will not benefit much from dietary supplements and a child whose diet has been deficient will, so an intellectually well-nourished child is not likely to benefit markedly from further intellectual enrichment whereas a deprived child will.

In large measure, all of these misunderstandings derive from a contemporary overemphasis on intellectual growth to the exclusion of the personal-social

128

side of development. Although I know it sounds old-fashioned to talk about the whole child and tender loving care, I strongly believe that many problems in child rearing and education could be avoided if concern for a child's achievement as a student were balanced by an equally strong concern for his feelings of self-worth as a person.

On the Value of Both Play and Structure in Early Education

WILLIAM FOWLER

In a recent article in YOUNG CHILDREN, Elkind (1970) has extolled virtues of the traditional nursery school and derogated limitations of the newer academic preschools. While I would agree that play and socioemotional development are at the heart of early educational processes, so too are cognition, organization of program and learning. Defining the field of early education in terms of two models may be useful to point up issues, but it may also oversimplify. The academic preschool model is not infrequently a set of techniques which are applied as one component in a context of typical nursery activities—free play, music, art, story time, etc.—in which general as well as cognitive development of the individual child are the objectives (Evans, 1971; Fowler, 1964, 1965a & b, 1970; in press a & b; Fowler & Burnett, 1967; Klaus & Gray, 1968; Leithwood & Fowler, in press; Moore & Anderson, 1968; Sigel & Olmstead, 1970; Smilansky, 1968; Weikart et al., 1970). What is stressed in the academic model is the importance of systematic attention to cognitive learning, *not* necessarily the unimportance of play and the other aspects of child development. It is easily conceivable that a field survey of current programs would show as much variation in the quality of play, social relations, *and program organization* between programs following the nursery school model as between programs following the two separate models.

In this paper I will present an orientation to child development, embracing both cognitive and socioemotional processes and stressing structured guidance and play. Both sets of dimensions are viewed as essential aspects of child rearing in the home and early education in the school. The discussion will be developed in three ways, namely,

YOUNG CHILDREN, 1971, Vol. 27, pp. 24-36.

through a conceptual framework, through discussion of methods and through presentation of some relevant findings.

Conceptual Framework

Competence and Coping

Human development may be seen as a process of acquiring, through activity, competence for coping in all aspects of living. Competence (or intelligence, ability) is the mental organization of rules for learned behavior. There are rules about the nature of the world and how it works. A second set consists of rules for representing and manipulating both the physical and social world and our activities in them. Generally speaking, all human functioning has both cognitive and affective aspects closely interwoven.

Piaget (1950, 1952) has furnished us with an intricate, general theory of the cognitive development of these two basic rule systems, i.e., the structure of the world and our operations in it. His theory has given form and function to mental processes, a gap in traditional stimulus-response theory which has tended to see the person as a passive victim of environmental forces. This gap also has served to retard our understanding of how the mind develops cumulatively and transformationally through experience acquired over long time spans.

Piaget has given less place to the utility of language rules, which appear to aid

William Fowler, Ph.D., is Associate Professor of Applied Psychology at the Ontario Institute for Studies in Education, University of Toronto, Ontario, Canada. He has just completed a three-year study on infant care and education and is now directing a five- to seven-year longitudinal educational investigation on children from early infancy through the preschool period.

comprehension and actions as early as the first year, even though language may not predominate as a guiding and representational tool until the late preschool period (Menyuk, 1964). He also has tended to overlook the role of rules specific to an activity or area of knowledge. There are, for example, rules specific to types of perceptual-motor activities (jumping, gymnastics, drawing, playing a musical instrument, etc.) and rules intrinsic to particular content areas of knowledge (plants, animals, cultural categories, etc.). Partly for this reason Piaget contributes little to our understanding of how enormous individual differences in competence come about.

Competence is, in the main, built around the organization of general rules about the world, around problem-solving strategies and around verbal, language rule systems. For more specialized types of activity, particularized language systems (e.g., mathematical, musical knowledge), perceptual-motor skills and certain analytic and integrative cognitive styles (tactics) essential for problem-solving also come into play. Individuals can differ greatly not only in their experience and hence their competence in general cognitive, problem-solving and language rules, but also in other language skills, perceptual-motor competencies (e.g., wine tasting), specific knowledge and tactical approaches to problem-solving. Intricately interwoven into the development of competence are hierarchies of emotional preference (values) for different kinds of things and activities. Feelings organized around types of rules, things and activities may be spoken of as areas of interest. The organization of enduring drive systems (strong interest areas) emerges through the satisfaction and dissatisfaction and sense of mastery (White, 1965) we encounter in learning the set of rules that defines the type of activity.

Source of Development

What is the source of development of competence and motivation? All kinds of experience, within the limits of biological potential, contribute to the development and differentiation of competence and interests—as hosts of studies relating social variables to IQ and other measures of ability repeatedly show (Anastasi, 1958; Deutsch et al., 1968; Fowler, 1962a, 1968; Hunt, 1961). The amount by which the expression of biological potential can vary is probably huge though difficult to plot, since there is so far no technique for measuring inherited intellectual potential. But we do know and can measure how differences in the amount and type of stimulation experienced over the life span can accumulate to make vast differences in the abilities a person may attain.

This great potential *in each individual* for widely different developmental outcomes, depending on his cumulative experiences, has two serious implications. First, it is essential to become more aware of the quality and variety of developmental experience from earliest infancy. Second, the risks of understimulation are at least as great as the risks of overstimulation for the development of competence and personality. We need to optimize stimulation to realize something approaching maximum potential— while using methods which minimize risks that could arise from the wrong kind of pressure. It is not that we can develop every child into a genius, but that 1) cognitive potential is widely underdeveloped even in the general population of the middle-class world, and 2) stimulation is not something artificially imposed from without; it is an essential catalyst without which development cannot occur.

Development may be defined as a process of developmental learning, in which the acquisition of personality, competence and interests evolve through the cumulative effects of thousands of encounters between the organism and the environment. In this process the organism is far from being a passive screen upon which stimulation is inscribed, as the early behaviorists were inclined to say. Developmental learning is a continuously active process in which experience structures the mind of the child as a system to select and organize all new stimulation to fit in with what he has already learned. As Piaget puts it, assimilation is as integral to the developmental process as accommodation. Piaget, however, and nursery school philosophy value mostly the active, self-regulatory processes of learning, the learning children get from self-initiated play and other exploratory-manipulative activities. The powerful role construction and sociodramatic play and autonomous activity serve in elaborating the cognitive and imaginative operations of the mind indeed appears vital, as many theorists hold and the investigations of Smilansky (1968) suggest. Yet the competence complexity and coping strategies a child acquires are just as dependent upon the information and the quality and quantity of verbal guidance and demonstrations made available by adults as upon the manner in which stimulation is presented. It is unfortunate that active experimentation (play) has become pitted against adult planning and guidance, both of which are in different ways essential to complex and rounded development.

Early experience is critical for development, in the sense that the fate of all later learning is irrevocably dependent upon the type of early experience. Because learning is cumulative, if the first three years have been spent productively in the acquisition of knowledge and effective problem-solving strategies, the child is better equipped to assimilate widely and deeply from all subsequent encounters. It makes a difference what kinds of approaches toward problem-solving become established in the early years—whether diffuse or analytic, scattered or integrated. If a young child fails to learn effective problem-solving styles at the beginning, he does not simply operate at a lower level of functioning. He in fact acquires *nonproductive* modes of coping to which he becomes emotionally attached and which are difficult to alter in later development, as our experiences with the socially disadvantaged tend to show. Although early established deficiencies can in most cases be later improved, it is undoubtedly advantageous to establish productive levels and styles in the first place.

Experience provides an amalgam of stimulation from multiple sources. Among these are 1) the patterning of the physical environment; 2) the child's own activity in manipulating the dimensions of the physical environment; 3) the world of stimulation from peers and adults; and 4) the child's own activity in interacting with these two social sources of stimulation.

Methods of Early Education and Child Rearing

Certain principles for facilitating the cognitive and socioemotional development of infants and young children appear to follow from the foregoing conceptual framework. Many of them are consonant with traditional practice in nursery school despite shifts in emphasis. In the first place, the child as an "actor" on the scene helps determine how and what learning occurs. Second, it is essential to present stimuli in patterns intrinsic to, though slightly in advance of, the child's acquired cognitive complexity level and familiarity patterns as Hunt (1964) has suggested. Similarly, it is equally desirable to present stimulation in the context of the sensorimotor and concrete modes which predominate in early development. Fourth is the importance of fluid, interactive relations between peers, and between adults and children, to develop personality, social mastery and coordination of actions between the social and physical world. Further, is the importance of play, fantasy, manipulation and experimentation.

Most of the above principles are well represented in the nursery school movement, but other equally important ones are usually underemphasized or overlooked. Of these, perhaps the most important is the notion of systematic planning. Few teachers (or parents) attempt to map what a child could acquire over the period from birth to six years of age. Long-range curriculum planning and teaching, even when employed, is constructed with reference to norms which represent cultural tradition, *not the potential which might be realized through planned socialization.* Individualizing the curriculum and interactive, play-oriented methods, while valuable (and, contrary to much opinion in the field of early education, are not in opposition to systematic, flexible planning of development curriculum), are insufficient in themselves to stimulate development optimally. We must make a more realistic developmental inventory of potential competencies, and design systematic, long-range developmental learning programs to develop optimum potential in *all* children.

Also typical of much nursery school practice is to take one's program cue mainly from the child's spontaneous interest of the moment. Insufficient thought is given, not only to where an instruction fits into either developmental or concept sequences, but to what happened the week before or what could happen the week after. Any laboratory or well endowed nursery school is well equipped with blocks, puzzles and a variety of construction and play materials; but few teachers are aware of the hierarchy of spatial rules by which building with unit blocks can be ordered. Lacking this information, teachers seldom know how to facilitate a child's progression from simple concepts to the more complex, combinatorial rules for constructing block structures. It is not that some children do not make progress spontaneously through their own activity and observations of other competent block builders. It is rather that there is always a substantial proportion of children (particularly girls for cultural reasons), in the nursery school who make little or no progression in mastering these forms of competence. Moreover, the level of all—even the most advanced—children could generally rise, given adequate perspective and guidance by the nursery school teacher (Fowler, 1965b).

I use the example of block building since it lies at the heart of the traditional curriculum and for good reason. It provides experience in integrative (creative) cognitive processes as well as in mastery of the rules of spatial organization. But the same lack of system permeates many other equally important areas including language development. Many children learn rules to manipulate language quite well through the spontaneous social interaction available in the home and nursery school. But the opportunity to hear and produce language in elaborative forms, through individual diagnosis and programming of each child, would greatly enrich the level of many underdeveloped children and raise the general level of preschool language development. If most preschoolers acquire the basic rules of language through the socialization ordinarily provided in any of the world's cultures (Lenneberg, 1964; Menyuk, 1964), there are nevertheless developmental variations in their rate of learning. Minimal competence also is not to be equated with the potential for expanded thematic and combinatorial richness in the refined rules and use of language which could be fostered by systematic attention. Language has many more dimensions as a complex problem-solving instrument and as an aesthetic literary tool than are usually made available for most young children. Psycholinguistic theories and research could be effectively applied to greatly enhance competence in language through day care and nursery school experience. In the same way, many additional concepts about the physical world could be systematically inventoried and developed in sequential curricula. Again, it is not that attention to concepts does not occur in current practice. It is rather that there is little detailed perspective of what comes next, of what series of steps leads to abstract logical thinking as, for example, what steps lead to the development of multiple classification and conservation competencies.

It is a mistake to think that there are typical forms of socialization employed in both the middle-class and nursery school worlds which already embrace most of the effective methods that can be discovered and applied. There are many variations among school methods and many of the wide individual differences in competence among children within the middle-class world have been shown to relate to differences between child-rearing techniques in the home (Cox, 1962; Fowler, 1962a; Freeberg & Payne, 1967). Similarly, I believe that nursery school curricula and methods will benefit the middle-class as well as the disadvantaged child far more, as current developments in our knowledge of cognitive development are incorporated as a basis for planning developmental learning strategies.

Interaction, Sequential, Developmental Learning Model

Over a number of years I have been developing methods for facilitating the cognitive and general development of children from infancy to school age. Many of the principles of this approach are similar to those employed in a good laboratory nursery school (Fowler, 1964, 1965a, b & c, 1966, 1967, 1970, in press a & b; Fowler & Burnett, 1967; Leithwood & Fowler, in press). Free play, cooperative social and warm emotional experience, experimentation in fantasy development and with construction toys, sensorimotor curriculum have been extensively used in every infant and nursery school program where I have taught or directed.

But I also have developed roles for teachers to guide young children sys-tematically yet interactively in concept learning in small groups. Concept learning programs in areas of knowledge (e.g., transportation, occupations) or language systems (e.g., math or reading) are individually sequenced, paced and presented in sensorimotor play and problem-solving activities. The significance of this approach is not restricted to the information imparted—although this has much value—but is considered to rest more in the development of learning sets and cognitive styles of inquiry as a foundation for learning later in development. It is the dual aspect of learning how to figure out problems, how to analyze and integrate relations in the context of acquiring knowledge, which imparts to children both the value of learning and the skills to acquire it.

Teachers are also trained to guide children in free play—on a more limited, yet still essential basis. The objectives of guidance in free play are to furnish occasional cues to help children discover critical relations in their construction, puzzle and sociodramatic play activities. Without cognitive guidance, along with occasional emotional support, children often fail to grasp essential operations, become discouraged and soon desert their play. Guidance in this form, used selectively and sparingly, far from creating dependency, is a useful and probably necessary means of fostering the development of cognitive as well as socioemotional autonomy at complex levels of experimentation and play. Children who need little or none of this type of guidance are already comparatively self-propelled at advanced levels because of a history of judicious guidance at home or in the neighborhood from parents or older peers (Fowler, 1962a). But many children—middle-class and otherwise—enter nursery school needing considerable guidance to advance further. Even the already well developed, independent players will develop more richly with some continuing guidance—if it is sensitive and knowledgeable.

The Concept of Structure in Learning

The importance of adults (or older peers) guiding the stimulation of children, that is, ordering and arranging environmental patterns and pointing out rules to facilitate problem-solving and learning, cannot be underestimated. Self-initiated exploration, inquiry and discovery alone is only one, albeit major source for the development of competence systems. Historically, there has been an unfortunate confounding of several essentially distinct dimensions of the concept of structure. There are first the structures of the physical world, which are of course the basis for the structure of knowledge. There is no effective knowledge which does not have a structure, whether derived through spontaneous interaction with an environment or through a teacher ordering and explaining patterns to facilitate discovery and learning on the part of the child.

But the sort of structure usually confused with these other two by nursery school traditionalists is the structure the instructional approach assumes. Strongly condemned are the formal, didactic and authority-centered forms of teaching prominent in education until the development of the nursery school and progressive education movements early in this century (Fowler, 1962a). Teachers are and ought to be legitimately concerned about the danger of stifling children's curiosity, active exploration and creativity in learning and problem-solving. Still another definition of structure, often attacked but frequently confused with other definitions, is the notion of structure as an abstract and symbolic type of curriculum.

This confounding of definitions has led to a confusion of method with substance. Few professionals anywhere still advocate the rigid methods of the old didacticism, in which the sole child-teacher interaction consisted of rote recitation. But to advocate direct experience and openness of teacher-child, child-environment interchange need not—indeed *can* not—eliminate the need for structuring information, simply because both the world and the intricate set of rules we call knowledge, problem-solving and constructing activity *are* ordered. There are only two ways in which method conflicts with the structure of knowledge: when methods and communication are either too rigid or too loose (as sometimes happens in nursery school practice). In either case, method is pushed at the expense of substance and less than optimal amounts of knowledge are exchanged—or opportunities for complex problem-solving provided. Adults cannot escape their role as a repository of information about the world, acquired through a lifetime of socialization in knowledge and institutions, which in turn have taken a long social history to develop, as Dewey (1943) long ago observed. The teacher, even with young children, must be a leader in guiding the child to acquire rules about how the world works and rules for creative problem-solving. He should not resort to "transmission belt" approaches to impart information. This is both too restricting of the child's mental processes and too abstract. But he does need gently to draw the child's attention to how environmental arrangements and processes *are* ordered. The child will also apprehend more readily and rapidly if a teacher has an ordered plan for pacing her guidance. She needs to follow some flexible scheme of levels of complexity, charted for each area of knowledge, like community relations, social concepts or geographical concepts. While she need not follow slavishly a point-by-point plan, she does need a map of the territory she plans to cover, which would spell out many examples of concepts roughly equivalent in level of difficulty for each level. For example, she should expect to explore with young children the names and prominent parts of flowers, and the setting, before getting too involved with analyzing complex organizations of flower structures, their functions, their relations to the environment, and the sequential transformations of growth processes. Again, sequential learning plans are essential; following them, on the other hand, is an exercise involving considerable flexibility and multiple interpersonal and communication skills.

The Use of Language

As far as the employment of language in early curricula, it has already been pointed out that, while the world of the young child is sensorimotor and literal, language plays an increasingly vital role in organizing and steering the child in his engagements with the environment. In many senses, it may be handicapping to defer concentration on language (including graphic forms, i.e., reading, mathematical operations and certainly music) from early periods of development. Anything but a rich exposure to language will deprive children of a complex foundation in the cognitive rule systems in which much of their later social experience will take place.

Developmental Learning Programs in Nursery School

Happily, teaching young children language rules in systematic programs, whether oral (verbal language), graphic (reading and writing), or in other systems (music and math), can be as productive and enjoyable to young children as experiences in any other domain. Using the sensorimotor play and interactive model mentioned earlier, the author has constructed a number of learning programs for infants and young children. These programs have generally led to the development of competence in the areas presented beyond norms usually encountered and, usually, has been accompanied by considerable enjoyment and curiosity. Each of the programs has been sequenced and tailored to individual children instructed singly or in groups of two to six children. We capitalize on children's delight in identifying and interacting with peers, yet groups are small enough to permit continuous individualizing of attention for every child.

In a series of studies on early reading, for example, culminating in a large scale three-year program at the University of Chicago Nursery School, over 80 percent, or 107 of 132, three- to five- year-old children learned to read with a moderate to high degree of fluency (Fowler, in press (b)). Programs of five to six months duration were built around sensorimotor play, interactive methods. Several points relevant to the value of this kind of play-oriented, early academic learning should be stressed:

1. The proportion of time spent in

learning to read. Reading activity consumed about 10 to 20 minutes per day for each child who participated, generally constituting one of three guided learning activities. The other two activities consisted of math, music, and/or natural or social science concept learning projects. The total time expended in guided learning projects, therefore, ranged from 30 to 60 minutes in a three-hour morning nursery school program. The balance of the time was spent in free play, indoors and out. The remainder of each child's day was spent in play at home or in the neighbourhood, together with varying amounts of the usual stimulation provided in middle-class homes.

2. Readiness and motivations for academic learning. The children had a mean IQ of around 120 and a mental age of about four years or over, a level at which research has consistently shown children taught with tutorial methods (in contrast to the mass methods of the elementary school system) can readily learn to read (Davidson, 1931; Durkin, 1966, 1969; Fowler, 1962b, 1965a, in press (b); Moore & Anderson, 1968). The high proportion and high level of successful readers underscores the appropriateness of early childhood as a period of cognitive developmental readiness for reading—at least for many cognitively advantaged children. Fluency was defined by the ease with which children meaningfully read test material. In addition, on a variety of letter and word recognition, and sentence and paragraph reading measures, performance levels typically reached 80 or more percent and rarely fell below 60 percent.

Another index of readiness, motivation, is suggested by the mean motivational level of 3.3 (on a 4-point scale) of the children in the program. This statistic is paralleled by observers' frequent characterizations of the children as enthusiastic and self-propelled in pursuing reading both at school and at home. Many of the reading activity games involved children working in pairs independent of continuous teacher guidance. Moreover, the 20 percent who were offered reading, but failed to continue, included children who (mistakenly) were not posttested, children who left school because the family moved in the course of the program, and children diverted to other projects because a teacher could not cope with a child's general behavioral style even though the child was making progress in and enjoying the reading process. Perhaps 10 percent were moved to other activities due to failure to develop interest or difficulty in learning. And this in turn was usually a failure of teachers to follow careful pacing and play-oriented methods. The freedom of teachers to discontinue reading instruction with any child at any time is believed to be in itself a good measure of the children's continuing high motivation.

3. The general cognitive nature of the process. The involvement of cognition is suggested by the 80 percent score level at which children were able to recognize unfamiliar words and combinations of words and the even higher level (around 90 percent) for reading and comprehending paragraphs of new material. Reading new words, new sentences and paragraphs involves cognitive processes of sequential integration in which the child must identify discrete elements in sequence and synthesize them into a new pattern from which he can then derive meaning. While this is anchored in perceptual processes the integrative conceptual act is clearly a cognitive process. The acquisition of these integrative operations, central to the process of learning to read, appeared to be facilitated by an analytic-synthesizing method which organized tasks to illuminate these operations, e.g., grapheme units to make words, and words to make sentences. While not at the more abstract, logical level of class inclusion-exclusion and conservation, it would seem that these should be defined as cognitive operations beyond the level of rote association which Elkind (1970) and White (1965) appear to believe are the limits of preschool cognitive competence.

The use of the concept "rote association" to characterize learning as a developmental universal for early childhood can be questioned even for infants. In an investigation on teaching problem-solving to 16- to 24-month-old infants, a student of the author succeeded in developing cognitively mediated problem-solving in a box-opening problem (significantly more than controls) with four of six infants (Henninger, 1968). Mediation was judged on the basis of ability to transfer across different box shapes, sizes and orientations, the infant operating purposively on relevant dimensions, ignoring distracting perceptual and positional cues. In another study, at the preschool level, 12 four-year-olds not only mastered complex gymnastic routines through a four-month program, while controls learned virtually none, but many went on to recombine components spontaneously to create new (to them) routines of considerable complexity (Leithwood & Fowler, in press).

In all of these studies and in fact, in creative social and construction play, children can be seen as learning rules.

Two sorts of rules are needed. One sort are the rules for making flexible mental constructs for how external structures are *generally* organized, regardless of many perceptual details—as in the foregoing cases, the nature of boxes, complex gross motor movements, graphic language, social roles, block structures, etc. The second sort consists of rules for operating on and combining elements to problem solve and create. It is doubtful if either of these classes of rule systems are limited to rote associational processes, given the variety of *intentional* constructions young children come to create which follow general rules and are not literal copies of models. While none of the situations described consist of a completely abstract framework of symbol systems, they appear to demand mental manipulation of concrete and semiabstract structures according to cognitively mediated rules.

4. Does early reading instruction limit creativity? That learning to read does not appear to inhibit creativity, curiosity or inquiry is indicated by the children's behavior in free play outside the various guided learning activities in which they participated. Highly elaborated, independently conceived and developed block structures, paintings, clay productions, sociodramatic play engagements, and so on, were typical in their play. Moreover, the level of participation, complexity and diversity of play among the children was substantially greater at the end than at the beginning of the program year. An interesting feature with respect to the potential value of guided learning was the extent to which themes in the children's play were found to reflect many features originating in but creatively varied from the guided learning activities. They constructed forms, used materials and concepts (e.g., vehicles, dinosaurs, community concepts, play with words and sentences, and reading itself) drawn from the content themes of the various guided learning projects.

Infant Developmental Learning Program

During the past two years I have been developing a similar general program in an infant day care center but adapted to the younger developmental period (Fowler, 1969). In a group of about 40 infants (cumulatively) ranging in age from approximately 3 to 30 months and consisting of children of advantaged working mothers and disadvantaged (usually) nonworking mothers, we have developed an all-day program of total care and developmental learning which includes parent guidance. The approach to child care and education is built around the same methods of flexible, interpersonal communication and stress upon autonomy, warmth, physical expression of tenderness (e.g., cuddling) and cognitive orientations toward the child's exploration of the world around him. There is considerable emphasis upon language, problem-solving and learning concepts in many spheres of activity, through the daily routines, extensive free play, indoors and out, and special guided learning activities.

While samples are still small, a recent testing (Fowler et al., 1970) shows a sample of disadvantaged children (N = 5) changed from a mean of 92 IQ points on the Bayley Mental Scale at age 5 months to 115 points at 13 months, a significant (p<.025) mean IQ gain of 23 points over a period of eight months. All pretesting was carried out only after a period of one to two months adaptation in the program.

Among the advantaged children we have an interesting comparison of the differential effects of age and duration of treatment. Six infants (Group A) whose mean age was 22 months at the time the program began had a mean IQ of 119 on the Bayley Mental Scale and a mean of 121 on the Binet seven months later when they were 29 months of age, an inconsequential change of only two points. In contrast, another sample of seven children (Group B), 11 months of age when the program began, changed from a mean IQ of 114 to 128 on the Bayley over six months, reaching a mean IQ of 143 on the Binet about nine months later when they were nearly 27 months of age. Not only are these total 29 point mean gains highly significant (p<.025) but the difference in the final score between Groups A and B, 121 versus 143, at about the same age, 29 versus 27 months, are also significant (p<.025), compared to their similar initial IQ levels 119 versus 114 (though at different ages, 22 versus 11 months). Five of the seven children in Group B attained a final Binet score of 140 or above and only one child failed to gain at least 12 points (he lost seven points, from 136 to 129).

Of equal interest, on preliminary measures (Schaefer and Aaronson's Behavioral Inventory, unpublished), the mean level at which our infants are rated on socioemotional items such as positive social response, inquisitiveness, perseverance, contentment, enthusiasm, and so on, is consistently high (14 to 15 on a combined 20 point scale) while ratings on negative-affect items such as monotonous behavior, self-consciousness, irritability, distractibility, passivity and so on, consistently fall at 10 or 12. These (and other) ratings are supported by manifold impressions of staff and visitors of the unusual competence and personal expressiveness of most of our children in social relations with both peers and adults, their ability to adapt to many adults and new situations readily, their general language competence (Kohen-Raz, 1967) and their high general interest and curiosity. In one instance, a child who was borderline autistic upon entering the program at ten months is now quite responsive, curious and active in cognitive learning. Final analysis (now in process) of cumulative findings embracing more children appear to show the same magnitude of cognitive gains and socioemotional adaption (Fowler, in press (a)).

Conclusion

The full implication of these findings must of course, wait upon the accumulation of larger samples (currently planned) and systematic follow-up research, in light of the relatively small samples and known instability of test scores in the early years. What is important at this stage of our knowledge (which rests mainly upon methods derived from untested theories, philosophies and convictions) is to leave open opportunities for systematic assessment of the differential effects of all sorts of programs and methods. Provided proper child welfare safeguards are always utilized, we must explore many avenues before we have anything approaching clear answers on what constitutes good programs for infants and young children. It is not unlikely that different combinations of approaches will be found to be suitable for different types of homes and children. Yet, on a broad plane our findings generally support the notion of the equal, indeed essential, value of *both* symbolic, guided, cognitive orientations and self-propelled, free play and flexible approaches toward early child care and education. The implications of our research to date suggest that, far from being uneconomic, integrated cognitive-interpersonal approaches to child rearing foster the development of competence, autonomy and personality development in children from many social backgrounds.

References

Anastasi, A. *Differential psychology.* (3rd Ed.) New York: Macmillan, 1958.

Cox, G. G. *The effect of Parent-Child Relationships on Intelligence and Achievement in Children.* Unpublished doctoral dissertation. Univ. of California, Berkeley, 1962.

Davidson, H. P. An experimental study of bright, average and dull children at the four-year mental level. *Genet. Psychol. Monogr.,* 1931, 9, 119-289.

Deutsch, M., Katz, I. & Jensen, A. R. (Eds.) *Social Class, Race and Psychological Development.* New York: Holt, Rinehart & Winston, 1968.

Dewey, J. *The Child and the Curriculum* and *The School and Society.* Chicago: Univ. of Chicago Press, 1943.

Durkin, D. *Children who Read Early.* New York: Teacher College Press, Columbia, Univ., 1966.

Durkin, D. A two-year language arts program for pre-first grade children: first year report. *Amer. educ. Res. Assoc.,* Paper Abstracts, 1969, 122-123.

Elkind, D. The case for the academic preschool: fact or fiction? *Young Children,* 1970, 25, 132-142.

Evans, E. D. *Contemporary Influences in Early Childhood Education.* New York: Holt, Rinehart & Winston, 1971.

Fowler, W. Cognitive learning in infancy and early childhood. *Psychol. Bull.,* 1962, 2, 116-152 (a).

————. Teaching a two-year-old to read: an experiment in early childhood learning. *Genet. Psychol. Monogr.,* 1962, 66, 181-283 (b).

————. Structural dimensions of the learning process in early reading. *Child Develpm.,* 1964, 35, 1093-1104.

————. A study of process and method in three-year-old twins and triplets learning to read. *Genet. Psychol. Monogr.,* 1965, 72, 3-89 (a).

————. Concept learning in early childhood. *Young Children.* 1965, 21, 81-91 (b).

————. Design and values in the nursery school. *Inland Architect,* 1965, 9, 12-15 (c).

————. Dimensions and directions in the development of affecto-cognitive systems. *Human Develpm.*, 1966, 9, 18-29.

————. The design of early developmental learning programs for disadvantaged young children. *Supp. to IRCD Bull.*, 1967, 3, 1A.

————. The effect of early stimulation in the emergence of cognitive processes. In D. Hess & R. M. Bear (Eds.), *Early Education*. Chicago: Aldine, 1968, chap. 2.

————. The patterning of developmental learning processes in the nursery school. In A. J. Biemiller (Ed.) *Problems in the Teaching of Young Children*. Toronto: Ontario Institute for Studies in Education, 1970, 27-43.

————. A developmental learning approach to infant care in a group setting. *Merrill-Palmer Qtrly.* (in press) (a).

————. A developmental learning strategy for early reading in a laboratory nursery school *Interchange* (in press) (b).

Fowler, W. & Burnett, A. Models for learning in an integrated preschool. *Elem. sch. J.*, 1967, 67, 428-441.

Fowler, W., Grubman, D., Hart, S., Rotstein, A. & Ward, S. *Demonstration Day Care and Infant Education Program: Interim Report*. Ontario Institute for Studies in Education, Toronto, 1970 (mimeo.).

Freeberg, N. E. & Payne, D. T. Dimensions of parental practice concerned with cognitive development in the preschool child. *J. Genet. Psychol.*, 1967, 111, 245-261.

Henninger, Polly. *Infant Problem Solving*. Unpublished master's thesis, Ontario Institute for Studies in Education, Toronto, 1968.

Hunt, J. McV. *Intelligence and Experience*. New York: Ronald, 1961.

————. The psychological basis for using preschool enrichment as an antidote for cultural deprivation. *Merrill-Palmer Qrtrly.*, 1964, 10, 209-248.

Klaus, R. A. & Gray, S. W. The early training project for disadvantaged children: a report after five years. *Monogr. Soc. Res. child Develpm.*, 1968,

33, (Whole No. 120).

Kohen-Raz, R. Scalogram analysis of some developmental sequences of infant behavior as measured by the Bayley Infant Scale of Mental Development. *Genet. Psychol. Monogr.*, 1967, 76, 3-21.

Leithwood, K. A. & Fowler, W. Complex motor learning in preschool children. *Child Develpm.* (in press).

Lenneberg, E. H. A biological perspective of language. In E. H. Lenneberg (Ed.), *New Directions in the Study of Language*. Cambridge: M.I.T. Press, 1964.

Menyuk, P. Syntactic rules used by children from preschool through first grade. *Child Develpm.*, 1964, 35, 533-546.

Moore, O. K. & Anderson, A. R. The responsive environments project. In R. D. Hess & R. M. Bear (Eds.), *Early Education*, Chicago: Aldine, 1968.

Piaget, J. *The psychology of Intelligence*. London: Routledge & Kegan Paul, 1950.

————. *The origins of Intelligence in Children*. New York: International Universities Press, 1952.

Schaefer, E. S. & Aaronson, M. *Infant Behavior Inventory*. Laboratory of psychology, National Institute of Mental Health, U.S. Dept. HEW, (unpublished).

Sigel, I. E. & Olmsted, P. The development of classification and representational competence. In A. J. Biemiller (Ed.), *Problem in the Teaching of Young Children*. Toronto: Ontario Institute for Studies in Education, 1970, 49-67.

Smilansky, S. *The effects of socio-dramatic play on disadvantaged preschool children*. New York: 1968.

Weikart, D. P. et al. *Longitudinal results of the Ypsilanti Perry Preschool Project*. Ypsilanti, Mich: High/Scope Educational Research Foundation, 1970.

White, S. H. Evidence for a hierarchical arrangement of learning processes. In L. Lipsitt & C. C. Spiker (Eds.), *Advances in Child Development and Behavior*. Vol. II. New York: Academic Press, 1965, 187-220.

Play, The Essential Ingredient

Ruth E. Hartley

THE VOICE OF THE HURRIER is being heard in the land. We have not come unscathed through the crippling attacks of the developmentally ignorant who so recently sought to set early childhood education back into the dark ages of the Dame schools and the horn book. Many of us, including parents, teachers and psychologists, are still anxious and uncertain about the values of child-oriented, rounded basic early education, of which the child's own eager play is the chief tool.

"Play," said Lawrence Frank, "is the way a child learns what no one can teach him." More than ever before, we need to deepen our understanding of the power of this spontaneous, absorbed activity. We need to see what enormous and necessary contributions play and creative activities can make toward the learning and thinking abilities of children —toward the desired cognitive growth that is currently being emphasized almost to the exclusion of all other facets of development.

COGNITION—PROCESSES AND CONCEPTS

First, perhaps we need to review briefly what cognition is and how it develops. During the child's early years we can identify a number of *processes*, through which learning takes place, and key *concepts*, the tools that are needed for thinking.

The processes make up a fairly long list: identifying, differentiating, generalizing, classifying, grouping, ordering or seriating, abstracting, symbolizing, combining, reasoning.

They involve a number of activities and abilities: attending, perceiving, remembering, recognizing, focusing.

The concepts needed for dealing with ideas are even more numerous. The simplest are concepts of objects, object-qualities, and characteristics of substances: form, color, texture, consistency, elasticity, permeability, solidity— the "thingness" of things.

Children also need to acquire many sorts of *relational* concepts—relationships of object to object, of part to whole, of part to part. Within these relational concepts are included quantitative relationships of number, ordination, cardination, equivalence, size, volume and conservation. These are based on such simple learnings as: what is more and what is less; what is larger and what is smaller, heavier and lighter; that a group is more than one; that a group of many is different from a group of few; that two small entities can equal one larger one; that objects can be arranged in an orderly progression; that a given amount remains the same no matter into how many parts it is divided or what shape it takes.

Young children need to learn about the qualities of space, which include *topological* aspects of proximity, order, continuity and enclosure, as well as the simpler relationships of objects in space: up-down, in-out, far-near. They must acquire concepts of time (today-yesterday, now-later, before-after), which depend on understanding sequences, beginnings and endings; and concepts of velocity, which depend on realizing the relationships between movement and space.

CHILDHOOD EDUCATION, 1971, Vol. 38, pp. 80-84.

143

They need to know about the functioning of natural forces: gravity, electricity, magnetism, air, fire and water. They need to comprehend natural processes: growth, birth, decay, death. Finally, they must begin to comprehend the relationships of event to event— causation, which forms the substratum of all logical thinking.

To acquire all these understandings, a child needs, first and most basically, a wide variety of *repeated, concrete* experiences. Both the variety and the chance for repetition are essential. Only in this way can a child master the quality of objects—through his own relationship to them. He has to taste, feel, smell, hear and manipulate as well as see them—and he has to do this over and over again until he knows the objects so well he no longer needs to have them physically present to know what they are like and how they will behave in a wide range of circumstances.

By giving the child access to many different kinds of materials (blocks, paints, sand, water, toys of different sizes and colors, objects of the same size and shape but differing in color, objects of the same color but differing in size and shape) and freedom to explore them in his own way, we make possible the first cognitive layer—his ability to recognize objects and actions, to distinguish them from each other, to become aware of similarities and differences, and finally to abstract, to classify and to symbolize. All this comes naturally and zestfully from a rich, active play life.

SOME PLAY ACTIVITIES

A most important step in the development of thinking lies in the direction of problem-solving. Skill in problem-solving involves attitudes as well as information—a willingness to ask questions, to experiment, to explore different ways of doing things, to try out alternatives. For the development of these attitudes the free give-and-take of the play world is the best of all contexts and the structured tasks of rote learning the worst. Let us look at some specific play materials to see how play serves these functions.

Fingerpainting and Mindbuilding

Few people consider fingerpainting a mind-building activity. But notice what is happening while a child fingerpaints. First he learns what the fingerpaint "feels" like—part of the multi-sensory input considered so important for getting children ready to learn in more abstract fashion. Then he notices that *he* is producing an effect, which has a visible form. At the same time he gets muscle-sensations from the movements he is making, so that the form he sees and the movement sensations he feels are connected; and he gets to know the forms he is producing in the most basic fashion, from the inside out. He then goes on to learn color differences and color-blending, how to create more subtle effects with colors and more complex and rhythmic designs than he can with any other means. His own intimate body rhythms and natural motoric responses become

144

externalized as aspects of the outside world, which he has produced. When the child can so easily create welcome impressions on the world, he is encouraged to keep on doing, trying, experimenting—all activities that go into making creative learners.

Playing with Water
Now let us look at waterplay, another too frequently disregarded form of play that packs a powerful intellectual punch if made available correctly. What can children learn from waterplay? What can they not learn?

First, of course, there is the lovely *feel* of the stuff—the sheer *pleasure* of playing with water. This pleasure is extremely important to learning because it encourages the child to explore, to try out different ways of handling it. Here at once we have two essentials of intellectual growth—*interest and experimentation*. This stuff we call water—probably the best thing we can find for lengthening the interest span of jumpy, short-spanned children—leads to spontaneous exercises in control and in estimating quantity. Waterplay offers, too, the kinds of experiences of reversibility that are essential to developing an understanding of conservation.

Blocks and Spaces
Wise teachers know that in manipulating objects and themselves in play children are laying the groundwork for mathematics, physics, geography. Blockplay, for example, offers opportunities for discovering equivalences (leading to understanding fractions); concepts of size, form, quantity, directionality, gravity (balance); and the whole gamut of spatial relationships. But always we must remember it is the child's spontaneous interest that furnishes the steam. And the teacher's knowledge gives

focus and form, by varying the materials made available and letting the child take them over in his own way.

While "playing" with blocks children are practicing seriation, gaining skills in the dynamics of balance, learning cause and effect in physical relationships. The properties of size and spatial relations are reinforced as they fit cylinders into each other, as they pile graduated blocks into towers and pyramids. The properties of space are most intimately learned as they climb jungle gyms, nets, ropes and ladders; as they guide wagons, platforms and tricycles around obstacles; as they swing their bodies through arcs, try to cram themselves into crannies too small for them, create spirals and serpentines as they twist and weave around the playground.

The World's a Stage
Dramatic play, perhaps the most prevalent type of play, is rarely appreciated for its mindbuilding functions. Yet we must realize that the child uses dramatic play to master the meaning of adult behavior. To this end he plays imitative sequences of family life over and over. He is mastering the ways of the adult world in the same way he earlier mastered the skills of walking and climbing and throwing —by sheer repetitive practice.

Another step in mental development, one we might call mental digestion, is taken when a child is able to express his perception of an object through action. The infant uses his body constantly to learn about the world: objects become meaningful to him only through sensory and manipulative experience of them. As part of his learning, he imitates them. Trying to open a box, he opens his own mouth. Getting to know a dog, he walks on all fours; if it licks him, he licks it back. He does not know that "a hole is to dig" until he has dug

145

one. So he must complete his perception of mothers and fathers, teachers and postmen by enacting them; and this often precedes being able to talk about them. Giving the child enough uninterrupted time for his spontaneous dramatic play may do more for his language development than any number of structured lessons.

Another aspect of dramatic play related to intellectual development is its service in helping the child maintain a sense of identity and of continuity in life. Events are fleeting and discontinuous. They are like hit-and-run drivers, with children the passive targets or victims. Without the power to foresee, an incident is over before they can fully realize what has happened. Only by reproducing and repeating an experience can the child build it into his life. Through dramatic play the child transforms himself from a passive target into an active participant and *integrates* into his life what was itself only an *intrusion*.

VALUES AND PLAY

Cognitive growth is only one kind of development play facilitates. When we consider *values*, we find play filling another extremely important role. The values we see emerging in children's play relate to courage and curiosity, commitment without reserve, self-acceptance, optimism, gaiety, cooperation and emotional maturity.

We do not always approve all the values play behavior expresses, but even those we disapprove are worth thinking about. Two spring to mind immediately: sex play and aggression. These are types of play that cause parents and teachers the greatest amount of discomfort. Yet, when we consider them calmly, what do they mean?

Sex Play
The little boy who explains to the male observer, "Now we show our pee-pees," in the same tone he might use to say, "Now we play with clay," is proposing neither a seduction nor a rape. He may be expressing self-acceptance, curiosity, growing fellowship with others of his own sex, trust in adults. He may also be asking for reassurance about his own adequacy or for more information about sex differences and attributes. So, too, the common games of "doctor," the toilet-room "peeking," the naptime masturbation reflect wholly reasonable urges to know and to experience, that in later guises are approved and are sought as positive values.

Aggression
Acts of aggression in play often cause real dismay. But they can be instrumental in building courage and cooperation. The toddler who strikes out in defense of a toy is showing a blessed self-confidence we would all like to see preserved. Even the unregimented snatcher, whose means we cannot condone, sometimes compels our admiration for his boldness, lack of fear, directness in approaching challenges. Every child who bounds up to a new piece of equipment to try it out, or who squeezes a handful of clay for the first time, is manifesting a flexibility and an affirmative spirit that call for cherishing. The tenderness with which a little girl puts her doll to bed, her devotion to the care of her "house" and the "daddy" bespeak a deep willingness to provide nurturance, to create order, to know joy in serving. No, it is not difficult to discover the basis for values in children's play. Our challenge is to *maintain* these so that they may find fruition in adulthood.

Finally, let me remind you that the utility of play does not end when academic learning begins. The core of play, the child's own intrinsic absorption in mastery, continues to provide energy for the learning enterprise. The ability of the teacher to prepare an evocative environment and to utilize the teachable moment gives guidance and form.

Research of D. E. M. Gardner

Research data and models are available for the teacher with courage to pursue a "play-centered" or "child-centered" program for systematic academic learning. Perhaps the most compelling research is that of Dorothy E. M. Gardner, who has received the Order of the British Empire for her contributions to education. She compared children who had spent their school lives in child-centered schools, where *their* interests largely served as drive and directive, with a carefully matched group of others from good traditional schools. She evaluated mathematical skills, language usage, science knowledge and creative abilities. She found that in none of the traditional subject matters were the pupils from the child-centered schools inferior, while they were clearly superior in activities calling for invention and originality. The relevance of this research is undeniable. Few will disagree that, of all things we need now and in the future, original thinkers and problem-solvers head the list.

THE PLAY WAY

Why, then, is play being derogated and opportunities for play destroyed, even by well-meaning teachers? Unfortunately, many who deal with children have not received the training to enable them to understand the kind of organic learning that proceeds from knowledgeable use of play and wise provision of play opportunities, including enough uninterrupted *time* for play. It is triply unfortunate that many persons who make policy in schools and centers and many who evaluate programs know even less about this aspect of child growth than those in direct contact with children. The ability to promote the optimal development of children through the "play way" requires deep understanding and sensitivity to the unique pattern of each child's abilities and interests at any given moment of contact. It is built by mastering the vast repertoire of materials that can help a child achieve more and more complex integrations of concepts while feeding his self-initiated enthusiasm. It demands true respect for the individual, with flexibility and patience to adapt to *his* rhythms and *his* idiosyncratic patterning of sequences.

Admittedly, preparing oneself for this service is not easy. Ignorance cannot, however, be accepted as justification for giving the child less than the best obtainable. If we accept responsibility for serving children, we also accept the moral imperative to prepare ourselves to serve them well. It is no accident that OMEP (World Organization for Early Childhood Education) sees need for play opportunities for young children as primary in every country in the world. Let us go a step further —to demand that all who voluntarily undertake to guide children acquire the knowledge needed to guard and to enlarge the precious right and necessity of childhood—the right to play richly, joyously and freely.

See also:
ACEI. *Play: Children's Business.* Washington, D. C.: The Association, 1963. Pp. 40. 75¢.
Davis, David. "Play: A State of Childhood." CHILDHOOD EDUCATION 42, 4 (Dec. 1965): 242-44.
Frank, Lawrence K. *Play Is Valid.* ACEI Position Paper. Washington, D. C.: The Association, 1968. 8pp. 10¢ ea.; 25, $2.
Hartley, Ruth E. "Toys, Play Materials and Equipment." CHILDHOOD EDUCATION 45, 3 (Nov. 1968): 122-27.
Scarfe, Neville V. "Play Is Education." CHILDHOOD EDUCATION 39, 3 (Nov. 1962): 117-21.

THE FUNCTION OF PLAY IN EARLY CHILDHOOD EDUCATION

LUCILE LINDBERG

IN one of the African countries, a country where they have barely established primary education, a group of mothers gather together to plan a kindergarten program for their children. It is a program where the natural sands and the twigs from the trees will provide the material and equipment.

In Ceylon, a tremendous effort is being made to establish nursery schools. In Japan, great thought is given to providing beautiful playgrounds for the very young. In Australia and New Zealand, young mothers are constantly seeking new revenues so that more early childhood centers can be developed.

In the Soviet Union, there are many remarkable kindergartens with high standards. Children attend 12 hours a day, 12 months a year. Since there are not enough places for all, parents are particularly anxious to enroll their children.

When they are asked, "Why do you want your child to go to kindergarten at age 3; why are you willing to have him out of the home for such long periods?" they are likely to reply, "We don't want him out of our home for that long. But we do want the advantages that he gets. He will learn better when he goes to school."

Some years ago, when Head Start centers in a large city were being evaluated, parents who were bringing their children in, were asked whether they liked the program. They gave such responses as, "My first child didn't have an opportunity like this. I can tell the difference already. He wants to arrive here at six in the morning. He likes school." Or, "He is interested in so many things. He keeps asking what this word means and that one and that one. He brings books for me to read. My other children didn't do that. He's

NATIONAL ELEMENTARY PRINCIPAL, 1971, Vol 51, pp. 68-71.

learning a lot."

This is the story, not just from the disadvantaged, but also from wealthy and middle-income families. It is currently a universal story.

What is it that so many wish to buy for their children at such a cost? And the cost *is* considerable, for early childhood education programs are expensive.

We watch the children at play—happy, vigorous play, on climbing frames, in sand piles. We watch them jump, run, tumble, tug. We see them turn out paintings at an easel and pound at clay. We see them build elaborate structures with blocks.

At the same time, they are developing strong bodies. We see that they are learning to play with other children. We notice that they reach out curiously to learn more and more. They are interested and excited by what they are doing.

In these times, it is difficult for many parents to provide the physical space in which children can develop healthy muscles and bone structure. In busy areas of the city, children often have no one to supervise them. In suburban areas, many young children find that grass is to look at, not to play on. The socialization processes achieved in early childhood centers also make them well worth the investment required.

However, much more is happening. Frequently, tremendous intellectual development goes unnoticed. As children play, they are building foundations—foundations that make it possible for them to bring a greater depth of understanding to their studies in the years ahead. They gain perceptions that can later help them in mathematics, science, history, geography, the arts, and in learning to read. In these early years, children undertake the kinds of explorations that enable them to see the meaning behind what they are learning. They benefit from experience with both people and things.

A child paints, enjoying the colors he uses. This enjoyment is enough to give the painting value, but he is actually learning much more than that. We need

only watch, for example, as he mixes paint. Red becomes deep pink, then pale pink, then still paler pink. As he places one line of each, side by side on his paper, he shows an appreciation of the subtle difference. Differentiation is an ability sought in determining whether or not a child is ready to go into formal reading.

He makes a wide line on his paper, then one that is narrower. Then he makes another wide line and another narrower one. Then he makes a large, unusual shape, a shape created by him. Isn't mathematics a study of shapes? But he is doing more than that as he sweeps the brush across the page. Here are the beginnings of writing and what could make writing an easy, natural process in the next year or so. Experience in grasping the brush gives background for holding the pencil. In dealing with space, he is working with geographic concepts as well.

Another child is pounding clay. He feels the texture; he manipulates it. As he pinches and pulls it apart and puts it together again, he is dividing, adding, subtracting in three dimensions. He does not label them as such, but he is developing the feeling of what these processes really are.

Another child plays with dough. He pounds and slaps it into interesting shapes. Then he reaches for the box of cookie cutters. He tries one after the other to see what the shape is. Then he begins to combine the shapes. He does not need workbook drill in configuration. He is getting it here. As the dough is mixed, flour, water, and salt combine, and he becomes acquainted with yet another chemical change.

We observe a boy doing a puzzle. He puts the pieces together perfectly. Then he takes them out and does it again, then again and again. He may do it 19 times before he wanders away to something else. He will probably do it on another day, too, again and again until he is comfortable enough with the puzzle and pleased enough with himself that he reaches for a more difficult one. He sets his own challenges. He doesn't need formal exercises in matching. He is developing an awareness of shapes and the spaces into which they fit.

Possibilities for learning are tremendous when children use blocks. They develop a sense of design and balance, as well as proportion. It takes two blocks like this to make one like that, and two of these to make that still longer one. Fractions, division at firsthand, are a part of his experience.

In one room, the children had built an elaborate house. Later they decided they would put some decorations at the top. They were to be small, colored blocks. But no one was tall enough to do it without running the risk of knocking them over. What should they do? They could pull a table over and stand on that. "What else could you do?" asked the teacher. "Maybe you could stand in the wagon and reach?" "Is there any other possibility?" the teacher inquired.

The teacher knew that even 4- and 5-year-olds had much to learn by searching for alternatives. "Which way do you think would be best?" was a question that moved them into an evaluation of each alternative. "What will happen if you do this? Or this?" It was not a trial-and-error procedure. Rather, they moved into solid decision-making processes on a project where they would be able to test the results of their planning at once. Procedures that will be used in attacking learnings in many academic areas have their beginnings at very early ages.

Two 3½-year-olds had built a bridge. The approach to it was not smooth, and the cars kept falling off. What could they do to make it even, to gain balance? Work habits of a lifetime are developing when children are very young. The bases for thinking can be developed when children have an opportunity to play in centers planned especially for them. Learning acquired through highly motivated play

becomes integrated into a child's behavior. They are put to real use for him when he does something he wishes to do.

Language development is stimulated through every part of the program. It is especially important in dramatic play. We watch two boys, with handkerchiefs tied to their backs, high on the climbing frame. A sign says, "Troop Plane." The boys jump and run and come back and jump again. We count 31 technical terms related to planes and parachutes that the boys use in their play. In the same center, the playhouse is labeled "Hospital." A small red wagon labeled "Ambulance" serves as a conveyance for bringing in patients. "Do you need a stethoscope?" the teacher asks. Then, "What kind of medication are you giving?" We count 43 technical terms as the children converse in their play, which is really their work. Vocabulary building takes place in context. Many complicated and unusual words become commonplace as they are used freely. Children reach for words, enjoying them, accepting new ones as they hear them, and they try them again and again.

Vocabulary is important in learning to read, as it is for moving into all of the academic subjects. Even more important for the reading is the flow of words. To enjoy language and feel power in using it is an ability children need if they are to move into reading without going through a jerky word after word approach.

Through the best in poetry, poems written for children by fine poets, children experience rhyme. They learn the structure of language, the ways of combining words to express thoughts. After hearing the teacher read the poems many times, they begin to be intrigued with "Godfrey, Gordon, Gustavus, Gore." Learning to hear such similarities is important in learning to read. But it is learned in an informal setting, as the child explores the artistic and unusual language.

Singing, too, provides an important way of developing facility in the use of language. Words need to flow in singing.

The language is used rhythmically, and this provides a background much needed by children entering first grade.

Not only are children in early childhood programs gaining intellectual development, but an important emotional development as well. They begin to think positively about themselves. They feel that they are learners. They expect to be able to learn well. In addition, they are gaining from being with adults who have faith in them. At a very early age, children learn to trust or to distrust. They learn to have confidence in themselves, or they develop negative self-concepts. They see themselves as either discoverers or merely as absorbers of knowledge. A child begins to develop standards of literature, music, art in these early years.

Children develop values and attitudes whether or not they are able to engage in an early childhood program. For this reason, it is important that they have the opportunity to do this in a setting where a wide variety of media is provided under the careful guidance of a teacher trained to help them.

There are differences of opinion concerning how these goals are to be attained. Obviously, the illustrations given here are based on the use of play as the basic medium of a child's instruction. From among the many activities made available to the child through the materials used and the way they are arranged, he engages in a self-selecting process. The teacher through careful observation tries to introduce appropriate questions or additional materials so that decision-making processes become an important part of the child's play. There is concern for achieving a maximum cognitive development, but this is done along with the concern for physical, social, and emotional development. Learning is a result of a child's own exploration and discovery. Emphasis is placed on a creative approach to cognitive learning, as well as to the arts.

Some who work in the field of early childhood insist on a considerably dif-ferent approach. They view play as merely a socializing, rather than a "solid" learning, process. They give systematic instruction in each item they think will be needed by the child when he enters first grade. Often this is done by drilling day after day. Although concrete objects are usually used to emphasize meanings, this is still learning by rote. Sometimes, they employ verbal bombardment in the hope of keeping the child attentive to what is being taught. Some methods are based on giving rewards for making correct responses.

Some of these methods are used in relation to play and fitted into carefully specified periods each day. Others are based on a given set of materials, arranged in certain proper ways, and used exactly as indicated by their originators.

There is no doubt that children learn through these approaches. However, in considering the methods to be used with young children, we need to think about their future learning, as well as what they gain now. What learning style do we wish to encourage?

There are those who feel this doesn't matter. First, teach the child what you think he needs to know. Let him gain confidence because he can do what you have asked of him. They maintain that there is enough time later to be concerned with exploration and discovery.

There are others of us who feel it makes a great deal of difference from the very beginning how we help a child learn. In these very early years, the child gains an impression of what learning is and the feeling of himself as a learner. If we wish to encourage thinking, self-evaluation, self-motivation, then that should be the approach used. If we think creativity is important, then it is important in every aspect of learning.

There are differences of opinion, too, about how learning to read should be dealt with in an early childhood program. In the illustrations of children at play given earlier, considerable emphasis was placed on the skills underlying reading and the experiences needed to understand what reading is. The best in literature was introduced through stories and poems. Children were stimulated to enjoy words. Many of them discover reading processes on their own. This approach is intended to give a child power in reading and to make it a valued skill.

Others wish to begin with children at an early age, with formalized drill to promote language development. Or they provide equipment such as a talking typewriter or programed materials so as to get letter and word recognition quickly.

In the great push to make early childhood education available to many children, however, we may lose some of the values we hope to attain. Work with young children requires the services of highly qualified teachers who understand learning processes and developmental patterns. They need to be aware of the various equipment, materials, and methòds available and understand the philosophies involved in their use. It is not enough that a commercial concern brings equipment and sets out a program. Teachers need to be knowledgeable about what they hope to do so that they can ask well-chosen questions and make appropriate choices.

Not only must a teacher understand children, but she must also know how to work with other adults. Usually, there will be more than one adult in a room. Often, the others involved will be paraprofessionals who are interested in young children and work well with them. But they depend on the teacher to supervise their work and participate in the planning. If maximum use is to be made of teacher aides, the teacher in charge must conduct careful inservice orientations. She must recognize which activities require the work of a trained person and which can be done well by a person with less educational background.

Parents play an important part in early childhood programs, both because many parents are eager to learn all they can about their children and because teachers need the help and insights they have to offer. Nonworking mothers often give volunteer help on certain days, and when care is given to their orientation, their services are valuable. Parents need to know what goes on in a center so that some of the activities can be continued in the home.

Many groups of young children meet for only half-day sessions, for full-day sessions are extremely expensive: More professional hours are needed, and provisions must be made for lunch. However, in areas where mothers work, all-day programs must be provided.

There are advantages, too, to a full-day program for children of nonworking mothers. They can learn much in the extra time, both through their outdoor and their indoor activities. Children learn to eat a variety of foods and gain from eating with other children in a social situation. Rest periods, too, provide learning opportunities.

In many instances, early education has been considered important for children from low-income homes, but little attention has been given to these opportunities for children from middle- or upper-income levels. Actually, these programs should be available for *all* children. Parents are recognizing this and increasing their demands.

Because good programs for young children are expensive, we are not meeting needs in this area. A concerted effort should be made to secure the advantage of these programs for all children. We have money for many luxuries in our society. The question is, when will we push for some of the necessities?

An Overview
of British Infant Schools

DONNA C. HETZEL

Even the briefest visit to an Infant School in England points to the need for a closer look at the innovations in their system. Five- through seven-year-olds all in one classroom? Totally free activity days? Thirty-five children to one teacher? Children indoors and out at the same time? Block building in the hallways? How can this be? All these atypical occurrences are characteristic of the vertically grouped Infant School. All are thought to be advantageous by those teaching in the open-plan school.

Faced with many of the difficulties found in American public schools today—teacher shortages, crowded classrooms, growing discipline problems, early school failures—the British government began a study of Primary School Education. Since the publication of the Plowden Report in 1967[1], the innovations of vertical grouping, gradual reception, open-school planning and free activity programs have grown in popularity. By 1964, over 90 percent of the Infant Schools in Bristol were vertically grouped to some extent. Programs including such practices can be seen throughout the country—in West Riding, Oxfordshire, Leicestershire, Bristol and even in the London suburbs. New ideas have taken hold in the more rural areas first and then have slowly influenced education authorities in the larger cities.

Vertical Grouping—What is It?

An Infant School which is vertically grouped may have from three

---

[1] *Children and Their Primary Schools: A Report of the Central Advisory Council for Education (England)*; in response to a request by the Minister of Education in 1963, "to consider primary education in all its aspects, and the transition to secondary education." First published by Her Majesty's Stationery Office in 1967. Lady Bridget Plowden, Chairman of the Advisory Council.

YOUNG CHILDREN, 1970, Vol. 26, pp. 336-339.

to 14 classes containing children ages five to seven-plus. A typical class has 35 to 40 children with only one teacher. At first this appears an impossible task for any one adult. But, as you will see, the age arrangement and gradual reception of the five-year-old make it quite workable.

At the beginning of the school year the teacher meets with those children returning to her class. This group of approximately 24 children includes those five- and six-year-olds from the previous term's class. The seven-year-olds have moved on to the Junior school (ages seven to 11-plus). As the year progresses, five-year-olds are received into the existing class during the term of their fifth birthday. There are three terms in the school year: September—Christmas, Christmas—Easter and Easter—July. By the third term, the class has again reached full size. In this system then, the child remains with the same teacher for the entire seven to nine terms in the Infant School.

A Look at the Classroom

Since each class is composed of the same age grouping of children, equipment and materials are similar from room to room. An open-plan school allows the children to use all available space for their learning activities. Hallways are often equipped with work benches and other materials for large-scale noisy projects. Cloakrooms are de-

Donna Hetzel, M.A., is an instructor in Child Development at Connecticut College. Concurrently, she has served as Director of a laboratory nursery school. She has traveled in London, Moscow and Leningrad for a study of comparative educational systems, and was Coordinator for a Special Studies Tour of British Infant Schools.

signed to leave space open for large block building or floor-work projects. The classroom itself is typically sectioned for activity in "maths," science, art, table-work, imaginative play and reading. The free activity plan allows the children to move from one area to another, from one learning task to another, throughout the day. Compulsory religious instruction, physical education and other events which require scheduling lend a stabilizing but not restrictive routine to the program.

From the Child's Point of View

The five-year-old attending school for the first time comes into a setting totally new to him. In a traditional arrangement, as we have in this country, he arrives at kindergarten with his mother to find a roomful of children all as bewildered as he and a teacher who is able to cope only with those whose needs are most urgent. Few children openly express their fears on the first day, even fewer the second day, still less the third. As the term goes on, these anxieties are internalized only to reappear the following September when the entire process begins again with a new teacher, a new classroom, a longer school day and, invariably, quite a few new children. Along with these superficial changes comes the increased pressure of formalized academic learning with reading, writing and arithmetic, all to be learned as if the kindergarten teacher had magically brought every one of her children to the same level of readiness.

In the vertically grouped classroom, the trauma of September is gone for the teacher as well as for the five-year-old. First of all, the classroom is filled with children who are comfortably busy and old hands at what to do and where to do it. The teacher is free to give the incoming five-year-old the time and support he needs. There is almost certain to be a sibling or neighborhood friend in the classroom who will take on the responsibility of helping the newcomer to become acquainted with the standard procedures such as where to put his things, where to hang his coat, how to find the bathroom and the playground. There is also someone to help with the stuck zipper and the shoe that needs tying. He is quickly absorbed into the existing class. Within a few days it is virtually impossible to pick out the newcomer. Throughout the year, the five-year-old benefits from the availability of classmates as models. His motivation is stimulated by observing his friends reading, working "maths" and writing stories. He may work at whatever pace he can sustain, finding materials geared for various levels of competence. There are no more upheavals.

As a six-year-old, this child returns to the familiar classroom secure in his knowledge of the teacher's ways, the jobs to be done, the materials to be explored. There is no interruption to learning. This increased physical and mental comfort allows him to accept greater responsibility for his own learning. The six-year-old benefits, too, from the teacher's more appropriate expectations. From working with the entire age range in the Infant School, she knows even more precisely the needs and abilities of the six-year-old. She also is more aware, from the start of the second year, of the individuality of the returning child.

By the time the child is a seven-year-old in the Infant School program, he is most able to benefit from the open-plan school and free activity program. He has acquired the skills and abilities to work independently, to accept the leadership role in the class and to assist the teacher. Aware of the demands to be made on the seven-plus when he moves on to the Junior school, the teacher carefully assesses and evaluates his progress in the third year. Filling in gaps and stretching and firming-up newly acquired abilities is her focus.

From the Teacher's Point of View

The teacher in such a classroom has a new and different role. She is no longer the central source of information. Rather, she is the preparer of materials, supporter to those working, source of guidance when specific skills or facts are needed, a questioner, listener, and most of all, an observer.

There are many advantages which have come to light from the practice and application of such an imaginative plan. Children helping children and smaller age groups ease some of the pressure on the classroom teacher. The urgency of the beginning reader, for instance, is easier to cope with if there are only 12 rather than 35 or 40. Having the oldest children working with investment for comparatively long periods of time sets a more leisurely pace than that which would exist in a roomful of active five-year-olds with short attention spans.

One of the greatest advantages gained is an opportunity to examine more closely the children's use of learning materials. Each teacher collects and constructs much of her own learning equipment. The chance to work through the series and schemes with so many children is ideal for assessing omissions, shortcomings and strengths. An alert teacher can spot points where children stumble in their thinking, then explain problems and amplify the concept with supplementary experiences.

The long line of "naughty big boys" no longer forms outside the headmistress' office. The characteristic bully groups of seven-year-olds are almost nonexistent, not only because their numbers have been decreased, but also because an atmosphere of cooperation rather than competition has been fostered throughout the Infant School years. Children who are allowed and encouraged to choose their own learning activities are not bored, restless and troublesome. Instead, their energies have been directed into constructive channels on their own initiative. An obvious decline in discipline problems has been noted throughout the entire program.

Finally, teachers feel that contact with a child and his family over such an extended period of time fosters good home-school relationships. Cooperation between parents and teacher lends consistency in the approach to any problem, be it academic or social.

I found visiting schools operating within the framework of the creative British system fascinating and thought-provoking. Anyone examining practices of early childhood education should not overlook the British Infant Schools.

A TEACHER SPEAKS OUT . . .
WHAT I LEARNED FROM THE BRITISH SCHOOLS

Donald S. Ulin

A SABBATICAL YEAR can be a very unsettling experience—especially for an American elementary teacher who spends it in Leicestershire, England. Previously well satisfied, perhaps a bit smug about my own teaching and my teaching situation, I have returned home shaken by a year of observation and teaching in some of the best British infant and junior schools. I find myself more critical both of myself and the educational system I work in. I will never be able to teach in quite the same way again.

What was so impressive about the teaching and learning I saw in Leicestershire? First of all, the enormous variety of activities which can go on simultaneously and productively under the aegis of a single good, but not necessarily extraordinary, teacher.

For example, in one typical "infant room" for five- and six-year-olds, I found children happily painting, drawing, pouring at the sink, reading, writing, constructing models from cardboard boxes, using Cuisenaire rods, weighing beans on a scale and doing puzzles, all at the same time. In another class, eight- and nine-year old youngsters were busy reading, drawing, writing, doing math and using building

GRADE TEACHER, 1969, Vol. 87, No. 6, pp. 100-103 ff.

blocks. These were not extraordinary situations. In practically every classroom I visited, at least two activities were going on simultaneously.

The classes are conducted in rooms about the size of those in the United States, and the number of youngsters per class runs from 35 to 40. The youngsters move about freely, work singly, in pairs, or in groups, and chat with each other during their work. Teachers are rarely at their desks, but are constantly on the move giving help where and when it's needed.

In some schools, the children are "family grouped", i.e., each class has a heterogeneous group of five- six- and seven-year-olds in one unit, and eight-, nine- and ten-year-olds in another. In other schools, the children are grouped by age as they are in the United States. A third kind of school combines both family-grouping and age-grouping.

English teachers generally prefer the family-group system. The youngsters, their teachers say, work freely together, the younger emulating the older. Older youngsters, already familiar with the school routine, help make new entrants feel at home. Often an older child is more successful than a teacher in getting a younger one to read, write, do arithmetic or put on his boots. The children in family-grouped classes get to know each other very well. Since they remain with one teacher for two years, what develops is a continuity impossible in classes that begin with 35 fresh new faces each year and end with 35 old ones. In family-grouped classes, there is actually no beginning or end, simply continuous learning.

Some schools allow children a continuous "free day" when children can work at whatever they please all day long. At Medbourne Junior and Infant School, a two-room building about 25 miles outside Leicester, a partially programmed, partially free day is the rule. Youngsters at Medbourne are required to do some mathematics during the morning, but otherwise, the day is their own. I have never seen children work with such joy, without complaint and utterly without confusion as I did in two eye-opening weeks at Medbourne.

At Thurmaston Junior School, on the other hand, classes are **more highly programmed. In a typical class, half the youngsters do math, while the other half work on reading and English from 9–10:30 a.m. From then until noon, those who have been working on math turn to reading and English, and the others change to math. Afternoons, the children have free choice. Pro**grams vary greatly from teacher to teacher and from school to school. Without exception, however, they are flexible. Even within prescribed activities, youngsters have a wide variety of choice.

One advantage of this system is the fact that complete sets of books and materials are unnecessary. Since not all the children do the same thing at the same time, schools need not purchase expensive sets of 35 English, math, social studies, reading and spelling books. With the same money, they can indulge in a much greater variety of materials. And they do. The extent and diversity of the art and math materials in these classes far surpass anything I have seen in American public school classrooms.

Maybe one of the first things that strikes an American teacher about these schools is how much better behaved these British youngsters are than ours, how little friction there is between pupils and teacher, how few class crises there are. Children stay out of each other's way. Teachers do not spend their day threatening students. The problem of discipline seems to have disappeared.

Another observation which American teachers invariably make is that British students are far more reliable and independent than our own. We are surprised to see English children working alone for long periods of time without prodding or help from their teachers. But from their first days at school, British pupils are taught to be independent in the best sense of the word. From the first, they are expected to choose for themselves what to do.

In the United States, we talk about independence and responsibility for children, but never really expect any. Generally, we tell children what things to do, when to do them, and how to do them, and then we explain why they have done them. We argue that to do otherwise, to allow as many activities to go on at once in a classroom as are allowed in England, would make a shambles of the room by the end of the day. Leicestershire teachers do not agree. They simply insist that children tidy up after themselves. They expect this, and the children oblige.

American teachers are finely attuned to what they judge to be the "limited attention span" of their pupils. At one fine private school on the outskirts of Boston,

teachers are actually warned not to keep youngsters below fifth grade at any kind of work for longer than 25 minutes. At one English school I visited, however, I can remember 20 busy five-year-olds painting, play-acting, clay-modelling, playing store, pasting and making designs on pegboards. Most were working indoors, but the clay-modellers worked outside on a little patio, and the dressed-up actors rehearsed in the corridor. Their teacher wandered from group to group, helping and suggesting while from time to time youngsters came to her. By my actual timing, the five-year-olds at the pegboard worked on their own designs for 45 minutes at a stretch. Other youngsters got on just as well by themselves for equally long periods of time. Evidently, when children do things they have chosen themselves and when they are expected to work by themselves, their involvement and staying power are greater than we have supposed possible.

Their self-discipline is better. One day Mr. Bradley at the Medbourne Junior School had to leave for a meeting. A half hour later one of the youngsters asked me where Mr. Bradley was. Until then he had not been missed. When I told him that Mr. Bradley had gone to a meeting, he simply said, "Oh," and went right on with what he was doing. The other youngsters kept working at what they were doing and 90 minutes later at 3:30 p.m. they all simply packed up and went home.

Were I to have left my own sixth-grade class alone for an hour, I would have returned to a sea of blood and bones.

In many of the schools I visited in Leicestershire, teachers periodically leave children unattended. In any one class, children may be spread about three or four different areas—some in the class itself, others in the hallway painting, some on the athletic field measuring, and still others working in other classrooms. Obviously, the teacher cannot be everywhere, nor does he try to be. These teachers trust their students, and their trust is rewarded. They see no need here to line children up by twos and warn them of the dire consequence of any misbehavior. The children walk off by themselves to the assembly hall or to buses, take their places and behave themselves.

To an American Teacher, this may all seem a bit unreal. So might another incident I recall during my stay at the Millfield Infant and Junior School in Braunstone. I was working with Kenneth, a little fellow in Miss Atkins' room of five- and six-year-olds. As usual, youngsters were moving about doing all sorts of things. Suddenly there was a tremendous crash. One of the youngsters had brushed up against a huge plant. Dust, dirt, and smashed bits of pottery were everywhere.

In most American schools I know, this would have been the end of a good day. Somebody would have heard about it in no uncertain terms. Instead, quietly, Miss Atkins merely turned and said, "Oh my, we'd better take care of this!" And they did. There was no fuss. There were no recriminations. The youngsters were quickly back at work and the teacher was still completely calm.

On another occasion, I remember helping in a room of nine- and ten-year olds at Millfield

School. I looked up to see one little girl whimpering. The boy next to her had been playing with an elastic band; it had snapped and hit her on the forehead. I waited for the shrill harangue and the punishment. The teacher merely said, "You know you have hurt Mary, and I'm sure you are sorry. Please let's not play with elastics again. They are dangerous. Would you like to apologize to Mary?" He did. That was that.

This ability to make light of untoward situations rather than exaggerate them makes for a serene classroom. Children have fewer difficulties and cope more easily with those they do have. Teachers don't rush youngsters off to the health room for every little bump, as we do. Little cuts and bruises are treated as little cuts and bruises. Since teachers pay scant attention to scratches and scrapes, children, too, make light of them.

A busy serenity pervades these Leicestershire classrooms. Youngsters walk about and talk to each other in low tones, eagerly and without anxiety. There is neither bedlam nor a pall of silence. Youngsters work, not for grades or gold stars or to beat out Johnny, but because they are seriously interested in what they are doing. Teachers, compared with their American counterparts, worry less about what parents think. They feel no compulsion to have Billy carry papers home to Mummy and Daddy every day to prove he is forging ahead.

Teachers in the Leicestershire schools have faith in the essential goodness of children, and their experiences bear out this faith. Youngsters are expected to be good and they are good. They are expected to be honest, and they are honest. In too many American schools, teachers really do not trust children so they are not to be trusted. They are not expected to be good, so they are often not good.

In a system in which everything the children do must be measured, we feel we cannot allow them to sit too close to one another. Our concern soon shifts from what each child is learning to the character of the competition being staged. Teachers distrust students, students distrust each other, and we live together in an anxious, fearful world where little goodness or learning can emerge.

In sharp contrast with the British students I observed, American children also no longer trust or like *themselves*. A set of letters I brought with me from American youngsters who wanted English pen pals, I found replete with recrimination and self-recrimination. These children write about both themselves and their mates disparangingly. It is my sense of the situation that the constant harassment to which they are subjected and the ever-present need they feel to measure up help make our children as self-critical and vindictive as so many of them are.

Again in comparison with our own, the English children I worked with seemed to be allowed to grow up at a leisurely rate. Leicestershire schoolmen work on the assumption that a happy, productive adulthood stems from a satisfying, reasonable childhood.

By contrast, we seem to feel that childhood is something to be done away with as quickly as possible, like the mumps. We rush children pell mell into adulthood. Parents worry more about a child's future than his present. Will he get into

the college or even *a* college? Will he become an engineer or a machinist? Parents are concerned with what their child *is* only as what he *is* predicts who and what he *will be*.

Since American parental concerns quickly reflect themselves in the curriculum, we find ourselves with all sorts of crash programs for instant scientists, instant mathematicians and instant scholars. We buy expensive packaged programs. Meanwhile, we go on teaching in the same old way, mouthing the same old platitudes —"whole child," "individual differences," "teaching children not subjects," etc. In Leicestershire, schoolmen have no packages or programs for sale, but they have developed a way of teaching that Americans should consider seriously.

Some comparisons

Educational statistics, particularly British ones, are hard to come by and are often deceptive. Determining how American and English children compare in the various subject areas is slippery business, especially since in many instances educators in the two countries are using different materials and seeking somewhat different ends. Nevertheless, some rough comparisons are possible.

In mathematics, it is obvious these British youngsters are well ahead of ours. Eight- and nine-year-olds can routinely handle multi-base problems in addition, subtraction, multiplication and division. Their teachers have at their disposal an enormous variety of materials and are able to cope with a wide range of individual learning. Through their use of this

161

assortment of manipulative materials, these British children learn to understand what they are doing. They are seldom found juggling numbers in a fumbling search for correct answers.

In language arts, British practices differ markedly from our own. For one thing, from the very beginning, English children do more writing. It is common practice for five- and six-year-olds first to draw pictures and then, with the help of their teachers, to write about them. In no school I visited did I find any study of formal grammar. By and large, the children's spelling is atrocious, but teachers are more concerned with the content of their writing than with mechanics or grammatical niceties. In general, one may judge from the products that English children write more easily than ours and certainly more creatively.

Social studies, British teachers approach only incidentally. The library and the classrooms contain books on the subject, but the curriculum entails no required reading. Teachers often preside over special projects, sometimes rather ambitious ones. For example, at Medbourne I found the eight-, nine- and ten-year-olds writing a 20-page history of their town and printing it on their own press. One Millfield teacher and his pupils had done an impressive study of a local stream, measuring the speed of the stream and studying the nesting and mating habits of the wildlife in the area.

Reading is seldom taught as a subject *per se,* and when it is, teachers use the same techniques we use—even the Dick and Jane materials. Good teachers try to listen to each student read once

a day, but with 35 to 40 in a class, they often find this impossible. More so than his American counterpart, the British teacher relies heavily on the child's natural desire to read and write. British teachers are almost always available for children who seek their help. And children constantly come to them. One may ask what a word in his reading book means. Another may want to know how to spell something for a story he is writing or for the personal dictionary he constructs of words he has found useful.

Still, English children are often behind our own in reading. If our problem is worrying too much about reading and spending too much time too early in the formal teaching of reading, the British probably err by doing too little too late. My impression is that the English teacher's reliance on a child's natural inclination to read is not always well founded. For many children, learning to read is difficult—very difficult—and children often find other more appealing things going on in a British classroom.

English teachers feel confident they can sense when a child is ready to read, and that this is the time to begin. But the fact is that there are far too many eight- and nine-year-old English children who cannot read and, because of embarrassment and an over emphasis on sight reaching as opposed to phonics, may never read well.

In art and music, Leicestershire youngsters do amazing things. The variety, originality and vitality of their art work is staggering. School orchestras and bands such as those I have seen at Thurmaston and Medbourne are, I believe, unparalleled in the United States.

Some caveats

Although much of what is happening in the Leicestershire primary schools is different and in many respects better than anything in the United States, several nagging problems remain.

First, in reading, it seems to me children should have reading periods set up for them, at least when nothing else is available.

Second, since classes are often overcrowded, it would be of enormous help if lay people were hired, particularly for work with slow learners.

Third, I have already mentioned the wide assortment of materials available to children for independent study. More would be useful—particularly puzzles, books and science materials.

Fourth, in language arts, anxious teachers might do well to restrain themselves from rushing youngsters into learning symbols before they can handle referents.

And, fifth, in mathematics, learning number symbols before one can count actual things seems to make little sense.

By American standards, Leicestershire schools are remarkably independent. An Advisory Centre gives advice, but each headmaster sets his school's policy. Teachers, too, have a freer rein than they do in the United States.

This independence can be invigorating, but it sets a burden on the headmaster and encourages teachers to develop a wide variety of approaches. One teacher may advocate "fire and brimstone," another may espouse a starry-eyed "just-give-them-their-freedom" approach. When youngsters move from an extremely rigid teacher to one who gives almost total freedom, it can be disconcerting, even destructive. More so, perhaps, than their American counterparts, British headmasters need to use great care in selecting teachers and in shaping in-service training programs. While some diversity is obviously desirable, a consistent atmosphere and a single instructional philosophy should prevail within each school.

Obviously, the British elementary schools I saw did not have all the answers. But it was exciting to discover in them educators who tackle their problems head-on and often with great success. These teachers have bought no packages and have none for sale —in fact, they abhor the idea of learning packages. What they have to offer is a new approach to teaching and learning, an approach which American schools might do well to adopt and adapt to meet American needs.

HEAD START:
NATIONAL FOCUS ON YOUNG CHILDREN

Jenny W. Klein

EARLY childhood education is not new to the United States. A glance at the past reveals the beginning of the kindergarten movement in the late 1800's and the growth of various types of nursery schools and day care centers from the 1920's through the early 1960's.

What is new, since the middle 1960's, is the discovery of the importance of early childhood education by a larger segment of the American public. Before then, education of children under 5 was a luxury primarily available to children of the affluent. Legislation of the 1960's introduced a means of extending the advantages of early childhood education to include children of the poor. Traditionally, federal legislation promoting education has been a response to national concerns and critical needs. Social crises of the last two decades have stimulated legislation to combat poverty, poor health, and unemployment.

In an attempt to break the crippling

cycle of poverty in America, planning officials considered numerous alternatives. The potential of early childhood programs as a form of intervention was reviewed. As a result, the Economic Opportunity Act of 1964 included Project Head Start, a comprehensive program addressing itself to the needs of young children and their families, as well as to the needs and resources of the total community.

In November 1964, an interdisciplinary planning committee was formed under the leadership of Dr. Robert Cooke, Chief Pediatrician of Johns Hopkins University Hospital. Community planning, funding, and staff orientation took place during the next four months. Three concepts were basic to the comprehensive approach taken by the Cooke Committee:

1. The poor are homogeneous only in their economic deprivation.

2. Effective programs would have to be tailored to individual, sociocultural, as well as geographic, differences.

3. Involvement of the immediate community in all phases of the program was crucial.

Jenny W. Klein is Senior Educational Specialist, Project Head Start, Office of Child Development, U.S. Department of Health, Education, and Welfare, Washington, D.C.

NATIONAL ELEMENTARY PRINCIPAL, 1971, Vol. 51, pp. 98-103.

The Cooke Committee carefully reviewed the intervention experiments of a number of eminent researchers and studied the deficits most noted in school-age children from poverty families. They then outlined a "total impact" approach for preschoolers, geared to the following objectives:

1. Meeting physical, nutritional, and dental needs
2. Strengthening emotional and social development by encouraging self-confidence, spontaneity, curiosity, and self-discipline
3. Stimulating mental processes and skills, with particular attention to conceptual and verbal aspects
4. Establishing and reinforcing patterns and expectations of success to promote self-confidence
5. Increasing the child's capacity to relate positively to family and community, while at the same time strengthening the family's capacity to contribute to the child's development
6. Fostering in the child and his family a responsible attitude toward society, while stimulating constructive opportunities for the poor to work together on a personal and community basis toward the solution of their problems.

The overall goal was to strengthen the sense of dignity and self-worth within the child and his family. Every child deserves an education conducive to growth and development within a family that is being helped to achieve a higher level of social effectiveness.

In 1965, a pilot Head Start project enrolling 561,000 children was launched with an initial appropriation of $96.4 million. The first program was an eight-week summer session for children who would enter regular school for the first time that fall. Centers opened in remote rural areas, suburban poverty pockets, inner-city ghettos, Eskimo villages, on Indian reservations, and among migrant groups.

Since then, Project Head Start has grown to include full-year programs for preschool children of age 3 and above. By 1970, Head Start had served more than 3,804,000 children from low-income families in 50 states, Puerto Rico, the Virgin Islands, and American Samoa. The project currently operates on a federal budget of $360 million.

Although 1965 is generally regarded as the beginning of Head Start, it was not until the following year that the program had explicit legal authority. The first summer program was essentially an experiment under the "War on Poverty" as part of the Office of Economic Opportunity's broad authority to give grants to communities for locally developed projects. Project Head Start remained under the Office of Economic Opportunity until July 1, 1969, when authorities were delegated to the Office of Child Development, U.S. Department of Health, Education, and Welfare.

Local Community Involvement

Under the direction of the Office of Child Development, Head Start has remained a uniquely local program, administered under the auspices of the Community Action Agency. The Office of Child Development has established regional offices and operates through a network of regional coordinators, community representatives, regional training officers in each state and territory, state technical assistance offices, numerous consultants in the various disciplines, including members of the American Academy of Pediatrics. The national headquarters staff in Washington, D.C., supports field operations, career development and training, research and evaluation, and program planning and innovation. The federal government issues the broad goals for Head Start, approves local program designs, and monitors local agencies to assure that grantees are operating high-quality, well-balanced programs. Implicit in the guidelines is the individualization of each program in terms of the community's perception of its needs and resources.

Participating in the largest program for young children ever sponsored by the U.S. Government, teachers, social workers, persons from the medical profession, parents, and volunteers combine their resources to accomplish Head Start goals. These goals do not stress academic achievement or the raising of IQ scores. Rather, they concentrate on providing many social, emotional, and intellectual experiences commonly available to most children but often not experienced by those in poverty families. Local determination, a fledgling concept when Head Start was conceived, is inherent. Head Start is the community's program—not a program *for* the community.

The most appropriate local programs

are determined by a group of parents and community representatives working in conjunction with interested professionals on a policy committee. These committees, which are part of every Head Start group, must have at least 50 percent membership of parents or parents' representatives and play an active role in program planning, operation, and evaluation.

A Comprehensive Approach

Because Head Start attempts to provide some of the medical, nutritional, and educational advantages experienced by children of more affluent parents, the program draws heavily on the professional skills of persons in health, nutrition, education, and social services. At the same time, it recognizes that nonprofessionals can also contribute meaningfully. The family is fundamental to the child's total development, and the role of the parents in developing policies and participating in the program is emphasized. Parents participate in the centers as volunteers, teacher aides, cooks, carpenters, bus drivers, secretaries, or other paid employees. Adult educational activities, which may range from basic literacy courses to consumer education, are part of the comprehensive plan for every program. Although such programs are not operative in all instances, they represent the total impact approach toward which program administrators are striving.

The Educational Component

Although the essence of Head Start lies in its comprehensive services, all programs revolve around the children's daily education program. Complementary or supporting services are essential to the total concept, but its core is educational.

Since all of the child's experiences while he is in the center contribute to his learning, his total experience in the program can be called the "curriculum" and must be carefully planned. The formal learning situations are, within broad guidelines, tailored to individual situations. A program for children of Mexican-American migrant workers, for example, grows out of different circumstances and faces different challenges from a program in a city ghetto. Aside from obvious geographical and social differences, effective programs attempt to remain alert to differences in children, family situations, and cultural attitudes. Thus, programs are individualized according to local needs and within

the general framework of a high-quality child development center. The most successful Head Start programs recognize the wide variations in children's behavior patterns, family situations, interests, and innate strengths and weaknesses, and they attempt to provide each child with the elements the home has had the most difficulty in offering.

Generally, educational goals for poor children cannot be distinguished from objectives for children from other segments of society. In spite of individual or social differences, all children must have opportunities to learn the skills appropriate to their age group. Recognizing these universalities, many Head Start classrooms have been patterned after the most successful kindergartens and nursery schools in the nation. Interrelated activities are offered in:

Language Arts: Providing experiences that 1) encourage children to learn to use language effectively as a means of communication, as a tool for thought and learning, and as a resource for self-expression; 2) begin to develop understanding of the relationship between the spoken and written word; 3) develop skills and concepts that form a basis for learning to read and write.

Mathematics: Incorporating into children's daily experiences many opportunities to explore, discover, and use number ideas as a foundation for understanding and later mathematical reasoning; to begin to appreciate numbers as a means of problem solving and communicating ideas.

Science: Extending the children's awareness and understanding of the natural environment in which they live, through opportunities for firsthand investigation; inspiring a sense of wonder and curiosity about the physical world; encouraging the development of skills with which to search for explanations; helping children to grow in ability to organize and interpret the facts they acquire.

Social Studies: Providing opportunities for extended personal relationships through which children 1) learn to live and work successfully with others; 2) identify within social groups; 3) have experiences in learning to think and act cooperatively.

Creative Arts: Enriching personal development through opportunities for creative expression in many forms and providing an atmosphere of respect for individuality and imagination.

Recently, increasing emphasis has been placed on experimentation to determine which educational strategies are most effective in dealing with disadvantaged children. A pilot program called Planned Variation has implemented 12 curriculum models in 37 Head Start programs. Planned Variation is designed to provide information about the impact on the Head Start child of various well-defined educational environments and learning situations. Other factors to be evaluated include the effect of continuity in early education, a comparison of the sustained effects of specific program approaches, and information about the most critical periods for intervention.

In these programs, the precise role of the teacher and other staff members varies. However, in all instances, warmth, support, encouragement, and perception are the characteristics that seem to contribute to the success of the educational component and to the total impact of Head Start.

Social Services

Social services are both a prelude to an effective Head Start program and an integral part of every operation. A primary task is to identify children with the greatest needs and encourage their parents to enroll them. As the child becomes a daily participant, the social service staff provides background information on the family to enhance the center's understanding of the individual needs or problems. Social services are a link to the larger community resources, referring parents to complementary services, stimulating development of more effective services, and interpreting available services to parents and other community residents.

Health and Nutrition

Health services follow the same comprehensive model and range from routine examinations, diagnostic techniques, and dental checks to provisions for special needs, such as remedial speech, hearing, vision, or psychological services. There is a commitment to make complete health and dental care available to the poor, to foster positive attitudes toward health services, and to assure the continuation of services for the child who progresses from Head Start.

Integrally related to health services is a broad nutritional program that provides at least one complete meal and one snack for each child daily. Although most low-income parents strive to feed their children as well as possible within a limited budget, Head Start assures a child at least one balanced daily meal. In addition to providing needed nutrients and teaching mothers sound nutritional patterns, Head Start mealtimes are opportunities for children to relate easily to the staff and peers.

Career Development

A training component that prepares parents and other community residents for dignified employment in local programs has been a required aspect of each program since the inception of Head Start. As Head Start evolves and as other federally sponsored programs address themselves to training the poor, this aspect has taken on even greater significance. More than 7,500 low-income employees of full-year Head Start programs are currently enrolled in college level training for two-year and four-year degrees at nearly 300 colleges and universities in the United States, Puerto Rico, and the Virgin Islands. Several organizations with substantial backgrounds in career development and other anti-poverty activities provide technical assistance and training for upgrading skills useful in Head Start and other local programs with critical manpower shortages.

The career development program improves job stability and provides advancement opportunities, while reinforcing changes in children that may accrue through Head Start. Local residents are utilized as change agents, while training increases family income, alleviates manpower shortages, and improves the quality of staff. Further reinforcement occurs through providing self-confident success-models to youngsters enrolled in the centers.

Research and Evaluation

Ultimately, long-range data will provide information on the success of Head Start. But for many teachers, physicians, social workers, parents, and others who participate actively in the program, the daily here-and-now experiences the children receive make the program successful. Focusing on social competence for every developing child, Head Start is interested in producing healthy, whole, productive human beings.

An extensive program is under way to

167

evaluate and assess the impact of Project Head Start. The Division of Research and Evaluation of the Office of Child Development is directing most of the study.

Major evaluational research studies on the effects of Head Start began in 1968 when the Office of Economic Opportunity funded two major studies. One, popularly termed the Westinghouse Study, was an attempt to assess, as quickly as possible and after the fact, the impact of Head Start on alumni in the first three grades of primary school. The major recommendation was that, "Large scale efforts and substantial resources continue to be devoted to the search for finding more effective programs, procedures, and techniques for remediating the effects of poverty on disadvantaged children."[1] In some ways, only a narrow range of Head Start's possible impact was investigated by this study, for human behavior encompasses far more than the cognitive and specifically school-rated capabilities that were measured.

A more comprehensive research effort was undertaken by the Educational Testing Service in 1969. This six-year investigation of 2,000 children is measuring Head Start children and a control group during each of the six years.

Kirschner Associates, Incorporated, a national research and consulting firm, conducted field research in 58 communities with full-year Head Start programs during the July 1968 through January 1969 period.[2] In contrast to other recent studies, which concentrated on academic achievement of Head Start children, the Kirschner Study focused on Head Start's effort to influence the entire community in ways that are beneficial to children of low-income families. The survey was designed primarily to determine what changes in local education and health institutions have occurred that are consistent with Head Start's goal of helping poor children and their families develop their capabilities more fully.

Head Start's influence in helping to bring about these changes was also studied. Major findings indicated an increased involvement of the poor with institutions, particularly at decision-making levels and in decision-making capacities. In the 58 communities studied, there were 1,500 identifiable changes in the educational system and the health delivery system to improve the lives of children. It was also found that Head Start made an impact on the institutional change process in the communities surveyed by working with the institutions, rather than by violent confrontations. The Kirschner Report concludes, "Head Start has indeed been a successful strategy in widely achieving the goal of modifying local institutions so that they are more responsive to the needs of the poor."

Several other evaluations of early intervention programs have been conducted. The bulk of available data indicates that Head Start and other early intervention programs show positive results, largely in children's achievement and general ability level.[3,4,5,6,7,8] In addition, we have some indications[9] that children's attitudes, motivation, and social behavior also change. However, the impact of Head Start as measured by these studies seems to decrease or disappear as the children go through the early grades in elementary school.

A variety of explanations has been given for this "leveling off" phenomenon.[10] One of the most commonly stated reasons is that the public school, because of large classes, low expectations, and incongruent philosophy, is at fault. It has been suggested[11] that in order to maintain the effects of early intervention programs, we must either change the elementary school's educational approach or provide children with preschool experiences that will better prepare them for existing school situations.

Debate as to the most appropriate educational methods or approaches is not restricted to Head Start but continues among those concerned with enhancing the development of all children. Considering all aspects of this debate, Head Start has been a successful intervention program. The intent of the program was not just to raise the IQ but to raise the quality of children's lives before the effects of poverty are reinforced into a self-perpetuating circle.

Effect on the Field
of Early Childhood Education

Project Head Start, during its six years of growth, has strongly influenced the interdisciplinary field of early childhood education. The impact of the program on many professionals, parents and their children, and the general public has been impressive. Perhaps the single most important effect has been that the project has inspired the nation to focus its attention on preschool education for all children.

The following represents a brief summary of significant implications of Project Head Start on early childhood education:

• Advocation of a comprehensive approach to programing that considers the total developmental needs of young children.

• Influence on professionals and administrators to design programs that are relevant to the cultural and ethnic backgrounds of children and their family lifestyles.

• Incorporation of parent involvement by bringing the total family unit into the learning process.

• Influence on the nation's kindergartens, day care centers, and nursery schools to maintain small adult-child ratios.

• Increasing acceptance of nonprofessional teacher aides by school systems, and social welfare and health aides by respective agencies.

• Advocation of career development for all staff in preschool programs.

• Development of new curriculum materials for both young children and for teacher education.

• Influence on institutions of higher education to include early childhood teacher education as part of their program. Institutions have been encouraged to develop innovative offerings for auxiliary personnel through extension services, as well as at the undergraduate and graduate levels.

• Encouragement of extensive research in areas related to early childhood, both within and outside the federal government.

• Extension of the concept of early evaluation of the growth and development of young children as it relates to their school experience. As a result, better cumulative record keeping and articulation between preschools and primary grades now exist.

• Demonstration that children of preschool and kindergarten age can learn more, faster, and at an earlier age than was thought previously. The result is an increasing demand for new and better teaching methods, provision of special services for early childhood programs, and high-quality experiences for young children.

Project Head Start has successfully and dramatically contributed to the professionalization of early childhood programs and their acceptance into the total educational system. From this point in time, programs for young children will expand and evolve in many forms. The continuing development of day care centers, family day care homes, and infant care is benefiting greatly from the experience and knowledge gained from this comprehensive national program for young children.

FOOTNOTES

1. Cicirelli, Victor G.; Cooper, William H.; Grange, R. L. The Impact of Head Start: An Evaluation of the Effects of Head Start on Children's Cognitive and Affective Development. Westinghouse Learning Corporation, June 12, 1969. OEO Contract No. B89-4536.

2. "Highlights of Kirschner Study of the Impact of Centers on Community Institutions," HEW/OCD/R&E, 1969.

3. Datta, Lois-ellin. A Report on Evaluation Studies of Project Head Start. Paper presented at the convention of the American Psychological Association, Washington, D.C., 1969.

4. Grotberg, Edith H. Review of Research, 1965-1969, OEO Pamphlet 1608-13, 1969.

5. Gray, Susan W. Selected Longitudinal Studies of Compensatory Education—A Look from the Inside. Paper presented at the Head Start National Conference, Washington, D.C., 1969.

6. Klaus, Rupert A., and Gray, Susan W. "The Early Training Project: A Report After Five Years." Monographs of the Society for Research in Child Development, 1968, 33 (4, Serial No. 120).

7. Weikart, David P., editor. Preschool Intervention: A Preliminary Report of the Perry Preschool Project. Ann Arbor, Mich.: Campus Publishers, 1967.

8. ————. A Comparative Study of Three Preschool Curricula. Paper presented at the meeting of the Society for Research in Child Development, Santa Monica, California, 1969.

9. See footnote 4.

10. See footnote 3.

11. Spicker, Howard H. "Intellectual Development Through Early Childhood Education." Exceptional Children 37: 629-40; May 1971.

ADDITIONAL REFERENCES

Forest, Ilse. Preschool Education: A Historical and Critical Study. New York: Macmillan Co., 1927.

Frost, Joe L., editor. Early Childhood Education Rediscovered. New York: Holt, Rinehart, and Winston, 1968.

Klein, Jenny W. "Planned Variation in Head Start Programs." Children 18: 8-12; January/February 1971.

Leeper, Sarah H. and others. Good Schools for Young Children. New York: Macmillan Co., 1968.

Zigler, Edward. Contemporary Concerns in Early Childhood Education. Address presented at the 1970 conference of the National Association for the Education of Young Children, Boston, Massachusetts, November 21.

FOLLOW THROUGH

ROBERT L. EGBERT

THE main purpose of the Follow Through experimental program is to develop evidence to help guide policy decisions in designing and implementing educational programs that will ease the impact and the consequences of poverty. Follow Through's most distinctive feature is the research and development approach that is used in a program that includes more than 170 projects in urban ghettos and isolated rural areas, from Van Buren, Maine; to San Diego, California; and from Hoonah, Alaska; to Miami, Florida. It is a program that offers comprehensive services and parent participation and, as a result of administrative decision, provides for extensive inter-project variation in program approach, usually instruction.

Follow Through's strategy of planned variation seeks to test the relative efficacy of a variety of social and educational programs in the natural laboratory of the public school and its community. Planned variation involves the association of a local community with a program sponsor which may be a university, regional educational laboratory, or other organization that has developed an especially promising approach for working with young children.

There are 20 program sponsors, each working with from one to 19 local projects. As a long-term undertaking, the Follow Through design recognizes that: 1) each local community-sponsor relationship requires a period of time to develop; 2) even where their goals are similar, various sponsors project different schedules for achieving the goals—for example, learning to read; and 3) the ultimate test of a program approach is the child's suc-

Robert L. Egbert is Dean, Teachers College, The University of Nebraska, Lincoln, Nebraska.

NATIONAL ELEMENTARY PRINCIPAL, 1971, Vol. 51, pp. 104-109.

cess after leaving the program, not simply while he is enrolled in it.

Developmental History of Follow Through

The Head Start Program, which was launched in the summer of 1965, focused national attention on the importance of child development in the early years most particularly for poor children. It soon became obvious that there was a need for a follow-up early elementary program. Head Start evaluation reports suggested that preschool gains tended to dissipate when they were not reinforced in the primary grades. During his address at the opening session of the Annual Meeting of the Great Cities Research Council in 1966, Sargent Shriver pointed to studies that indicated Head Start gains were being nullified. He stated that, "The readiness and receptivity they had gained in Head Start has been crushed by the broken promises of first grade."

President Johnson first proposed the Follow Through Program in his State of the Union Message on January 10, 1967. During fiscal year 1968 funding, under the Economic Opportunity Act, he asked for $120 million to operate Follow Through programs for up to 200,000 children. In his February 8, 1967, Message on Children and Youth, the President voiced a concern:

Head Start occupies only part of a child's day and ends all too soon. He often returns home to conditions which breed despair. If these forces are not to engulf the child and wipe out the benefits of Head Start, more is required.

Follow Through was intended to be the "more" referred to in this message. Designed to answer the "What next?" question, it was launched as a pilot venture in the fall of 1967.

Although Follow Through was later authorized by the Economic Opportunity Act, the Administration decided that the program would be administered under a delegation of authority from the Office of Economic Opportunity to the U.S. Department of Health, Education, and Welfare. Within HEW, the specific unit directed to administer the program was the Division of Compensatory Education of the U.S. Office of Education.

Pilot Phase

In anticipation of legislative authorization by the Congress, the Office of Economic Opportunity transferred $3.5 million to the U.S. Office of Education to fund 40 school systems that would serve as pilot Follow Through centers in the school year 1967-68.

An advisory committee with broad representation from early childhood education, the social sciences, and school administration met to make recommendations on program content. The early work of this committee formed the basis of *Preliminary Thinking Related to Follow Through,* a document that guided pilot communities in designing the first Follow Through projects.

On December 23, 1967, the Congress acted on the amendments to the Economic Opportunity Act. Section 222 (a) (2) of P.L. 90-22 authorized Follow Through. Title II—Urban and Rural Community Action Programs Section 222 (a) reads:

(1) A program to be known as "Project Headstart" focused upon children who have not reached the age of compulsory school attendance which (A) will provide such comprehensive health, nutritional, education, social, and other services as the Director finds will aid the children to attain their full potential, and (B) will provide for direct participation of the parents of such children in the development, conduct, and overall program direction at the local level.

(2) A program to be known as "Follow Through" focused primarily upon children in kindergarten or elementary school who were previously enrolled in Headstart or similar programs and designed to provide comprehensive services and parent participation activities as described in paragraph (1), which the Director finds will aid in the continued development of children to their full potential. Funds for such program shall be transferred directly from the Director to the Secretary of Health, Education, and Welfare. Financial assistance for such projects shall be provided by the Secretary on the basis of agreements reached with the Director directly to local educational agencies except as otherwise provided by such agreements.

This legislative language is simple and straightforward, and Congressional intent is clear. Follow Through was to be a comprehensive, developmental program for elementary school children who had been enrolled in Head Start. Their parents were to participate in the development, conduct, and overall program direction at the local level. However, in the fall of 1967, before the legislation was enacted, it became known that the Office of Economic Opportunity would probably receive substantially less money than had been requested and that Follow Through, as a new program, would receive little, if any, funding. The decision was therefore made that, for the time being, Follow Through should be an experimental program designed to produce information that would be useful "when" the program was expanded to nationwide service proportions.

At the federal level, decision makers need information about program impact and cost; for example, whether any program approach produces sufficient results to justify authorizing and funding a Follow Through type effort and, if so, how much money would be needed to fund a nationwide effort. At the local level, decision makers need information to facilitate their decision whether to introduce a Follow Through type program and, if their decision is positive, what sort of program they should develop. At the federal and state levels, program personnel need information that permits them to provide both leadership and technical assistance. At the local level, personnel need information that permits them to secure appropriate assistance to plan and to operate their program.

Despite the modification in program emphasis from a service program to an experimental program, the Follow Through legislation was not changed, the expectations of people in the field—for example, Office of Economic Opportunity regional offices and local Community Action Agencies (CAA's)—were not changed, nor did Follow Through deviate from the requirements attached to other fully operational Economic Opportunity Act Title II programs; for example, urban-rural distribution of funds, state-by-state allocation of funds, nonfederal share, private school participation, involvement of local CAA's project planning, involvment of regional OEO personnel in project planning and approval, and uniformly high emphasis on parent participation.

Although these requirements, designed as they were for fully operational service programs, presented special problems to Follow Through as an experimental undertaking, the Follow Through staff felt that it was appropriate to maintain them since they represent the kinds of problems that a service program must meet and hence constitute legitimate hurdles for an experimental program ultimately intended as operational.

The Follow Through program has been developed, not only in compliance with the legislation, but also to produce information for program decision makers and implementers.

Experimental Phase

As a result of its new program emphasis, Follow Through focused its attention on developing, refining, and examining alternative approaches to the education and development of young, economically disadvantaged children. In preparation for such a program, the U.S. Office of Education sponsored a series of meetings that included persons who had gained recognition for planning, describing, and initiating new program approaches that appeared to be promising. In these meetings, each program developer described what he was doing and outlined an approach he might like to use in Follow Through. From the presentations at these meetings, it was obvious that despite the growing interest in this field and despite the extensive publicity given various new programs, no one was fully prepared to move into the primary grades with a completely developed, radically different program. For example, the exciting and highly publicized Engelmann program was developed partially for preschool (kindergarten), but not beyond. A number of approaches, however, including Engelmann's, seemed to be sufficiently well developed and to have enough institutional support to justify including them in Follow Through.

At the same time that these meetings were taking place, procedures were initiated to identify new communities that would be willing to participate in a cooperative enterprise to develop and evaluate comprehensive Follow Through projects, each one of which would incorporate an alternative program approach as part of its comprehensive program. From approximately 225 school districts nominated jointly by state education agencies and state economic opportunity offices and reviewed by regional selection panels, 51 communities, in addition to the pilots, were invited to participate in Follow Through's program of planned variation. Two meetings were held in Kansas City, Missouri; on February 20-24 and on February 25-28, 1968. The first was for representatives from the 40 pilots; the second, for representatives from the prospective sites. The Kansas City meetings were designed to acquaint participants with the program approaches. Pilot projects were permitted to choose a sponsored approach or to continue with their original project plans. New communities were required to select one of the available 14 program approaches.

In succeeding years, additional communities—approximately 50 in 1969 and 12 in 1970—were brought into the program, following procedures paralleling those used in 1968. At the present time, Follow Through makes 158 grants in support of more than 160 local projects.

In addition to the 14 sponsors that began with Follow Through in 1968-69, six entered the program in 1969-70. These new sponsors provided somewhat different approaches to working with children, and five also gave three different groups —state education agencies, minority colleges, and profit-making companies—not included in the first set of sponsors an opportunity for representation. These five sponsors are: the California State Education Agency, Hampton Institute, Center for Inner City Studies, Southern University, and Responsive Environments Corporation. The sixth new sponsor, Georgia State University, has a combined parent education and a classroom model that utilizes a diagnostic prescriptive approach to teaching, whether the teaching occurs in the home or in the classroom.

A Follow Through grant is normally made to the local education agency, and Follow Through projects are funded at the rate of approximately $750 for each poor child enrolled in the project. Half of the children in each Follow Through project must have completed a full-year Head Start program or a similar preschool program. Each Follow Through project begins with the earliest grade level in that particular school and adds one grade each year up to the third grade. In other words, if children enter school in kindergarten, they proceed, grade by grade, to the third grade, with a class being added behind them each year.

Follow Through Sponsorship

The Follow Through Program cannot be understood without careful consideration of the function of program sponsors. In the school year 1970-71, there were 20 individuals and institutions acting as Follow Through sponsors. By having a program sponsor in a community, several essential functions are served: *First,* the sponsor provides the community with a well-defined, consistent, and coherent approach on which adaptation to local conditions may occur. *Second,* the sponsor continually provides the technical assistance, training, and guidance needed to implement his approach locally. *Third,* the sponsor exercises a "quality control" function by constantly monitoring the progress of implementation and by providing information on the degree of implementation and necessary adjustments. *Fourth,* the sponsor, who has an important stake in the full and adequate implementation of his approach, serves as an outside agent, a source of program constancy, to help the community maintain a consistent focus on the objectives and requirements of the approach.

Any attempt to group Follow Through approaches is difficult, but the following characterizations may prove helpful. Follow Through models reflect a broad spectrum of theoretical positions, from highly structured instructional approaches that stress cognitive skills to far more informal child-centered approaches that, in addition to curriculum content, emphasize the development of the child's confidence and other behavioral traits. Two approaches are not directly concerned with classroom instruction. One trains parents, particularly in rural areas, where there is often a teacher shortage to supplement their children's education at home. The second emphasizes a more active role for parents in school decision making about how and what their children learn.

1. *Parent Education Approaches.* The primary emphasis is on providing parents with the skills needed to become better teachers of their own children, to continue or better support the child's learning in the home.

2. *Parent Implementation.* Major discretionary and decision-making powers are transferred from established authorities to a parent group that is charged with designing and managing a program.

3. *Highly Structured and Sequenced Curriculum Approaches.* In these approaches, there are few curriculum choices for the child or the teacher. The curriculum is predetermined, and the teacher uses prescribed procedures. The range of instructional materials may be limited to specific, sequenced material. Departure from these materials or a fixed schedule is either discouraged or is not allowed. Although all approaches advocate positive reinforcement to support a child's motivation, this group requires

173

reinforcement that includes a systematic use of material rewards, based on an analysis of the child's behavior.

4. *Structured Curriculum Approaches.* Curriculum objectives are predetermined. Sequenced procedures and materials may be required, but the teacher has a measure of choice among suggested procedures and materials in attaining these objectives. Although options for the teacher are increased, the child is granted little choice in what he will do.

5. *Less Structured Curriculum Approaches.* The teacher has a wider range of choices of materials and procedures for designing an instructional program for individual children based on his diagnosis of the child's own choice of learning task or interest. There are increased opportunities for the child to explore different options.

6. *Open Classroom Approaches.* Curriculum principles and instructional philosophy are defined, but precise structure for classroom management and teacher behavior is not predetermined. The child has the highest degree of choice in determining his own curriculum. Material and equipment emphasize the importance of intrinsic motivation. The teacher's options for supporting the child's learning are limited only by her imagination within the context described.[1]

Evaluation

The aim of Follow Through, as a program of service to children, is to increase the life chances of those enrolled; that is, to increase the probability that Follow Through children will be developmentally successful and that they will become productive, happy adults. The aim of Follow Through, as an experimental program, is to produce information about alternative approaches that show promise of increasing the child's life chances. It is the task of the longitudinal evaluation to gather, analyze, and interpret the relevant data.

The Follow Through longitudinal evaluation focuses on the child—the personal attributes he brings to the program, the attributes that characterize him as he leaves the program, and those that characterize him some time after leaving the formal Follow Through Program. The evaluation also recognizes that the child's development is influenced by certain critical elements of his environment— family, school, neighborhood, community —and that the school is but a part of this

life space. The program elements of Follow Through explicitly acknowledge this by defining comprehensive services to include instructional, physical, and psychological services so that parent and other nonschool adult participation in policy making and program implementation is encouraged. Recognizing the importance of these environmental influences, the evaluation describes at the entry level the child, his family characteristics, and his community. Data are also collected on the instructional program, the personal characteristics and attributes of teachers and aides, the nutrition program, the health services, and the parent involvement program.

The Follow Through Program is interested in producing institutional changes that will benefit children who are currently enrolled in the program. It is concerned also that these changes be permanent and thus affect future classes of Follow Through children. Therefore, in addition to information about children, their background, the instructional program, and so forth, the Follow Through evaluation gathers data intended to indicate the permanency of changes that Follow Through produces in educational systems.

As stated previously, children enter Follow Through at the earliest elementary grade level (K or I) and remain in the program through grade 3, or the equivalent age level. Entry data are gathered in the fall of the child's first year in the program. Sample data are collected at the end of each grade until the third grade, when comprehensive data will again be gathered.

Although Follow Through is a research and development program, the absence of a systematic experimental design deserves special attention. In Follow Through, neither communities, schools, classrooms, nor children were randomly assigned to either "treatment" and to "control" groups or to a specific approach within Follow Through. Thus, there will always be some basic uncertainty about its findings—an uncertainty that may be reduced but that can never be entirely eliminated by sophisticated statistical treatments or other instruments.

The control group problem has two aspects: One has to do with the family and community characteristics of the children; the other, with the nature of the institutional services. Both are important. However, the first contains the really key issue: Given evidence of the very strong relationship between family characteristics and measures of children's performance, with what standards can the progress of Follow Through children be appropriately compared?

The attempt to resolve this dilemma has been cumbersome and expensive, but it appears to have a greater "margin of safety" than any proposed alternative. The chosen approach involves, first, selecting for each Follow Through project a set of comparison classrooms in which the characteristics of the children are believed, on the basis of available information, to approximate those of the Follow Through children. In most cases, these have been located in the same school district as the associated Follow Through project, thus, it is hoped, controlling interdistrict differences in the basic educational program or in the availability of other services. In a few places, where Follow Through serves all or most of the poor children in the district, arrangements have been made to gather data in comparison classrooms in a neighboring community.

Evidence from the Coleman Report and other studies has shown that family characteristics almost overwhelm all other variables in accounting for children's performance in school. In the face of this evidence and the dangers of regression effects inherent in ex post facto analyses, so well documented by Campbell and others, measures of family background and home circumstances, provided by interviews with mothers (or mother surrogates), were incorporated in the study. Preliminary analyses reveal rather substantial differences between Follow Through and comparison group families in socioeconomic status and other characteristics. And as expected, other analyses confirm that performance on conventional tests is highly related to family traits.

Program evaluation is always fraught with difficulties. In addition to the issues already raised, the very nature of Follow Through causes normal evaluation hazards to be multiplied. The program is large (over 60,000 children in 1970-71), and its projects are widely scattered (over 150 separate locations in each of the 50 states). The projects are diverse: urban ghetto to isolated rural; English as a first language or Spanish, French, Portuguese, and various American Indian tongues as a first language; large public school systems or tiny private schools; a complete spectrum of ethnic backgrounds. In addition, the program has many "stakeholders" with differing concerns: a range of sponsors, different minority groups, local school systems, local community action agencies, state education agencies, and so forth. And, finally, the program is comprehensive: instruction, health, nutrition, parent involvement, and so forth. Follow Through, both as a program and in the evaluation, has attempted to be responsive to each of these issues and groups.

Follow Through is a program in transit. Local projects, in association with program sponsors, are under way and functioning effectively. Extensive data have been gathered on two experimental classes of children and on their parents, teachers, and other program participants. Mid-passage data are being gathered, and within two to three years, extensive end-of-program data will be available. Although it is too early to predict detailed program outcomes, available evidence suggests that Follow Through results will be of major importance to elementary education, especially education for poor children, for many years to come.

FOOTNOTE

1. The complete list of Follow Through Program sponsors is as follows (the name of the current project leader appears in parentheses): Afram Associates, Inc., New York, New York 10035 (Preston Wilcox); University of Arizona, Tucson, Arizona 85712 (Joseph Fillerup); Georgia State University, Atlanta, Georgia 30303 (Walter Hodges); Bank Street College of Education, New York, New York 10011 (Elizabeth Gilkeson); California State Department of Education, Sacramento, California 95814 (James Jordan); Education Development Center, Newton, Massachusetts 02160 (George Hein); Far West Laboratory for Educational Research and Development, Emeryville, California 94608 (Glen Nimnicht); University of Florida, Gainesville, Florida 32601 (Ira Gordon); University of Georgia, Athens, Georgia 30601 (Charles Smock); Hampton Institute, Hampton, Virginia 23368 (Mary Christian); High/Scope Educational Research Foundation, Ypsilanti, Michigan 48197 (David Weikart); University of Kansas, Lawrence, Kansas 66044 (Donald Bushell); New York University, New York, New York 10003 (Jack Victor); University of North Dakota, Grand Forks, North Dakota 68201 (Vito Perrone); Northeastern Illinois State College, Chicago, Illinois 60653 (Nancy Arnez and Edythe Williams); University of Oregon, Eugene, Oregon 97403 (Siegfried Engelmann and Wesley Becker); University of Pittsburgh, Pittsburgh, Pennsylvania 15213 (Lauren Resnick and Warren Shepler); Responsive Environments Corporation, Englewood Cliffs, New Jersey 07632 (Fairfid M. Caudle); Southern University and A & M College, Baton Rouge, Louisiana 70813 (Edward Johnson and Anne Price); Southwest Educational Development Laboratory, Austin, Texas 78701 (Juan Lujan).

The Case for the Academic Preschool: Fact or Fiction?

DAVID ELKIND

Over the past few years there has been a remarkable growth of professional interest in young children and in the preschool education they receive. In part, this new interest in young children derives from research (some of which is reviewed by Scott, 1968, and by Stevenson, Hess & Rheingold, 1967), which suggests that the preschool years are of great importance not only for social and emotional but also for intellectual growth. While the research findings came as no surprise to nursery school teachers, they seem to have come as something of a revelation to many educators and psychologists (e.g., Bruner, 1960; Fowler, 1962; Hunt, 1961).

This "new" recognition of the importance of the preschool years for mental growth has had two major consequences. One of these is a movement (that has or will soon succeed in states such as California, Massachusetts and New York) to provide preschool education for all children whose parents desire it. The second major consequence of this new focus upon the preschool child is a growing sentiment towards changing the character of preschool education. While the advocates of change in preschool education (e.g., Berlyne, 1965; Fowler, 1962; Hunt, 1961; Sava, 1968) are somewhat vague in their specifications, it seems fair to say that they appear to advocate more formal, academic types of instruction. In the present essay, 1 want to deal primarily with this second consequence and to examine some of the arguments for the formalization of preschool education.

Those who advocate more structured nursery school instruction (e.g., Sava, 1968) seem to base their position on four types of argu-

YOUNG CHILDREN, 1971, Vol. 26, pp. 132–140.

ments: a) The earlier we start a child in the formal academic path, the earlier he will finish and the cheaper the total educational cost; b) learning comes easy to the young child and we should take advantage of the preschooler's learning facility and eagerness to learn; c) intellectual growth is rapid in the preschool years and instruction will help to maximize that growth while failure to provide appropriate intellectual stimulation may curtail the child's ultimate level of achievement and d) traditional preschool experience is too soft, too directed towards emotional well-being and too little concerned with cognitive stimulation. Let us take up each of these arguments in turn.

Is the Academic Preschool Economical?

There is certainly a sense in which preschool instruction may be more economical than later educational interventions. In the case of disadvantaged children who do not profit from what Strodtbeck (1964) called "the hidden curriculum of the middle-class home," there is a real need for more structured learning experiences such as those provided by Bereiter and Englemann (1966); Kami and Radin (1967) and Blank and Solomon (1968). To the child who comes from the often chaotic stimuli of the ghetto, the structure of a formal instructional program is a needed counterpoise to his experience at home. The structured preschool experience offered to the disadvantaged child helps compensate for the cognitive and linguistic preparation that the middle-

David Elkind, Ph.D., is Professor of Psychology at the University of Rochester and has served as psychological consultant to various institutions. His many published books reflect a broad range of interests in psychology and education.

class child receives in the home. In the case of disadvantaged children, then, preparation is certainly cheaper in the long run than reparation or remedial education later.

The advocates of preschool instruction have not, however, limited their sights to the disadvantaged child only, but aim their arguments at the middle-class child as well. There is so much to learn these days, it is argued, that we need to start children earlier if they are to complete their education while still young. Besides it is more economical to educate at the preschool than at the college level. While these arguments seem to have merit, they do not really hold up under careful scrutiny.

It is true of course that we are living in an era of explosive increases in knowledge and that our highly technical civilization will require ever more highly trained individuals. Our task is thus to speed up the educational process. Such a speedup, however, can be accomplished in several ways just as it can be done in industry. If a manufacturer wishes to speed up his production, he can either get his workers to work longer hours or make his production facilities operate more rapidly and efficient. In most cases, the latter solution results in a more economical manufacture and a better product. The same probably holds true in education.

Our educational system today is really not geared to the needs of young people growing up in today's world. Too much of it is geared to the acquisition and storing of information and too little to teaching young people how to retrieve information. By the time we are adults most of us have forgotten about four-fifths of what we learned in school. That, after all, is a pretty poor yield.

177

Our educational system, thus, has a lot of dead wood and could be streamlined so there would be no need to start children at the preschool level in order to complete their education in a reasonable time. Children in Western Europe often do not begin school until age six or seven but are better educated than our young people when they complete high school. In any case, if we taught children to read and write at the preschool level there would still have to be a total change and reorganization at all educational levels. It might be more profitable in the long run to streamline our existing instructional institutions before creating new ones.

Formal instruction of the middle-class child does not appear, then, to have any economic advantages. Nor does it have the necessary preparatory quality it has for the disadvantaged child. The typical middle-class home provides a good deal of structure and instruction. Middle-class parents are constantly conversing with their children, labeling things for them, answering their questions, providing them with "educational" toys and instilling them with the idea that they, the parents, look favorably upon academic achievement. In the context of this structured tutelage in the home, additional instruction in the preschool would merely gild the lily. We shall, at a later point, return to the role of the preschool for middle-class children. At this point, it is only necessary to say that formal instruction of the middle-class preschool child is probably a less effective procedure than streamlining the educational system as a whole.

Is the Academic Preschool Efficient?

Those who advocate preschool instruction for the middle-class child ar-gue that the preschool youngster is an eager and facile learner. While both of these contentions are true, they do not necessarily imply the efficacy of preschool instruction in the formal sense. Let us look first at the young child's eagerness to learn. This eagerness is present in his constant questions, his curiosity and exploratory behavior. Actually, this eagerness is present at the kindergarten and first grade levels as well. But by the time children reach the fifth and sixth grade, more than 50 percent of the children once eager to learn dislike school, the prime agency of instruction. *It is at least possible that the dislike of school and of learning is a direct result of our lock step instructional processes which kill spontaneous interest.* The introduction of formal instruction at the preschool level could thus well have the effect of bringing children's eagerness to learn to an earlier grave than heretofore.

If we look now at the young child's facility in learning, it too offers no direct invitation for formal instruction. The young child learns quickly but what he learns, he learns by rote—not by reason and thought. Read a story to him several times and he will know it by heart. But in problem solving and in other types of learning situations, he has great difficulty and uses trial and error. In all but rote situations he is a terribly inefficient learner. This observation has now been substantiated by evidence from many different kinds of studies (White, 1965), which strongly suggest that something happens between the ages of four and seven which transforms the young child who learns merely on the basis of association to an older one who learns with the aid of language mediation and with deductive reasoning.

These data are important because as the writer has argued elsewhere (Elkind, 1969a), most of the tool skills required of the young child, such as reading and arithmetic, require the logical and linguistic structures that usually do not emerge until age six or seven. Accordingly, if we try to teach children to "read" and "do math" while still at the preschool level, they may learn by different means than they will at a later time. Such training could actually produce difficulties later and interfere with the successful mastery of these tasks at the cognitive level. Moreover, since such skills cannot be easily learned by rote means, children will have to invest much more time in the preschool learning to read than they would have to invest had they waited until they were older before learning this tool skill.

This is not to say—I want to emphasize—that the preschool period is not a very important one in preparing children for formal instruction in tool subjects. Listening to stories, learning the alphabet and familiarity with numbers and quantitative relations are all important preparatory education for formal instruction. Preparing children for reading and mathematics is, however, different from teaching them reading and arithmetic, which should be delayed until the child gives evidence of having attained mediational learning—the ability to learn with the aid of rational and linguistic formulae. Of course, no blocks should be placed in the path of the exceptional child who learns to read and do math through his own efforts and interest. Accordingly, while it is true that the young child is an eager and facile learner, this does not imply that he be given formal instruction in tool subjects. Such instruction could well stifle his spontaneous interest in learning because the skills themselves call for learning abilities the young child does not yet possess. His facility in rote learning is of little help in learning skills such as math and reading that require rational learning processes. In view of these considerations, it makes more sense for preschool education to focus upon preparation for formal instruction than upon formal instruction itself.

Does the Academic Preschool Maximize Mental Growth?

Those who argue for an academic preschool suggest that early childhood is a "critical period" in mental growth. The idea of critical periods in human development derives from analogies with animal studies. Such studies show that during certain periods in their development, animals are particularly susceptible to environmental influence. Young chicks, to illustrate, become attached to the prominent object about them approximately 17 hours after birth. Thereafter, the chick responds to this object as if it were his "mother," whether it is a box, balloon or graduate student (Scott, 1968). In humans, the period of primary socialization appears at the last quarter of the first year, when the infant gives evidence of fear of strangers and anxiety over the mother's departure (Schaeffer & Callender, 1959).

While there is thus some evidence for a critical period for human socialization, there is no unequivocal evidence for such periods in *mental* development. The evidence adduced by those who favor the critical period hypothesis is of three sorts: a) mental growth curves, b) case histories and c) data from academic preschools. Let us examine the evidence.

The argument for critical periods based on mental growth curves derives from the writings of psychometricians such as Bloom (1964). Bloom suggests that half the child's intellectual capacity is attained by age four and another 30 per cent by age eight. There is, therefore, evidence that early childhood is a period of very rapid intellectual growth. This evidence, however, does not necessarily imply that the period is critical in the sense that if stimulation is not received during this epoch, later stimulation will not be able to accomplish the same result. Let us look at the mental growth curves in more detail since they appear to be the primary basis for the critical period notion with respect to mental growth.

Unlike growth curves for height and weight, which involve merely recording the successive measurements on the same individuals across time, mental growth curves involve the correlations between test scores at successive age levels. What mental growth curves really tell us is not how much of a child's total mental capacity he has at any given time, but only how much of his total intellectual ability we can predict at any age. To illustrate, from a child's IQ score at age four, we can predict with 50 percent accuracy what his IQ will be at age 17. That is the *only* straightforward interpretation of the mental growth curves report by Bloom (1964).

Suppose, however, that we accept the interpretation that ability to predict is related to total ability, and that a child does attain half his total mental ability by age four and 80 percent by age eight. Does this imply we ought to start academic instruction early to capitalize on this rapid growth period? Not at all! In the first place, the rate of mental growth

appears to decline as the rate of formal instruction increases. That is, almost 75 percent of a child's mental growth takes place before he receives formal schooling and the rate of mental growth declines as the amount of formal schooling increases—only 20 percent growth between eight and 17. There is, in effect, *a negative correlation between mental growth and formal instruction!* Looked at in this way, one could legitimately argue that formal schooling ought to be *delayed* rather than introduced early to maximize mental growth.

Another argument for the criticalness of early childhood for mental growth comes from the writings of Fowler (1968), who states:

"The unvarying coincidence of extensive early stimulation with cognitive precocity and subsequent superior competence in adulthood suggest that stimulation is a necessary if not sufficient condition for the development of his abilities" (p. 17). What Fowler forgets, however, is that correlation is *not* causation. It is true that many great scientists and artists received early instruction, but it is also true that they had gifted parents and were genetically well endowed. Furthermore, and more importantly, what of all those children whose parents stimulated and instructed them almost from the day of their birth and who did not achieve later eminence? In science, it is necessary to acknowledge negative as well as positive instances, and my guess is that the negative instances far exceed the positive. I have seen one such product of early stimulation, an autistic (schizophrenic) boy who believed he was a tape recorder. When he was an infant, his mother bathed him in a sea of tape-recorded

180

sound to stimulate his musical talents. In arguing about the benefits of early instruction, it is only fair to report the possible costs of intense instructional pressure at home and at school.

Finally, a third argument for the criticalness of the preschool period comes from those who cite the effects of preschool instructional programs, such as those of Head Start, Bereiter and Englemann (1966), and so on. To the extent that these programs are directed at disadvantaged children, the gains may be very real indeed but are probably of smaller magnitude than they appear (Jensen, 1969). This is because when the children take the initial pretest before the training, they are strange to the situation and examiners, whereas afterwards they feel at home and their test performance reflects that fact (Zigler & Butterfield, 1968). As I indicated earlier, however, there may be real benefits for disadvantaged children in an academically oriented preschool.

The question I wish to raise is whether such instructional programs would equally benefit middle-class children. Recently, Gottesman (1968) reviewed some of the animal and human research relevant to this issue. In general, the studies show that enriched environments benefit disadvantaged or deprived subjects to a much greater extent than they do advantaged or non-deprived subjects. As Jensen (1969) suggests, there seems to be a minimum level of stimulation necessary for children to realize their abilities. If the actual level is below that minimum, they do not realize their full potential. If, however, the environment is richer than necessary, it does not further implement their growth. If this view is correct, mental growth would have to be regarded as analogous to physical growth. Poor diet can stunt a child's height, but an abundantly rich one will not increase his ultimate height beyond a certain limit. If this analogy holds true, the level of stimulation children need to maximize their intellectual growth may be far less than we imagine and excessive enrichment wasteful.

Indeed, most middle-class preschool children are probably over- rather than understimulated. Such overstimulation occurs because we frequently overestimate the young child's ability to assimilate new experience. Most parents have had the experience of taking their preschoolers to the circus, carnival or zoo. Children are usually more interested in the food than other attractions. Usually it is not until weeks later that the youngster will begin to talk about or draw the events which transpired at the event. Children cannot assimilate new experiences in as large a dose or as rapidly as adults, and protect themselves by tuning out the stimulation they cannot process.

In summary, we have reviewed three arguments for the criticalness of early childhood intellectual stimulation and have not found any one of them entirely satisfactory. I do not wish, however, to deny the importance of the early childhood period for intellectual growth. The preschool period is important, even critical, but not because growth is most rapid at the time, or because great men received early stimulation, or because there is evidence to show the lastingness of early instruction. No, the preschool period is important for a simple reason, namely, mental growth is cumulative and depends upon what has gone before.

Whether we are talking about Piagetian stages, the acquisition of a skill such as playing the piano or knowledge in a particular area, there is a cumulative learning aspect. What the child learns in the preschool period must adequately· prepare him for what he is to learn later. It is in this sense, and this sense only, that early childhood is a critical period in intellectual development. In the next section, we will deal in more detail with the preparatory role of the preschool.

Is the Academic Preschool Superior to the Traditional Preschool?

The advocates of an academic preschool see little of intellectual value in traditional preschool education perpetuated by, as Sava (1968) derogatorily put it, the "child lovers." Such attitudes seem to reflect a boundless ignorance of what is accomplished in the traditional preschool and of the skill required to run such a school effectively. What the supporters of the academic preschool fail to realize is that the preschool child is a very different psychosocial being than the school-age child, and that the traditional preschool is well suited to his intellectual and emotional needs.

In the first place, emotions and intellect are not as separate at ages three and four as they will be later and an emotionally distraught preschooler is cognitively disorganized as well. The preschool teacher's concern with and response to the young child's feelings have cognitive as well as emotional benefits. Then too, preschool represents the child's first separation from home, his first experience with a peer group and a substitute mother figure. The preschool child still has a lot of social learning to do, and the traditional preschool pro-

vides the opportunity, security and structure for such learning.

Secondly, and more importantly, the traditional preschool does provide for cognitive stimulation and instruction in the most general and significant sense of that term. Play is, after all, the child's work and much of his motor play is preparatory to later cognitive developments. In stacking and building with blocks, the child learns about spatial relations, balance, weight and gravity. Likewise in large motor play such as climbing, swinging, running, he learns the motor and perceptual coordinations that are essential to later fine motor coordinations involved in reading and writing. Those who deride play in the preschool ignore the fact that all play has a cognitive component and role in all creative endeavor, whether it be intellectual or artistic.

Finally, the traditional preschool program has incorporated for many years some of the most innovative ideas in educational practice today. The traditional nursery school has, to illustrate, always sought to *individualize instruction* and allow each child, in today's lexicon, to do "his thing" whether it be carpentry, doll play, painting or block building. Also, *discovery learning* is built into many preschool activities, such as dramatic play. When a child play-acts roles with other children, he is learning about adult roles and reciprocal rules of behavior. He is, moreover, engaging in the social interchanges with peers that Piaget (1948) regards as so important to the overcoming of egocentrism. Finally, in providing a range of materials and allowing the child to engage in those which sent him at the moment, the traditional preschool capitalizes upon *intrinsic motivation* to learn in the best sense of that term (Elkind, 1969b).

The traditional preschool, thus, does much more than the advocates of the academic preschool credit. Indeed, the traditional preschool already embodies ideas that are only now beginning to appear at higher education levels, such as individualized instruction, discovery learning, peer group stimulation and use of intrinsic motivation. This is not to say, of course, that the traditional preschool is perfect and that there is no room for improvement. For one thing, the value of the preschool will vary with the quality of the teacher. Teacher variability at the preschool level is as great as at every other level of education and can always stand improvement. For another thing, traditional preschools may have too little material for spontaneous practice in logical and mathematical thinking and teachers might benefit from our new knowledge about the thinking capacities of preschool children (Inhelder & Piaget, 1969).

In short, with respect to middle-class children, the traditional preschool still appears to be consonant with the maximum benefit to intellectual and emotional growth of the preschool child. While the traditional preschool can probably increase considerably its effectiveness in preparing children for academic instruction, there is no strong evidence for exposing young, middle-class children to academic instruction itself. Indeed, it would be ironic if, in the name of progress, preschools were forced to adopt the lock step curricula already being given up at higher levels of education.

Summary and Conclusions

In this essay I have discussed four of the arguments for introducing an academic curriculum into preschool education. These arguments are that academic instruction is : a) more economical; b) more efficient; c) more necessary and d) more cognitively stimulating than the traditional preschool. I have tried to show that each of these arguments is weak at best and that there are stronger arguments for not having an academic preschool, at least for the middle-class child. There is no preponderance of evidence that formal instruction is more efficient, more economical, more necessary or more cognitively stimulating than the traditional preschool program. Indeed, while there is room for improvement in the traditional preschool, it already embodies some of the most innovative educational practices extant today. It would, in fact, be foolish to pattern the vastly expanded preschool programs planned for the future upon an instructional format that is rapidly being given up at higher educational levels. Indeed, it is becoming more and more apparent that formal instructional programs are as inappropriate at the primary and secondary levels of education as they are at the preschool level.

References

Bereiter, C. & Englemann, S. *Teaching Disadvantaged Children in the Preschool.* Englewood Cliffs, N.J.: Prentice Hall, 1966.

Berlyne, D. E. Curiosity and education. In J. D. Krumboltz (Ed.), *Learning and the Educational Process.* Chicago: Rand McNally, 1965, 67-89.

Blank, Marion & Solomon, Frances. A tutorial language program to develop abstract thinking in socially disadvantaged preschool children. *Child Develpm.*, 1968, 39, 379-390.

Bloom, B. S. *Stability and Change in Human Characteristics.* New York: Wiley, 1964.

Bruner, J. S. *The Process of Education.* Cambridge, Mass.: Harvard Univ. Press, 1960.

Elkind, D. Developmental studies of figurative perception. In L. P. Lipsitt & H. W. Reese (Eds.), *Advances in Child Development and Behavior.* New York: Academic Press, 1969, 1-28a.

—————. Piagetian and psychometric approaches to intelligence. *Harvard educ. Rev.*, 1969, 39, 319-337b.

Fowler, W. Cognitive learning in infancy and early childhood. *Psycholgl. Bull.*, 1962, 59, 116-152.

Gottesman, I. I. Biogenetics of race and class. In M. Deutsch, I. Katz & A. Jensen (Eds.), *Social Class, Race, and Psychological Development,* New York: Holt, Rinehart & Winston, 1968, 11-51.

Hunt, J. McV. *Intelligence and Experience.* New York: Ronald Press, 1961.

Jensen, A. R. How much can we boost IQ and scholastic achievement? *Harvard educ. Rev.*, 1969, 39, 1-123.

Kamii, C. & Radin, N. A framework for a preschool curriculum based on some Piagetian concepts. *J. creative Behav.*, 1967, 1, 314-324.

Piaget, J. *The Moral Judgment of the Child.* Glencoe, Ill.: The Free Press, 1948.

—————. *The Early Growth of Logic in the Child.* New York: Norton, 1969.

Sava, Samuel G. When learning comes easy. *Saturday Rev.*, Nov. 16, 1968, 102-119.

Schaffer, H. R. & Callender, W. M. Psychologic effects of hospitalization in infancy. *Pediatrics,* 1959, 24, 528-539.

Scott, J. P. *Early Experience and the Organization of Behavior.* Belmont, Calif.: Wadsworth, 1968.

Stevenson, H. W., Hess, E. H. & Rheingold, Harriet L. (Eds.). *Early Behavior.* New York: Wiley, 1967.

Strodtbeck, F. L. The hidden curriculum of the middle-class home. In C. W. Hunnicutt (Ed.), *Urban Education and Cultural Deprivation.* Syracuse: Syracuse Univ. Press, 1964, 15-31.

White, S. H. Evidence for a hierarchical arrangement of learning processes. In L. P. Lipsitt & C. C. Spiker (Eds.), *Advances in Child Development and Behavior,* Vol. 2. New York: Academic Press, 1965, 187-220.

Zigler, E. & Butterfield, E. C. Motivational aspects of changes in IQ test performance of culturally deprived school children. *Child Develpm.*, 1968, 39, 1-14.

'SESAME STREET' CAN'T HANDLE *ALL* THE TRAFFIC!

Gary M. Ingersoll

To a generation of parents who grew up watching "Howdy Doody" and "Ding-Dong School," "Sesame Street" provides a welcome addition to children's television programming. The fast-paced, entertaining, instructional sequences seem to have unusual appeal to both adults and children. However, the biggest asset of "Sesame Street" is that children are apparently *learning*.

The overall popularity of "Sesame Street" has assured its continuance and has encouraged its financial supporters to underwrite more endeavors of the same type. Those funding agencies which provided the Children's Television Workshop with $8 million for the initial 26 weeks of production were undoubtedly gratified to see that the Educational Testing Service gave this ambitious undertaking such high grades. Samuel Ball and Gerry Ann Bogatz, authors of the ETS report, concluded that "Sesame Street" had indeed demonstrated that television could be an effective medium for mass education of pre-school children. Further, on the basis of their study, Ball and Bogatz conclude that the more children saw of "Sesame Street," the more they learned.[1]

Recently, however, the early verdict on "Sesame Street" has been questioned. Some authors are arguing that the series is not as successful as initial reports would lead us to believe. John Holt,[2] for example, criticizes the producers for their choice of objectives. Holt claims that a variety of objectives which he feels are valuable for the pre-schooler were excluded. This form of criticism has doubtful value, since it really fails to consider what "Sesame Street" *has done*. The original Children's Television Workshop people were modest in their selection of objectives. By so doing, they guarded their ability to test the effectiveness of an experimental program in achieving a set of goals defined *a priori*. (See Joan Tierney's article in the January, 1971, *Kappan* for a review of the CTW's procedures.[3])

"Sesame Street" should be evaluated in terms of the objectives stated by the CTW. The degree to which those objectives were or were not met should serve as an index of the value of the "Sesame Street" approach to pre-school education. We should thus direct ourselves to a careful consideration of the accomplishments and/or failures of the "Sesame Street" producers in terms of their own goals.

The first major source of doubt concerning "Sesame Street"'s accomplish-

PHI DELTA KAPPAN, 1971, Vol. 53, pp. 185-186.

ments is a rather unheralded study by Herbert Sprigle, director of the Learning To Learn School in Jacksonville, Florida. Sprigle[4] tested the premise of the CTW that "Sesame Street" would reduce the gap between disadvantaged and advantaged pre-school children, putting them on an equal footing as they enter school. After matching 24 pairs of children on a variety of measures, Sprigle assigned one member of each pair to an "experimental" group which viewed all the "Sesame Street" episodes and were provided with all of the curricular activities suggested by the CTW. The matched children were assigned to a "control" group which did not view "Sesame Street" but spent an equal amount of time in activities using similar content but emphasizing emotional and social development. Sprigle's results are surprising because, on the basis of performance on the Metropolitan Readiness Test and the Draw-a-Man test, the control group scored significantly higher than the "Sesame Street" group. Further, when compared with classmates in the first grade, the experimental group failed to show any substantive advantage over an unprepared control group. While Sprigle's results are shocking, they should be noted with some caution, since the "control" group was not really a control in an experimental sense. Sprigle gave his "control" group another but different concentrated instructional sequence which reflected *his* biases. It is probably safe to conclude that there are other treatments equally effective or perhaps more effective than "Sesame Street."

What, then, of the ETS report which offers such praise for "Sesame Street"? Fortunately, ETS provides complete enough information that one is able to give the results careful scrutiny. Thus the interested educator can use much of the same data on which their evaluation is based to see whether the conclusions are valid.

The major portion of the ETS study used a rather simple experimental design to test the hypothesis that "Sesame Street" is an effective agent in producing change. For the purposes of this review, the major results can be viewed as a function of two of Ball and Bogatz' dimensions. The sample population was selected to satisfy certain criteria. First, children were selected from either advantaged or disadvantaged social backgrounds, with the overwhelming majority of cases falling into the latter category. All children were given a pre-test on the evaluational instrument. Following the presentation of the series of "Sesame Street" programs, ETS divided children into four stratified groups as a function of viewing patterns; i.e., Group average less than once per week, Group Q_2 viewed it two to three times per week, Group Q_3 viewed it four to five times per week, and Group Q_4 viewed it more than five times per week (this was possible since "Sesame Street" was shown twice a day). The stratification presents some sampling problems. The children were assigned to treatments (or samples) on a *post hoc* basis as a function of their viewing patterns. Assignment of learners to viewing treatments was clearly not random. Thus, of the three statistical assumptions necessary for most parametric statistics (independent, random sampling from a normally distributed population),[5] only the assumption of normality may have been met. However, the patterns of means and standard deviations presented show that there are several measures on which the distributions of scores are sufficiently skewed that the standard deviation exceeds the mean. Thus, even the assumption of a normally distributed population is questionable.

The selection procedures might further indicate external sources of contamination to the data. That is, there may be population differences other than the treatment of concern which could account for the differences in performance. Indeed, the pre-test data clearly demonstrated that those children who watched "Sesame Street" most were those who started with higher scores on the pre-test. The assignment of subjects would, therefore, make the ETS study, at best, a quasi-experimental design with a variety of plausible alternative explanations of the data available.

For example, the Ball-Bogatz report is quick to conclude that those who watch "Sesame Street" most gain the most. It is, however, equally plausible to attribute the gains to a function of pre-test performance. If the pre-test scores are viewed as an aptitude measure, one might then conclude that smart children learn more. Given that hypothesis as unsatisfactory, one might argue that "Sesame Street" offers the greatest educational value for those children who start with the most developed cognitive base. That is, there may be some prerequisites necessary for learning the skills taught on "Sesame Street." If socially advantaged children start off with higher pre-test scores, it would be expected that they would show greater gains than their disadvantaged counterparts. That is precisely what occurred. Thus, rather than diminish the deficit for disadvantaged children, "Sesame Street" may have increased it. As Sprigle noted, in gained points the advantaged child showed an increase of *15% more* than the disadvantaged child. Further, if the four groups are qualitatively different on some variable other than viewing time, the validity of a comparison between the gains of disadvantaged children in Q_4 with advantaged children in Q_1 is questionable. It is on the basis of such a comparison that Ball and Bogatz made some of their inferences.

This paper should not be interpreted to imply that "Sesame Street" should be abandoned nor that evaluations of the type provided by ETS are without worth. Rather, the educational community should maintain several avenues open to the solution of the problems of pre-school education. The ETS evaluation indeed opens new questions that need to be answered; e.g., What characteristic(s) of the Q_1 group account(s) for the fact that children in it are reluctant to view "Sesame Street," and what are viable alternative models of instruction that will benefit that portion of the pre-school population?

In addition to the sampling problems just described, the possibility exists that the selection of "advantaged" and "disadvantaged" groups may imply that the study might function as an aptitude-by-treatment interaction study. That is, since the differentiation of groups was on the basis of social class, the groups may differ in the type of cognitive functioning used. If, for example, the Arthur Jensen hypothesis of different categories of intelligence in different social groups[6] has any validity, it might be suggested that the same treatment for each group would have differential effects.

Finally, most of the ETS data are themselves of questionable validity. All conclusions made by Ball and Bogatz are based on analysis-of-gain scores. Gain scores notoriously have a large component of measurement error.[7] Lee Cronbach and L. Furby[8] have recently considered measuring change with a variety of sophisticated statistical techniques to partial out that error. Even with such techniques available (Ball and Bogatz apparently did not use them), Cronbach and Furby strongly discourage the use of change scores.

Any program having the impact of "Sesame Street" is certain to draw criticism from a variety of sources. Indeed, this article was partly intended to serve as a demurrer to the lavish praise offered by the ETS report. The ETS report is so enthusiastic in its support of "Sesame Street" that there is the danger that the educational community will be lulled into tacit acceptance of the series, or its future imitators, as the "best" form of education for the pre-school disadvantaged. The abandonment of existing pre-school programs or the discouragement of future innovations on the basis of the ETS report would be premature and a disservice to the whole area of pre-school education.

1. Samuel Ball and Gerry Ann Bogatz, *The First Year of Sesame Street: An Evaluation.* Princeton, N.J.: Educational Testing Service, October, 1970.

2. John Holt, "Big Bird Meets Dick and Jane," *Atlantic Monthly,* January, 1971.

3. Joan Tierney, "The Miracle on Sesame Street," *Phi Delta Kappan,* January, 1971, pp. 296-98.

4. Herbert A. Sprigle, "Can Poverty Children Live on 'Sesame Street'?" *Young Children,* January, 1971, pp. 202-16.

5. B. J. Winer, *Statistical Principles in Experimental Design.* New York: McGraw-Hill, 1962.

6. Arthur R. Jensen, "Social Class, Race and Genetics: Implications for Education," *American Educational Research Journal,* January, 1968, pp. 1-42.

7. Carl Bereiter, "Some Persisting Dilemmas in the Measurement of Change"; and Frederick M. Lord, "Elementary Models for Measuring Change," both in Chester W. Harris (ed.), *Problems in Measuring Change.* Madison: University of Wisconsin Press, 1963.

8. Lee J. Cronbach and Lita Furby, "How Should We Measure Change — or Should We?" Technical Report No. 6. Project on Individual Difference in Learning Ability as a Function of Instructional Variables, Stanford University, 1969.

Cognitive Performance in Montessori and Nursery School Children[1]

ALBERT S. DREYER

DAVID RIGLER

THIS REPORT represents a pilot study in a larger investigation comparing the approach of contemporary nursery schools and the Montessori approach to preschool education. The use of Montessori methods in preschool is highly controversial, and sharply criticized by nursery school adherents (15). In their turn, Montessori supporters attack the educational approach of the nursery school (16). A review of the writings of adherents of the differing positions, however, suggests that there is apparently less conflict between these two factions about long range *goals* than about *methods* employed to attain these goals.

One aspect of the disagreement may be illustrated by nursery school teachers who despair of "ambitious" or "uncomprehending" parents who demand academic content in a preschool program. In their turn the puzzled parents are themselves upset by a school where children only "play," and "teachers" fail to teach. Beneath this kind of disagreement, at least in part, is a conflict such as that recently described by Baldwin, a conflict between values placed upon cognition and upon personality adjustment:

"The term cognition is made synonymous with intellectuality, with deductive thinking, with knowledge of the facts and principles underlying the number system, space, time and other academic subjects. Personality adjustment refers to feelings, motives and effective interpersonal relations. . . . Some people argue that knowledge and academic skills are the important thing—that such matters as personal adjustment and effective functioning are important luxuries, as far as education is concerned. Others, in precisely the opposite camp, feel that emphasis on academic

THE JOURNAL OF EDUCATIONAL RESEARCH, 1969, Vol. 63, pp. 411-416.

instruction will at best have no effect on important aspects of human behavior, but worse yet, it may make children into intellectualizers—cold analytic computer-like machines, rather than warm sentient friendly human beings" (2:584–5).

Nursery schools in the United States have tended to adhere to an orientation concerned with personality adjustment. Centers that train nursery school teachers and textbooks used in training are based upon concepts of child development that are consonant with such an approach. As a result, nursery school teachers in this country have tended to decry the introduction of academic content into the preschool classroom. Instead, their principal concerns have been with social adjustment, with provision for emotional expression and support, and with opportunities for play with relatively unstructured materials. By contrast, programs oriented to a more cognitive approach, such as the Montessori program, appear to be less concerned with social and emotional adaptation of the child than with the provision of disciplined opportunities in which the children may acquire sensory discriminations and cognitive skills. Materials have been designed for work rather than for play, and program content has been both specific and academic. The interpersonal relations of the child have certainly not been the central concern of the teacher.

The resurgence of interest in Montessori has resulted in the generation of much heat but not much light concerning the relative advantages and disadvantages of each approach. Methods in the nursery school have the advantage, in this controversy, of support from a tradition of practice and from widely disseminated theories of child development. But the Montessori movement is growing rapidly, and some of its supporters, too, have sought support in psychological theory (7). Ultimate resolution, if at all attainable, appears to be dependent upon empirical findings. But Edmonson (6) has pointed out recently in a paper on the Montessori program that ". . . there are few references to comparative education approaches of any type. There are no follow-ups of Montessori trained children. In the absence of comparison and longitudinal studies, our educational theories are doctrinal and we believe what we believe as a matter of faith." Edmonson went on to suggest that the Montessori method warrants careful study which should include research comparison of several preschool educational approaches. Among Montessori contentions she suggests as worthy of examination are: (a) that young children do acquire the cognitive constructs which the materials were designed to provide; (b) that creativeness and problem-solving ability result; (c) that gross and fine motor coordinations are accelerated; (d) that initiative, purposiveness and perseverance, outgoingness, fair play and altruism are significantly fostered; (e) that later cognitive and social learnings are fostered by this early childhood foundation.

This paper is an attempt to present some empirical data on these issues. It is concerned with two questions. First, is there evidence of a selective process determining the kind of parents that choose to send their preschool age children to a Montessori rather than a traditionally oriented nursery school? Secondly, and more important, what are the cognitive consequences upon children of these contrasting approaches to preschool?

Methods

Parent Procedures

To control for the effects of the home environments upon children in the differing school contexts, it seemed necessary to ascertain whether there was a selective process which determined the kind of school to which parents sent their children. Were the ideologies, attitudes, and value orientations of parents choosing to send their children to a Montessori school different from those choosing a traditional nursery school for their children? Were the expectations for children different for these two groups of parents, and did they differ in the sanctions that were employed to enforce socialization demands?

To answer these questions a questionnaire battery was given to each mother and father in a Montessori preschool and in a cooperative nursery school. These schools each appear to be fairly characteristic of their types. The Montessori school is one that is committed to abide by Montessori principles, is well stocked with the appropriate materials, and is taught by teachers trained by Montessori teachers. The cooperative nursery school, with its multiple opportunities for "unstructured" play is probably representative of modern "progressive" nursery schools. A cover letter emphasized the necessity for independent response, and from the parents' reports and inspection of the data we have the impression the

191

questionnaires were indeed taken independently. The parental cooperation was remarkable in that completed questionnaires were received from both mother and father of fifty-four of the sixty couples in the Montessori schools with an additional five mothers only completing the questionnaire. In the cooperative nursery school thirty-seven of thirty-eight couples returned the questionnaires with the additional one mother only completing the material.

The questionnaire consisted of several sections which included the following:

1. Parental Ideology:

A Likert scale consisting of several sub-scales was used to tap parental ideological, attitudinal, and value structure. The items, their sources, and rationale for inclusion are as follows: (a) *F scale* —10 items from the well-known scale of general authoritarian orientation (1) were included to determine whether the two groups of parents differed as to their concern with conventional mores, submission to authority, and power orientation. (b) *TFI scale*—11 items from the Traditional Family Ideology scale (11) were included to determine if the two groups of parents differed with respect to husband and wife roles, concepts of masculinity-femininity, and the problems of authority, power, and responsibilities involved with child-rearing. (c) *Dogmatism scale*—4 items from Rokeach's Dogmatism scale (17) were included as a measure of a degree of openness or closedness of the belief systems of the parents. (d) *Anomie scale*—4 of Srole's (21) 5 Anomie items were included to see if the two groups of parents differed with respect to the degree they felt an absence of structure and support from society with its effects on the individual of feelings of helplessness, defeat, and meaninglessness. (e) *Low F scale*—2 items from the 5-item scale of Couch and Keniston (4) were also included to see if the two groups of parents differed in their readiness vs. unwillingness to respond to environmental forces i.e. their "agreeing" or "acquiescent tendencies." (f) *Achievement scales*—several sub-scales dealing with various facets of achievement—related attitudes and values were also included to tap what differences there might be between these parents regarding standards of excellence and accomplishment. These sub-scales included *Activistic value complex*—6 items (18); *Importance of knowledge*—3 items (13); *Independence*—2 items (13); *Achievement orienta-*

tion—9 items (13).

A score for each sub-scale consisted of average agreement (on a scale of 1 to 7), with each of the items in the sub-scale.

2. Parental Values:

We also wanted to assess the value system of these parents with regard to what has variously been termed "fun morality vs. work morality" (27), and "entrepreneurial vs. bureaucratic orientation" (14). To do so we adapted the list of values Kohn (9) used in his study of social class differences in values. From this list, we selected five child behaviors that were reliably judged by Brim (3) to be problem and task centered or "instrumental" characteristics and five child behaviors that were judged to be socio-emotional or "expressive" characteristics. The five instrumental characteristics are (a) able to defend himself, (b) self control, (c) finish what he starts, (d) serious about things, (e) able to play by himself. The five expressive characteristics are: (a) obey his parents, (b) popular, (c) cheerful, (d) affectionate, (e) considerate of others.

The parent was told that this part of the questionnaire dealt with the type of person that in general he thought his own child's age ought to be. He was asked to indicate how important he thought each of the characteristics presented is in a child of his own child's age. One of the measures obtained from the parent's response to this part of the questionnaire was the degree of importance of instrumental or expressive traits to the parent. This was determined by assigning a weight of 0 where a response of "not important" was given, a weight of 1 to a response of "somewhat important" and a weight of 2 to a response of "very important." The possible range of scores, therefore, for the instrumental and expressive characteristics was from 0 to 10.

3. Parental Childrearing Patterns:

Schaefer (19) has indicated that parental behavior can be organized around two basic dimensions of autonomy versus control and love versus hostility. A part of the questionnaire was designed to assess these qualities of parental nurturance and control.

Torgoff and Dreyer (24) view parental orientations towards control and autonomy not as polarities but as two independent dimensions. One component, achievement-inducing (A), refers to the degree to which the parent encourages the child to master modes of behavior the parent sees as

193

appropriate for the child's age and sex. The other component, independence-granting (I), refers to the degree to which the parent is willing to permit the child to make his own decisions, to grant autonomy, and to accept child-determined directions. A measure of over-all control, the I/A ratio, is obtained from responses to a section of the questionnaire consisting of 12 achievement-inducing and 12 independence-granting items for each sex separately. The score for a subject on each I/A sub-scale consists of the mean of the ages given in response of the items in the sub-scale. The I/A ratio consists of the mean age for the I items divided by the mean age for the A items. The higher the ratio the greater the over-all control. A series of studies reported since 1958 have demonstrated the reliability and validity of this measure of parental control (5, 10, 22, 23, 24).

Child Procedures

The sample of children was selected from the two settings by matching seven pairs of boys, and seven pairs of girls from these schools on socio-economic status, age, and Stanford–Binet IQ. Matching was closer for some of these variables than for others: Parents were homogeneous with respect to social class, being middle class—predominantly professional and managerial; deviation in age ranged from 0 to 6 months; deviation in IQ modally was 3 IQ points. The mean age of the children was 5 years, 1 month; the mean IQ was 125.3. The children in the two preschool settings had about the same exposure to their educational environments at the time of testing.

In order to assess the effect of these diverse educational experiences on the children, four instruments were administered to each child. First was an adaptation of the Vocal Encoding Test of the Illinois Test of Psycholinguistic Abilities (ITPA) (12) used to measure the concepts selected by the child in his verbal description of the world. After being taught the nature of the task with a blue marble, the child was presented with seven additional objects and asked to tell the experimenter all about each object. The objects consisted of a red rubber ball, a green wooden cube, a short length of rope, a steel mirror, a piece of rectangular clear plastic, a piece of chalk, and a short length of plastic tubing. The child's descriptions were recorded verbatim. The description of each of the objects was scored as to whether it was a functional, that is, a use description, or whether it was a description of the physical characteristics of the objects. These physical characteristics involved shape, composition, color, and so forth. The percent of Functional and the percent of Physical Characteristic descriptions over the seven objects was calculated for each child and was then normalized using an arc-sign transformation.

A second measure attempted to tap the child's degree of creativity, an area hotly disputed as an outcome variable of the nursery school. The Picture Construction Test (PCT), one of the non-verbal tasks of the Minnesota Tests of Creative Thinking developed by Torrance and his associates (25) was used. The child was presented with a blank sheet of paper, a piece of red gummed paper and a pencil. He was asked to think of and draw a picture in which the colored paper, in the shape of a curved jellybean, would be an integral part. The child's construction was scored, using the test manual, for degree of originality, elaboration, activity, and title adequacy. Inter-judge reliabilities for the categories ranged from 80–100 percent agreement. Each of the scores was weighted according to the manual and a sum score derived.

A third measure represented something of a bridge between these first two, being concerned with characteristics, preferred styles of response. The Children's Embedded Figure Test (CEFT), developed by Karp and Konstadt (8) in their work with Witkin (26) on cognitive style was administered to each child. In this task, the child is first presented with a stimulus figure (a *tent* in one series, and a *house* in another), and he is then requested to locate a similar figure located in an embedding context. Two scores were derived over the series of trials—one consisting of the number of times the child correctly located the embedded figure and the other score consisting of the total time to perform the entire task.

A final instrument was included to determine what the children would do with a task in which they could determine some of the structure. Each child was asked to draw a picture of anything he desired. The pictures were coded as to the presence or absence of people in the drawings, and the presence or absence of geometric figures in the drawings.

Results

The mean scores between the groups of fathers and the groups of mothers on each variable was

195

compared by using the parametric t-test. Since the child data were considered ordinal, non-parametric tests of significance were regarded as appropriate. The Wilcoxon matched-pair signed-ranks test (20) was used to determine the difference between the two matched groups of children. The Fisher exact-probability test (20) was used with the frequencies of the free drawing categorization. Although the means of the children's scores are not used in the calculations, they are reported to indicate the extent of differences between measures.

As can be seen in Table 1, the parents of the children in Montessori and of the nursery school did not differ on any of our questionnaire measures of authoritarianism, traditional family ideology, achievement orientation, dogmatism, and anomie. They did not differ with respect to the degree to which they held instrumental or expressive values to be of importance as characteristics they would want for their children. Neither did they differ on the measure of parental control behavior also included. From these data it would seem, that at least for this sample, there was no selective process as to which parents were sending their children to Montessori schools. It was not feasible to systematically interview the parents as to why they sent their children, but informal talks with the parents indicated they were excited about the educational prospects that Montessori preschools could provide. Perhaps a more focused interview might reveal some systematic basis for selection among parents. The differences that we did obtain in the children and which follow were therefore attributed to the differing educational environments.

The results reported in Table 2, indicate no differences between the Montessori children and the Nursery School children in the error score on the CEFT. Both groups were equally capable of locating the stimulus figure in the embedding context. The Montessori groups, however, did spend significantly less time on the test. Not only is the mean time for the Montessori children significantly faster than the mean time for the Nursery School children, but in each of the fourteen matched pairs without exception, the shorter time was achieved by the Montessori child.

The non-verbal measure of creativity, the PCT, significantly discriminates between the Nursery School children, and Montessori children. As can be seen in Table 2, the mean weighted creativity

Table 1.—Mean Scores of Parents of Montessori and Cooperative Preschool Children on Specified Variables

Characteristic	Mothers				Fathers			
	Mont. N=54	Coop. N=37	t	p	Mont. N=54	Coop. N=37	t	p
Attitude Scales								
Authoritarianism	3.14	2.89	0.55	N.S.	3.28	2.89	0.71	N.S.
Traditional Family Ideology	3.41	2.51	1.04	N.S.	3.21	2.64	1.05	N.S.
Dogmatism	3.10	2.66	0.78	N.S.	3.19	2.97	0.21	N.S.
Anomie	1.76	1.74	0.23	N.S.	1.82	2.06	−0.65	N.S.
Acquiescence	3.31	3.47	−0.65	N.S.	2.98	3.76	−0.53	N.S.
Activism	1.78	1.83	−0.07	N.S.	1.80	1.96	−0.37	N.S.
Importance of Knowledge	4.96	5.02	0.11	N.S.	5.14	5.23	−0.24	N.S.
Independence	4.60	5.48	−0.46	N.S.	5.10	5.11	−0.46	N.S.
Achievement Orientation	4.04	3.35	0.73	N.S.	3.96	3.37	0.73	N.S.
Value Orientation								
Instrumental	6.38	6.03	0.27	N.S.	6.08	5.27	0.36	N.S.
Expressive	6.58	6.27	0.30	N.S.	6.50	5.90	0.43	N.S.
Index of Control								
Boys	2.30	2.04	0.75	N.S.	2.15	1.95	0.73	N.S.
Girls	1.83	1.54	0.79	N.S.	2.31	1.88	0.73	N.S.
Boys and Girls	1.99	1.74	0.77	N.S.	2.21	1.90	0.73	N.S.

score 18.8 for the Nursery School group is significantly different from the mean weighted creativity score of 10.8 for the Montessori group.

There were further indications from the results that style of approach to tasks might be critical in differentiating outcome from the two educaional environments. The Montessori children used significantly more physical characteristics to describe the commonplace objects presented in the Vocal Encoding Subtest of the ITPA, whereas significantly more functional terms were used by the Nursery School children in their descriptions. To illustrate this difference, for example, one Montessori child when presented with the green block said, "It's square, it's made of wood, and it's green." In contrast, the most frequently functional characteristic for an object like the green block used by the Nursery School children was, "You can play with it."

And finally the free drawings of the Montessori children included people present significantly less often and geometric forms significantly more often than the Nursery School children. The people drawn by the Nursery School children were, parenthetically, depicted in very vibrant and lively activities.

Table 2.—Cognitive Scores of Matched Pairs of Children from Montessori and Cooperative Nursery Schools (N=14 Pairs)

Cognitive Measure	Montessori	Cooperative	P*
Children's Embedded Figures Test:			
Total mean number correct_____	12.0	12.4	N.S.
Total mean time—minutes_____	18.1	25.3	.05
Picture Construction Test:			
Total mean creativity score_____	10.4	18.8	.02
Vocal Encoding—ITPA:			
Physical characteristics—			
mean percent_____	50.6	36.9	.05
Functional characteristics—			
mean percent_____	39.2	53.7	.05
Drawing:			
People present—percent_____	21.4	78.5	.01
Geometric forms present—percent	85.7	14.3	.01

*P values determined by Wilcoxon matched-pair signed-ranks test and Fisher exact-probability test (20).

Discussion

Generalization from this study is limited due to its pilot character. It should be noted, for example, that this sample of children are homogeneously middle class. The Montessori program may be more salient for economically disadvantaged children and the effects more easily discernible and apparent. The study does, however, support the notion that differing preschool educational environments yield different outcomes. Although this appears obvious, there has not been a good body of research to support this conclusion in this area. Montessori children responded to the emphasis in their program upon the physical world and upon a definition of school as a place of work; the Nursery School children responded on their part to the social emphasis and the opportunity for spontaneous expression of feeling. The findings on the CEFT are particularly dramatic in this respect. Although the two groups did not differ in the traditional achievement score, they did differ on the time they took to accomplish the task. The examiner reported that the Montessori children were highly task oriented, while for the Nursery School children it was an opportunity to be involved socially with the examiner. Whether a predominant task orientation or social orientation is a more desirable outcome of the preschool experience is a value question. We would hope, ourselves, for some efforts to optimally balance these outcomes for children. Empirically we do have some indication that the children in these two different environments are moving in these two differing directions.

It seems to us that it is necessary to raise the issue of the need for longitudinal study of the effect of these educational experiences. While it is commonplace in research articles to conclude that "more research is necessary," it would seem particularly appropriate in this context, considering the dearth of empirical work in the area. Several dimensions of the problem need emphasis. We would, first, stress the need for study of both the short term and the long term effects of children's educational experiences. Secondly, more adequate definition of classroom procedures and atmospheres is indicated. This latter articulation of variables would enable us to answer the most intriguing educational question, that dealing with interactive effects. Why do certain children flourish in certain types of classrooms and not in others?

FOOTNOTE

1. This study was reported in a paper read at the Eastern Psychological Association meeting, April 1967, Boston, Mass.

REFERENCES

1. Adorno, T. W., Frenkel–Brunswik, E., Levinson, D. J. and Sanford, R. N. *The Authoritarian Personality* (New York: Harper, 1950).
2. Baldwin, A. "A is Happy—B is Not," *Child Development*, XXXVI (1965), pp. 583–600.
3. Brim, O. G., Jr. "Family Structure and Sex-Role Learning by Children: A Further Analysis of Helen Koch's Data," *Sociometry*, XXI (1958), pp. 1–15.
4. Couch, A. and Keniston, K. "Yeasayers and Naysayers: Agreeing Response Set as a Personality Variable," *Journal of Abnormal and Social Psychology*, LX (1960), pp. 151–174.
5. Dreyer, A. S. and Wells, M. B. "Parental Values, Parental Control, and Creativity in Young Children," *Journal of Marriage and the Family*, XXVIII (1966), pp. 83–88.
6. Edmonson, B. "Let's Do More Than Look—Let's Research Montessori," *Journal of Nursery Education*, XIX (1963), pp. 36–41.
7. Hunt, J. Mc. "How Children Develop Intellectually," *Children*, XI (1964), pp. 83–91.
8. Karp, S. A. and Konstadt. N. L. *Manual for the Children's Embedded Figures Test* (Brooklyn. New York: Cognitive Tests, 1963).
9. Kohn M. L. "Social Class and Parental Values," *American Journal of Sociology*, LXIV (1959), pp. 337–351.
10. Lansky, L. "The Family Structure Also Affects the Model: Sex-Role Identification in Parents of Preschool Children," *Merrill–Palmer Quarterly*, X (1964), pp. 39–50.
11. Levinson, D. J. and Huffman, P. "Traditional Family Ideology and Its Relation to Personality," *Journal of Personality*, XIII (1955), pp. 251–273.
12. McCarty, J. N. and Kirk, S. A. *Examiner's Manual, Illinois Test of Psycholinguistic Abilities* (Urbana, Illinois: Institute for Research on Exceptional Children, University of Illinois, 1961).
13. McClelland, D., Rindlisbacker, A. and deCharms, R. C. "Religious and Other Sources of Parental Attitudes Toward Independ-

ence Training," *Studies in Motivation,* edited by D. C. McClelland. (New York: Appleton–Century–Crofts, 1955).

14. Miller, D. R. and Swanson, G. E. *The Changing American Parent* (New York: Wiley, 1958).

15. Pitcher, E. G. Review of *Learning How to Learn—An American Approach to Montessori,* by N. Mc. Rambusch, *Harvard Educational Review,* XXXIII (1963), pp. 259–264.

16. Rambusch, N. Mc. *Learning How to Learn— An American Approach to Montessori* (Baltimore: Helicon Press, 1962).

17. Rokeach, M. *The Open and Closed Mind* (New York: Basic Books, 1960).

18. Rosen, B. "Family Structure and Value Transmission," *Merrill–Palmer Quarterly,* X (1964), pp. 59–76.

19. Schaefer, E. S. "A Circumplex Model for Maternal Behavior," *Journal of Abnormal and Social Psychology,* LIX (1959), pp. 226–235.

20. Siegel, S. *Nonparametric Statistics for the Behavioral Sciences* (New York: McGraw-Hill, 1956).

21. Srole, L. "Social Integration and Certain Corollaries: An Exploratory Study," *American Sociological Review,* XXI (1956), pp. 709–716.

22. Torgoff, I. "Some Correlates of Parental Developmental Expectancies," *American Psychologist,* XIII (1958), p. 319.

23. Torgoff, I. "Synergistic Parental Role Components: Application to Expectancies and Behavior Consequences for Child's Curiosity," *American Psychologist,* XV (1960) pp. 394–395.

24. Torgoff, I. and Dreyer, A. S. "Achievement-Inducing and Independence-Granting Parental Role Components: Relation to Daughters' Parental Role Orientation and Level of Aspiration," *American Psychologist,* XVI (1961), p. 345.

25. Torrance, E. P. *Guiding Creative Talent* (Englewood Cliffs, N. J.: Prentice–Hall, 1962).

26. Witkin, H. A., Dyk, R. B., Faterson, H. F., Goodenough, D. R. and Karp, S. A. *Psychological Differentiation: Studies of Development* (New York: John Wiley, 1962).

27. Wolfenstein, M. "The Emergence of Fun Morality," *Journal of Social Issues,* VII (1951), pp. 15–25.

DAVID ELKIND

Piaget and Montessori

In recent years there has been a renaissance of American interest in the work
of two Europeans, Jean Piaget and Maria Montessori. Although the reasons
for this rebirth of interest are many and varied, two reasons appear beyond
dispute. First of all, both Piaget and Montessori have observed hitherto unexpected and unknown facets of child thought and behavior. Secondly, and
in this lies their impact, both of these innovators have derived the general
laws and principles regarding child thought and behavior which were implicit in their observations. In the case of Piaget, these observations led to a
new philosophy of knowledge while in the case of Montessori, they led to a
new philosophy of education.

Unfortunately, it is not possible, in a presentation such as this one, to do
any sort of justice to the contributions of these two innovators. Under the
circumstances, all that I would like to do is to describe, and to illustrate with
research data, three original ideas about child thought and behavior which
Piaget and Montessori arrived at independently but share in common. Before turning to those ideas, however, it seems appropriate, by way of introduction, to note some of the parallels and divergences in the Piagetian and
Montessorian approaches to child study.

PARALLELS AND DIVERGENCES

Among the many parallels between the work of Piaget and Montessori, one
of the most pervasive is the predominantly biological orientation which they

HARVARD EDUCATIONAL REVIEW, 1967, Vol. 37,
pp. 535-545.

take towards the thought and behavior of the child. This is not surprising in view of their backgrounds. Piaget, for example, was publishing papers in biology while still in his teens and took his doctorate in biology at the University of Lausanne. Likewise, Montessori was trained as a physician (she was, it will be recalled, the first woman in Italy to receive a medical degree) and engaged in and published medical research (cf. Standing, 1957). This shared biological orientation is important because both these workers see mental growth as an extension of biological growth and as governed by the same principles and laws.

In addition to, and perhaps because of, this shared biological orientation, both Piaget and Montessori emphasize the normative aspects of child behavior and development as opposed to the aspects of individual difference. Piaget, for example, has been concerned with identifying those mental structures which, if they hold true for the individual, also hold true for the species. Likewise, Montessori has been concerned with those needs and abilities that are common to all children such as the "sensitive periods" and the "explosions" into exploration. This is not to say that Piaget and Montessori in any way deny or minimize the importance of individual differences; far from it. What they do argue is that an understanding of normal development is a necessary starting point for a full understanding of differences between individuals.

The last parallel in the approaches of Piaget and Montessori which I would like to mention is of a more personal nature. Both of these workers manifest what might be called a *genius for empathy with the child*. When reading Piaget or Montessori, one often has the uncanny feeling that they are somehow able to get inside the child and know exactly what he is thinking and feeling and why he is doing what he is doing at any given moment. It is this genius for empathy with the child which, or so it seems to me, gives their observations and insights—even without the buttressing of systematic research—the solid ring of truth.

Despite these parallels, Piaget and Montessori also diverge in significant ways in their approaches to the child. For Piaget, the study of the child is really a means to an end rather than an end in itself. He is not so much concerned with children *qua* children as he is with using the study of the child to answer questions about the nature and origin of knowledge. Please do not misunderstand; Piaget is in no way callous towards the child and has given not a little of his considerable energies and administrative talents to national and international endeavors on the part of children. He has not, however, concerned himself with child-rearing practices, nor—at least until recently and only with reluctance—has he dealt with educational issues (e.g. Piaget, 1964). There is only so much any one person can do, and Piaget sees his contribution primarily in the area of logic and epistemology and only secondarily in the area of child psychology and education.

Montessori, on the other hand, was from the very outset of her career directly concerned with the welfare of the child. Much of her long and productive life was devoted to the training of teachers, the education of parents, and the liberation of the child from a pedagogy which she believed was as detrimental to his mental growth as poor diet was to his physical growth. Montessori, then, was dedicated to improving the lot of the child in very concrete ways.

The other major divergences between these two innovators stem more or less directly from this central difference in approach. Piaget is primarily concerned with theory while Montessori's commitment was to practice. Moreover, Piaget sees his work as being in opposition to "arm chair" epistemology and views himself as the "man in the middle," between the arch empiricists and the arch nativists. Montessori, in contrast, saw herself in opposition to traditional Herbartian pedagogy, which she regarded as medieval in its total disregard for the rights and needs of the child.

CONVERGING IDEAS

I hope that I will be excused if I focus upon Montessori's ideas rather than her methods, for that is where the convergence of Piaget and Montessori is greatest and where the available research is most relevant. Definitive research with respect to the effectiveness of Montessori's methods seems, insofar as I have been able to determine, yet to be completed.

Nature and Nurture

It would be easy, but unfair and incorrect, to contrast Piaget and Montessori with those who seem to take a strong environmentalist position with respect to mental development. Even if we start with writers at the extreme end of the environmentalist camp such as Watson (1928) or more recently, at least apparently, Bruner (1960), it would be a misrepresentation to say that they deny the role of nature in development. The real issue is not one of either nature or nurture but rather one of the character of their interaction. One of the innovations of Piaget and Montessori lies, then, not so much in their championing of the role of nature as in the original way in which they have conceived the character of nature-nurture interaction.

As was mentioned earlier, both Piaget and Montessori see mental growth as an extension of physical growth, and it is in the elaboration of this idea that they have made their unique contribution to the problem of nature-nurture interaction. Their position means, in the first place, that the en-

204

vironment provides nourishment for the growth of mental structures just as it does for the growth of physical organs. It means in addition, and this has been stressed particularly by Montessori, that some forms of environmental nourishment are more beneficial than others for sustaining mental growth just as some foods are more beneficial than others for sustaining physical growth. The "prepared environment" in the Montessori school is designed to provide the best possible nourishment for mental growth.

The relation between nature and nurture in mental growth is, however, not as one-sided as that. Not only does the child utilize environmental stimuli to nourish his own growth, but growth must adapt and modify itself in accordance with the particular environment within which it takes place. Of the many possible languages a child can learn, he learns the one to which he is exposed. The same holds true for his concepts and percepts which are, in part at least, determined by the social and physical milieu in which he grows up. Both Piaget and Montessori recognize and take account of this directive role which the environment plays in the determination of mental content. Indeed, the beauty of the Montessori materials (such as sandpaper letters, number rods, form and weight inset boards) lies in the fact that they simultaneously provide the child with nourishment for the growth of mental capacities and with relevant educational content. In short, for both Piaget and Montessori, nature interacts in a dual way with nurture. As far as mental capacities are concerned, the environment serves as nourishment for the growth of mental structures or abilities whose pattern of development follows a course which is laid down in the genes. Insofar as the content of thought is concerned, nurture plays a more directive role and determines the particular language, concepts, percepts, and values that the child will acquire.

What evidence do we have for this conception of the dual character of nature-nurture interaction? With respect to the environment as a provider of nourishment for an inner-directed pattern of structural development, there is considerable evidence[1] from Piaget-related research. In a study by Hyde (1959) for example, children of different nationalities—British, Arab, Indian, and Somali—were given a battery of Piaget-type number and quantity tasks. Regardless of nationality and language, these children gave the same responses as Piaget had attained with Swiss children. More recently, Goodnow and Bethon (1966) found little difference between Chinese and American children with respect to the age at which they manifested concrete reasoning. These cross-cultural findings suggest that children can utilize whatever stimuli are available in their immediate environs to foster their mental

[1] For a more complete summary of this evidence see J. H. Flavell, *The Developmental Psychology of Jean Piaget* (New York: Van Nostrand, 1963).

growth just as children all over the world can utilize quite different diets to realize their physical growth.

At the same time, there is also considerable evidence with respect to the directive role which environmental stimulation plays with respect to the content of thought. In a cross-cultural study by Lambert and Klineberg (1967) for example, there were differences even at the six-year-old level in response to the question "What are you?" Most American children thought of themselves primarily as "a boy" or as "a girl" while Bantu youngsters usually described themselves in terms of race. Furthermore, Lebanese children, frequently responded to the question in kinship terms and gave responses such as "the nephew of Ali." This study amply illustrates the role of the physical and social environment in shaping the child's self-concept.

For both Piaget and Montessori, then, nature-nurture interaction has a dual character. In the case of mental capacities, nature plays the directive role and nurture is subservient, while just the reverse is true with respect to the content of thought. It is in their emphasis upon the dual character of nature-nurture interaction that Piaget and Montessori have made their signal contribution to this age-old problem.

Capacity and Learning

Within experimental psychology, the child is generally viewed as a naive organism. That is to say, a child is one who is lacking in experience although his capacity to learn is no different from that of the adult. If differences between children and adults exist, then they reside in the fact that adults have had more opportunity and time to profit from experience than have children. For both Piaget and Montessori, however, the child is a *young* organism which means that his needs and capacities are quite different from those of the adult. This issue can be put more directly by saying that for the experimental psychologist capacity is determined by learning, whereas for the developmental psychologist learning is determined by capacity or development.

To make this point concrete, let me use a crude but useful analogy. Over the past ten years, we have seen several "generations" of computers. The early computers were relatively slow and quite limited in the amount of information which they could store. The most recent computers, on the other hand, are extremely fast and have enormous memories. Even the earliest computers, however, could handle some of the programs that the high-speed computers can. On the other hand, no matter how many programs were run on the early computers, their capacity was not altered but remained fixed by the limits of their hardware. To be sure, by ingenious programing, these early computers were able to do some extraordinary things, but their limitations in terms of hardware persisted.

As you have anticipated, the several generations of computers can be likened to the several stages in the development of intelligence. Just as the hardware of the computer determines its memory and speed, so the mental structures at any given level of development determine the limits of the child's learning. Likewise, just as the number of programs run on a computer leaves its speed and memory unaltered, so does the number of problems a child has solved or the number of concepts attained not change his problem-solving or concept-learning capacities. Furthermore, just as we can, with elaborate programing, get the computer to do things it was not intended to do, so we can with specialized training get children to learn things which seem beyond their ken. Such training does not, however, change their capacity to learn any more than an ingenious computer program alters the speed or memory of the computer. This is what Piaget and Montessori have in mind by the notion that capacity determines learning and not the reverse.

This idea is frequently misunderstood by many advocates of Piaget and Montessori. Indeed, and here we must be frank, much of the acceptance of Piaget and Montessori in America today seems to be based on the promise which their ideas hold out for accelerating growth. Nothing, however, could be further from their own beliefs and intentions. Piaget was recently quoted as saying, "Probably the organization of operations has an optimal time.... for example, we know that it takes nine to twelve months before babies develop the notion that an object is still there even when a screen is placed in front of it. Now kittens go through the same stages as children, all the same substages, but they do it in three months—so they are six months ahead of babies. Is this an advantage or isn't it? We can certainly see our answer in one sense. The kitten is not going to go much further. The child has taken longer, but he is capable of going further, so it seems to me that the nine months probably were not for nothing" (Jennings, 1967, p. 82). In the same vein, Montessori wrote, "We must not, therefore, set ourselves the educational problem of seeking means whereby to organize the internal personality of the child and develop his characteristics: the sole problem is that of offering the child the necessary nourishment" (Montessori, 1964, p. 70).

The view that capacity determines what will be learned has been supported in a negative way by the failure of many experiments designed to train children on Piaget-type reasoning tasks[2] (e.g., Greco, 1959; Smedslund, 1959;

[2] Most of these tasks deal with conservation or the child's ability to deduce permanence despite apparent change. For example, the child might be "shown" two equal quantities of colored water in identical containers one of which is emptied into two smaller containers before his eyes. Since the child has no way of measuring the equality of the liquid in the large container and that in the two smaller containers, he must—if he can—*deduce* the equality on the basis of their prior equality and his awareness that pouring does not change amount.

Wohlwill, 1959; 1960). In addition, however, there is also evidence of a positive sort which substantiates the role of capacity in the determination of what is learned. In one of our studies, for example, we demonstrated that while six-, seven-, and eight-year-old children could all improve their perceptual performance as a result of training, it was also true that the oldest children made the most improvement with the least training (Elkind, Koegler, and Go, 1962). We have, moreover, recently shown (Elkind, Van Doorninck, and Schwarz, 1967) that there are some perceptual concepts—such as setting or background—which kindergarten children cannot attain but which are easily acquired by second-grade youngsters. In the same vein, we have also demonstrated that there are marked differences in the conceptual strategies[3] employed by children and adolescents and that these strategies limit the kinds of concepts which elementary-school children can attain (Elkind, 1966; Elkind, Barocas, and Johnsen, forthcoming; Elkind, Barocas, and Rosenthal, forthcoming). Similar findings have been reported by Weir (1964) and by Peel (1960).

There is, then, evidence that capacity does determine what is learned and how it is learned. Such findings do not deny that children "learn to learn" or that at any age they can learn techniques which enable them to use their abilities more effectively. All that such studies argue is that development sets limits as to what can be learned at any particular point in the child's life. These studies are in keeping with the positions of Piaget and Montessori. As we have seen, neither of these innovators advocates the acceleration of mental growth. What they do emphasize is the necessity of providing the child with the settings and stimuli which will free any given child to realize his capacities at his own time and pace. Such a standpoint is quite different from one which advocates the acceleration of mental growth.

Cognitive Needs and Repetitive Behavior

One of the features of cognitive growth which Piaget and Montessori observed and to which they both attached considerable importance, is the frequently repetitive character of behaviors associated with emerging mental abilities. Piaget and Montessori are almost unique in this regard since within both psychology and education repetitive behavior is often described pejoratively as "rote learning" or "perseveration." Indeed, the popular view is that repetition is bad and should be avoided in our dealings with children.

What both Piaget and Montessori have recognized, however, is the very

---

[3] In a problem-solving task, for example, once a child sets up an hypothesis, he continues to maintain it even when the information he receives clearly indicates that it is wrong. The adolescent, on the other hand, immediately gives up an hypothesis that is contradicted by the data and proceeds to try out a different one.

great role which repetitive behavior plays in mental growth. In his classic work on the origins of intelligence in infants, Piaget (1952a) illustrates in remarkable detail the role which primary, secondary, and tertiary circular reactions play in the construction of intellectual schemas. Likewise at a later age, Piaget (1952b) has pointed out the adaptive significance of children's repetitive "Why?" questions. Such questions, which often seem stupid or annoying to adults, are in fact the manifestation of the child's efforts at differentiating between psychological and physical causality, i.e., between intentional or motivated events and events which are a consequence of natural law.

Montessori has likewise recognized the inner significance of repetitive behavior in what she calls the "polarization of attention." Here is a striking example with which, I am sure, many of you are familiar:

> I watched the child intently without disturbing her at first, and began to count how many times she repeated the exercise; then, seeing that she was continuing for a long time, I picked up the little arm chair in which she was seated and placed chair and child upon the table; the little creature hastily caught up her case of insets, laid it across the arms of the chair and gathering the cylinders into her lap, set to work again. Then I called upon the children to sing; they sang, but the little girl continued undisturbed, repeating her exercise even after the short song had come to an end. I counted forty-four repetitions; when at last she ceased, it was quite independently of any surrounding stimuli which might have distracted her, and she looked around with a satisfied air, almost as if awakening from a refreshing nap. (Montessori, 1964, pp. 67-68)

The role of repetitive behavior in intellectual development is not extraordinary when we view mental growth as analogous to physical growth. Repetitive behavior is the bench mark of maturing physical abilities. The infant who is learning to walk constantly pulls himself into an erect position. Later as a toddler he begins pulling and dropping everything within reach. Such behavior does not derive from an innate perversity or drive towards destruction but rather out of a need to practice the ability to hold and to let go. What the child is doing in such situations is practicing or perfecting emerging motor abilities. Mental abilities are realized in the same way. In the course of being constituted, intellectual abilities seek to exercise themselves on whatever stimuli are available. The four-year-old who is constantly comparing the size of his portions with those of his siblings is not being selfish or paranoid. On the contrary, he is spontaneously exercising his capacity to make quantitative comparisons. The Montessori child who repeatedly buttons and unbuttons or replaces inserts into their proper holes is likewise exercising emerging mental abilities. Piaget and Montessori see such repetitive behaviors as having tremendous value for the child and as essential to the full realization of the child's intelligence.

Although there is not a great deal of research evidence relevant to the role of repetition in mental growth, I would like to cite some findings from one of our studies which points in this direction. In this study (Elkind and Weiss, 1967), we showed kindergarten-, first-, second-, and third-grade children a card with eighteen pictures pasted upon it in the shape of a triangle. The children's task was simply to name every picture on the card. The kindergarten children named the pictures according to the triangular pattern in which the pictures were pasted. That is to say, they began at the apex and worked around the three sides of the triangle. This same triangular pattern of exploration was employed by third-grade children and to some extent by second-grade children. First-grade children and some second-grade youngsters, however, did a peculiar thing. *They read the pictures across the triangle from top to bottom and from left to right.*

Why did the first-grade children read the pictures in this clearly inefficient way? The answer, it seems to me, lies in the fact that these children were in the process of learning the top to bottom and left to right swing which is essential in reading English. Because they had not entirely mastered this swing, they spontaneously practiced it even where it was inappropriate. Viewed in this way, their behavior was far from being stupid, and the same can be said for older slow-reading children who read the pictures in the same manner as the first-graders.

These findings thus support the arguments of Piaget and Montessori regarding the adaptive significance of repetitive behavior in children. Repetitive behavior in the child is frequently the outward manifestation of an emerging cognitive ability and the need to realize that ability through action. It was the genius of Piaget and Montessori which saw, in such repetitive behaviors as sucking and putting insets into holes, not stupidity, but rather, intelligence unfolding.

Summary and Conclusions

In this paper I have tried to describe and illustrate with research data, three original ideas about child thought and behavior which Piaget and Montessori arrived at independently but which they share in common. The first idea is that nature and nurture interact in a dual way. With respect to the growth of abilities, nature provides the pattern and the time schedule of its unfolding while nurture provides the nourishment for the realization of this pattern. When we turn to the content of thought, however, just the reverse is true; nurture determines what will be learned while nature provides the prerequisite capacities. A second idea has to do with capacity and learning. For both Piaget and Montessori, capacity sets the limits for learning and capacity changes at its own rate and according to its own time schedule. Finally, the third idea is that repetitive behavior is the external manifestation of cognitive growth and expresses the need of emerging cognitive abilities to realize themselves through action.

The recent acceptance of Piagetian and Montessorian concepts in this country is gratifying and long overdue. It would be a great loss if within a few years these ideas were once again shelved because they failed to accomplish that which they were never designed to achieve. To avoid that eventuality, we need to try and accept Piaget and Montessori on their own terms and not force their ideas into our existing conceptual frameworks, or distort them for our own pragmatic purposes. Only in this way can we hope to gain lasting benefit from the outstanding contributions which Piaget and Montessori have made to the study of the child.

REFERENCES

Bruner, J. S. *The process of education*. Cambridge, Mass.: Harvard Univer. Press, 1960.

Elkind, D., Barocas, R. B., & Johnsen, P. H. Concept production in children and adolescents. *J. Exp. Child Psychol.*, (forthcoming).

Elkind, D., Barocas, R. B., & Rosenthal, R. Concept production in slow and average readers. *J. Educ. Psychol.*, (forthcoming).

Elkind, D., Koegler, R. R., & Go, Elsie. Effects of perceptual training at three age levels. *Science*, 1962, 137, 755-756.

Elkind, D., Van Doorninck, W. & Schwarz, Cynthia. Perceptual activity and concept attainment. *Child Develpm.*, (forthcoming).

Elkind, D. & Weiss, Jutta. Studies in perceptual development III: perceptual exploration. *Child Develpm.*, 1967, 38, 553-561.

Goodnow, Jacqueline J. & Bethon, G. Piaget's tasks: the effects of schooling and intelligence. *Child Develpm.*, 1966, 37, 573-582.

Greco, P. L'apprentissage dans une situation à structure opératoire concrète: les inversions successives de l'ordre lineaire pare des rotations de 180°. In J. Piaget (Ed.), *Études d'epistemologie genetique*. Vol. 8. Paris: Presses Universitaires de France, 1959, 68-182.

Hyde, D. M. An investigation of Piaget's theories of the development of the concept of number. Unpublished doctoral dissertation, Univer. of London, 1959.

Jennings, F. G. Jean Piaget: notes on learning. *Saturday Rev.*, May 20, 1967, p. 82.

Lambert, W. E. & Klineberg, O. *Children's view of foreign peoples*. New York: Appleton-Century-Crofts, 1967.

Montessori, Maria. *Spontaneous activity in education*. Cambridge, Mass.: Robert Bentley Inc., 1964.

Peel, E. A. *The pupil's thinking*. London: Oldhourne Press, 1960.

Piaget, J. *The origins of intelligence in children*. New York: International Universities Press, 1952 (a).

Piaget, J. *The language and thought of the child*. London: Routledge & Kegan Paul, 1952 (b).

Piaget, J. Development and learning. In R. E. Ripple & V. N. Rockcastle (Eds.), *Piaget rediscovered*. Ithaca, N.Y.: Sch. of Educ., Cornell Univer., 1964.

Smedslund, J. Apprentissage des notions de la conservation et de la transitivité du poids. In J. Piaget (Ed.), *Études d'epistemologie genetique*. Vol. 9. Paris: Presses Universitaires de France, 1959, 85-124.

Standing, E. M. *Maria Montessori*. Fresno: Academy Library Guild, 1957.

Watson, J. B. *Psychological care of infant and child*. New York: Norton, 1928.

Weir, M. W. Developmental changes in problem solving strategies. *Psychol. Rev.*, 1964, 71, 473-490.

Wohlwill, J. F. Un essai l'apprentissage dans le domaine de la conservation du nombre. In J. Piaget (Ed.), *Études d'epistemologie genetique*. Vol. 9. Paris: Presses Universitaires de France, 1959, 125-135.

Wohlwill, J. F. A study of the development of the number concept by scalogram analysis. *J. Genet. Psychol.*, 1960, 97, 345-377.

Home Visiting Programs for Parents of Young Children

SUSAN W. GRAY

This paper will describe some of the work we have been doing over the years with parents at Peabody College, now in the Demonstration and Research Center for Early Education, and before that in the Early Training Project. Specifically, I shall report on certain studies which have used a procedure based on visits to the home, and shall try to pull out from these some general threads which characterize the particular approach which we use. Our approach is far from unique. It does have a certain flavor of its own, however, and it is that flavor which I shall attempt to describe.

Our first entry into the field of home visiting was rather casual in inception. In the Early Training Project, which Rupert Klaus and I began in 1961, we provided, for the children with whom we were working, an intensive program for ten weeks during the summer.[1] This program was planned to extend through three summers beginning at age three and one half. Because we were well aware that much forgetting could take place when the child was sent back for nine and a half months to the limited environment from which he came, we planned a bridge from one summer to the next. We met with the children once a month on Saturday mornings; we sent monthly newsletters to the parents. Our most important step, however, was the introduction of a home visiting program. In this endeavor, a skilled individual, with preschool and social-work training, met in the home with each mother for approximately an hour a week. She brought materials, and showed the mother how to use them effectively with the child. We had one interesting and unexpected finding. At the home visitor's suggestion we tested the younger siblings of the children with whom we had been working and compared them

[1]Susan W. Gray and R. A. Klaus, "The Early Training Project: A Seventh Year Report," *Child Development*, XLI, 4 (December 1970).

PEABODY JOURNAL OF EDUCATION, 1971, Vol. 48, No. 1, pp. 106-111.

to younger siblings in the local and distal control groups we had set up for our study. Here we found that the younger siblings of the more extensive experimental treatment showed IQ's approximately 13 points higher than those in the two control groups.

Because of this finding, our next study, under the direction of James O. Miller and Barbara Gilmer, was one in which we tried systematically to separate possible effects of a home visiting program from those of an assembled program. Our earlier study had confounded the two. This second study, now in the follow-up stage, involved three differential treatments for the children. In one group the children were enrolled for two and one half years in a special program every day for forty weeks a year. This was in the years just prior to entrance to first grade. There was no particular attention given to the parents. In fact, we did as little as might be considered decent with this particular group. In the second group, the children came to a specially planned preschool in the same fashion as the first group; in addition the mothers were involved once a week in a carefully scheduled sequence of training experiences. These activities were designed to enable the mothers to take on some of the functions of the assistant teachers in the assembled preschool and also to work more effectively with their young children. There was a third group in which no one came to an assembled program but in which there were weekly home visits during the year. The whole study is a massive one and the findings are highly complex. There are three very interesting findings, however, that I will mention briefly.

With the so called target-aged children, the age group with which we worked in the assembled preschool, the additional involvement of the mother did not increase the children's performance on usual tests of intellectual ability. Both groups, however, were superior to the home visitor group and to a comparison group that functioned roughly as a control group.

With the young siblings, however, superiority was shown in the performance of the younger children in the group in which mothers were involved along with the target-aged children and also in the group in which only home visits were made. Both of these groups were superior to the group in which there was no involvement of the parent and to the comparison group. The highly economical treatment, then, of the home visits appears to function as well for the younger children as one in which the mother is involved for half a day and in which the older sibling is involved for five half days a week. A third finding which is only beginning to emerge is a difference in the school careers of the two groups in which the children met in an assembled program. The IQ's of the group in which both mothers and children were involved in the preschool have tended to remain relatively stable—at least they are not significantly different—after the children have gone through their first two years of school. In the group in which the mothers were not involved, however, there has been a decline in IQ. Whether this sustaining effect will hold up still remains to be seen, but it does suggest to us that working with mothers may be valuable not only from the standpoint of immediate cost efficiency, but also it may have a more lasting effect.

Two follow-up studies of this large project have been concerned with training the mothers from the earlier study to function themselves as home visitors.[2] In a subsequent year they have been trained to work as trainers of home visitors. The effects on parent and child in these two programs are modest, but have been measurable.

Currently we are working with the mothers of very young children indeed. Twenty mother and infant pairs are involved. This work with infants fits with an emphasis we have always attempted to maintain in our work, that of making our intervention programs *developmental* rather than *remedial*. We do not yet have data to report on our work with infants, but to date it seems both feasible and promising.

As a research area, home visiting, as we do it, is extremely difficult. The most obvious problem is the wild heterogeneity in family groupings. This is an acute problem when one is dealing with children under five years. There are extremely few measures that are comparable from age to age for this age span. In addition, home visiting programs are carried out over a period of time—generally eight months or more. Thus one has problems of attrition, problems of major changes in the family group, such as the birth of a new sibling or the desertion of a father, which disrupt the effectiveness of a treatment program. We are enthusiastic enough about the promise of the approach, however, to find it well worth exploring in a research context, even if it does present a fearful array of problems in developing an adequate research design.

This brief paper is not the place to go into great detail about the specific content of our home visiting program, in terms of activities, which are carried out with the child and with the parent. These are important but we think they are more appropriate for description in guides and manuals for parent workers or for parents themselves. We are actively involved in preparing such materials, and have just completed a guide for home visitors which tries to express in considerable detail what we consider the important aspects of home visiting with mothers of young children.[3]

[2]C. R. Barbrack and Della M. Horton, *Educational Intervention in the Home and Para-professional Career Development: A First Generation Study*, DARCEE Papers and Reports, V, 3, 1970; *Educational Intervention in the home and Paraprofessional Career Development: A Second Generation Mother Study with an Emphasis on Costs and Benefits*, DARCEE Papers and Reports, V, 4, 1970.

[3]Rosemary Giesy, ed., *A Guide for Home Visitors* (Nashville, 1970).

Instead it would seem useful to list what may be considered as the common threads in the approach that we have used at the Demonstration and Research Center for Early Education in our work with parents of children as old as five or six, or as young as six months.

1. There is a common general goal in our programs—that of enabling the parent to become a more effective educational change agent with her young children.

2. Our general handle to the situation is the basic interest of the parent. Our parents want what is best for their children, but are often lacking in the knowledge of the instrumental steps. If we can enlist a mother's interest in learning these instrumental steps, our battle is half won. Equally important, in our approach, is the need for respect for the dignity of the parents and a recognition of the basic worth of the child himself or herself. This sounds fairly easy, but such an awareness is sometimes difficult for an inexperienced person working in a home that is dirty and disorganized, with an apathetic or distracted parent. Creating such an awareness is often the first hurdle with a home visitor trainee.

3. Our focus is on the parent rather than the child. Our reason is that, if an hour or so a week is to have any lasting effect, there must be some way to sustain this work over the remaining hours and days between. The parent is the most available sustaining agent, and normally the one who is most interested in the child's welfare.

4. It has been our approach not to exclude any family member from the lesson during the home visit. This sometimes makes the visit difficult but we feel it is necessary for two reasons. There is obviously an important factor of rapport; often the parent cannot avoid including younger siblings. It is unfair to expect her to make special babysitting arrangements for a home visit. Our second reason is of course that of the spread of effect. Other children, either joining in or watching, benefit from the lesson, and themselves, if old enough, learn new ways of interacting with younger siblings.

5. We have concentrated on the use of easily available and easily constructed materials. We use a few purchased materials such as wooden puzzles and one-inch cubes. Typically, however, we use materials constructed either out of inexpensive items such as outing flannel, or the things that are around the home such as discarded coffee cans and plastic containers. Our reason for this takes us to our next point.

6. We attempt through a sequence of home visits to move the parent towards increasing initiative and independence in planning the educational stimulation of her child. For example, a typical procedure with us has been for the home visitor to leave with the mother each week a series of activities for

the remainder of the week. At first, the activities are supplied for the entire week; then a fading technique is used, with the parent initiating and developing the activity for the last day, then for the last two days, and so on. Ideas of parents are not rejected, even if sometimes they are inappropriate. Although certain activities suggested by the parent may not be particularly educational for the child, they may have enormous value in developing the parent's initiative and independence; over time we can lead the mother to develop more appropriate activities.

7. We help the parent to understand and to use simple reinforcement procedures. Thus, parents can learn and see the effects of their own behavior. They can begin to reward the behavior in children which they wish to promote rather than paying attention only to the negative behavior, a common temptation to all of us when busy. We felt we had reached an important milestone with one parent when, after about six months of work, she said to us, "I've found out that you don't have to beat kids to get them to learn." Unfortunately, the implicit learning theory of many of these parents seems to have been one of viewing punishment as the way to change behavior. We believe some concentration on the effective use of positive reinforcement is of particular importance for this reason.

8. Using the work with her own children as the starting point, we have been concerned with helping the parent toward better coping skills in all of her life experiences. For example, if she is going to have some time to spend with her children, she has to plan her schedule for the day, rather than living from minute to minute, a procedure which seems fairly characteristic in some of our homes. If we can teach her to handle what little money she has more effectively in planning her food purchases, not only will this have a direct nutritional value for the children, but it will help develop in the mother a sense of competence in her ability to cope with life's demands. This increased confidence in turn spills over to other areas of her life.

9. Our program is a highly individualized one; a major attempt is always made to adapt the home visit and the suggested activities to the parent's particular life circumstances. Most of our parents, being of fairly low education and limited experience, need suggestions that are concrete and highly specific to their own situation. Our home visitors have become past masters at working with parents to show them how they can interact in an educational way with their young children while they are peeling potatoes, washing clothes, or cleaning house.

10. Our major effort as home visitors is to help provide more options for the mother to enable her both to take advantage of the options that are available and to develop new ones for herself. Some of these options relate

to her whole life circumstances. Many of the objectives which have been our direct focus of concern, however, have related to her interactions with her children and to her increasing ability to shape the child's behavior rather than simply to cope with it from minute to minute.

Our program is certainly not unique. We believe that it does have some particular strengths, however, based upon our focus on enabling the parent to become an effective change agent in realizing her goals and aspirations for her child and her family.

With few exceptions the parents with whom we have worked have wanted what is best for their children. They have not always been entirely sure of what is best for them—who is in these days? For the most part, our parents include in their aspirations such things as having a child do well in school, having him able to get a good job when he grows up, and in general, his being a decent human being. The difficulty, however, is that the parents often lack the knowledge of the instrumental acts involved in realizing the goals that they see as important for their children. For example, when we asked the mothers in the Early Training Project what they could do to realize one of their stated aspirations—for their children to do well in school—the most typical answer was that they could send the child to school clean and with his lunch money. No one will deny that these are worth doing but this limited perception certainly opens up a wide field for helping the parent become a more effective educational change agent.

A second major recommendation for a home visiting program is that of cost efficiency. We have found that paraprofessionals with appropriate—and extended —training, and with a sufficient amount of consultation and supervision, can become highly effective home visitors. A home visitor, on the basis of hourly visits, can handle as many as fifteen or twenty visits a week. Furthermore, we have data in our studies which show that one can, by such technique, affect not only a given child in the family and the child's mother, but also other members of the family group, most conspicuously the younger children.

Certainly, home visiting is not a panacea for the problems of the low-income family in our present day society. Enabling the parent to become a more effective educational change agent, however, can have an important contribution to make toward improving the life style and general welfare of such low-income families.

PARENT INVOLVEMENT IN EARLY CHILDHOOD EDUCATION

Ira J. Gordon

With the current emergence of a variety of approaches to early childhood education programs, some of which take place outside the formal classroom setting, public school people are now faced with a new set of issues concerning their roles and responsibilities. They have always recognized that nonpublic agencies such as church-related and private schools are centers for education. However, they have never been faced before-- at least to the extent that they currently are--with rival public and semipublic agencies heavily engaged in the business of education.

School people used to assume that the years before 5 did not belong to them and therefore worried little about private or welfare-type day care or nursery schools or the Montessori school down the block. Now, however, early childhood education is recognized as being a significant time to begin formal instruction and to provide comprehensive services to children whose families are economically unable to do so. As a result of Head Start (and it is really a sign marking the success of Head Start), parents now seek not only earlier education for their children but also some responsible, organized, institutional role in such education. This comes sharply into focus in the individual public school. Consequently, the principal is faced with the dilemma: Whom does he serve? What is his constituency? How does he respond to the pressure in the field of early childhood education?

Until as recently as half a dozen years ago, administrators, teachers, and professors of education held the commonly accepted view that the role of parents in public education was: 1) to drop their children at the door of the school, and 2) to vote for the bond issue. Parents were, of course, welcome to observe during American Education Week or become active in the PTA or even on occasion serve as chaperons on a field trip . But no one argued seriously that parents or parent organizations connected to individual schools had any decision-making role to play except to be voters in those places where boards are elected or to be clients. Yet, in the nursery school movement reaching back as far as the 1930's, if not before, consistent and well-organized efforts had been made to develop cooperative nursery schools in which parents performed many critical roles as decision makers, staff volunteers, and learners about child development. The abrupt shift came when the child entered the public school.

For most parents, however, no preschool education of any sort was available, so that their only role was that of silent partner. They were told rather emphatically by school people that it was neither wise nor desirable for them to attempt to teach their own children. Teaching belonged to the teacher, and it was separate and distinct from child rearing. Woe to the parent who proud- *(continued on the next page)*

NATIONAL ELEMENTARY PRINCIPAL, 1971, Vol. 51, pp. 26-30.

ly told the first-grade teacher that she had taught her child to read.

This separation of home and school, child rearing and education, was to some degree a natural outgrowth of the old theory of learning and development that placed heavy emphasis on maturation and innate biology of the child, on a fixed view of intelligence and development, rather than on the current view of both cognitive and emotional development. This current view recognizes the significance and importance of experience in the home as well as in the neighborhood as being effective precursors of formal schooling. Formerly, teachers were well aware that children came into their classrooms with different expressed capabilities to learn and were also well aware that home conditions often influenced the child's attitudes toward learning. Nevertheless, the prevailing attitude was that all education should take place within the confines of the school, under the control and direction of the professional.

With Head Start, life began to change. Our concerns for "compensatory education," beginning about 1964, emphasized our changing understanding about the nature of learning and development. It also presented to the general public the work of such key psychologists as Hunt, Bruner, Bloom, and Piaget, who indicated how important the early years were for intellectual growth. Head Start and other compensatory education programs, such as those financed by Ford, and research projects with NIMH and Children's Bureau support, began to concern themselves with parent involvement as soon as it became understood that the home was a potent influence on the child.

These early attempts to involve parents in childhood education were based on the idea that if the child were doing poorly, the fault lay at home. Thus we have the interesting paradox that up until the mid-1960's, school people had said to parents, both rich and poor, that responsibility for education rested on the professional in the classroom. As it became

clear that many children were not learning, particularly the children of the poor and minority groups, responsibility was shifted, and blame was assigned to the years before school and to the home as an inadequate learning environment. Parent involvement and parent education were designed to educate parents to deal with their children in a way that professionals thought would enhance growth. These efforts were based on a deprivation theory, in which the home was seen as inadequate either because of emotional instability, lack of consistent treatment, lack of materials, or lack of teaching skill on the part of the parents, all of which limit children in reaching their potential.

As professionals began to interact with parents in Head Start, Follow Through, and various research projects, educators realized that while these homes did indeed lack the characteristics we associated with good learning environments, so did the schools. We discovered that in order to create an effective learning environment, we had to bring about a new alignment and a new relationship between home and school—one in which each would move toward recognizing the strengths as well as the weaknesses of the other. This new relationship would replace the assignment of blame to one institution or the other and bridge the split between home, as child rearer, and school, as teacher.

The field of early childhood education seems to me to be moving toward this new home-school partnership. We recognize that children learn in all settings throughout the day and that motivation to learn, as well as actual learning success, requires a total living situation in which parents and school work together. Parents shift from being clients, or silent partners, to becoming full partners in the education of their children.

This is the path we have taken in the University of Florida Follow Through Program. Our basic assumptions about the learning situation are: "1) Attitudes toward learning are learned primarily at home, and the home is thus a central learning place; 2) the parent's self-esteem, attitudes toward school, expectations for success, and provisions of experience influence a child's performance, attitudes, and self-esteem; 3) children learn best when home and school share in the educational experience; 4) children learn best when their own subculture is respected and finds potency both in the classroom and in the general operation of the school; 5) parents themselves gain in self-esteem and feelings of competence when they see themselves able to teach their own children, to teach others, both adults and children, and to function as decision makers in all aspects of the program; 6) when parents are actively involved in the education of their children, they will continue to enhance the child's growth and their own activity after the formal program ends."[1]

In our Follow Through Program, the major elements are: 1) training the mothers (two to each classroom) in the role of combined parent-educator and teacher auxiliary, 2) training the teacher in the use of paraprofessional personnel, 3) developing the materials for family use that take into account not only the school's goals for the child but also, and equally, the family's expectations, goals, life-style, and value system, and 4) involving the policy advisory committee in all phases of the program. About once a week, each home is visited by a paraprofessional parent-educator who brings to the home a learning task that has been developed in the local community by teachers and parent-educators. This task reflects both school and home concerns. Parents are involved and encouraged to visit the school and classroom and to work with children in the classroom. They are not regarded as observers or bystanders but as people who contribute to the education of all children.

The policy advisory committee is involved in developing the basic program budget, developing the criteria for the selection of pertinent staff, and developing all of the various phases of the operation of the program. There are elements, then, in our Follow Through model, and in many of the others, of mixtures of new arrangements between professional and parent in which power and responsibility are not as settled as they once were.

In our program, we expect that both home and school will change in the direction of a greater understanding of how children learn, especially in the areas of language and cognition; increased understanding of the importance of self-esteem and ways to enhance it; better understanding of the mutual concerns for the health and well-being of the child and ways to achieve them. The success of such a program requires principals who accept these tenets, who see parents as people to whom they are accountable, who discover the power of parent support.

We have learned that the paraprofessional home visitor, bringing learning ideas from the school and carrying back the family's ideas, is a potent force in suburbia and in middle-class homes, as well as in the inner city and among the poor. The middle-class parent has also been isolated from the school, alienated from his children, and left virtually powerless to influence the system. The parent education approach we have developed for early childhood and primary education meets these parents' needs and thus transcends the earlier notions of "compensatory education."

When parent education and parent involvement mean more than teaching parents what school people want or encouraging parents to participate in parent-teacher associations which, while useful agencies, are not normally centers of power, a new set of problems is created for the school principal. To whom is he accountable? While he has always responded to the individual vociferous parent who most often was from the same

1. Gordon, Ira J. "An Instructional Theory Approach to the Analysis of Selected Early Childhood Programs." *Early Childhood Education*, Seventy-First Yearbook, National Society for the Study of Education. Chicago: University of Chicago Press, 1972. Chapter 10. (In press)

background as he and who was used to dealing with authority, he nevertheless saw himself primarily responsible to someone at a higher level of authority within the school system. His orders came from above, his budget was developed above, his raises and promotions in the system were governed by how well he accounted to his superiors.

We hear much these days about "accountability," and a whole new mythology of measurement is being created around this word. But the simple fact in early childhood education is that accountability for the school principal now means that he serves several kinds of groups. He is accountable and responsible directly to the parents as much as he is responsible to the school system authorities. He wasn't trained, however, to cope with this shift. If he was asked a few years ago who runs the school, the answer was clear. If he was asked who made curriculum decisions or instructional decisions or hiring decisions, the answer was clear. If he was asked who controlled access to classrooms, the answer was clear. But none of these answers is that simple any more.

Every parent in the suburbs or the inner city, black or white, now has, or should have, the belief that the school building is his and not the professional's. He should feel that professionals are his employees and not feel that he is the client. This is a drastic shift in attitude and responsibility. It can be accomplished with relatively little friction, or it can cause chaos and hostility. Where the principal sees the parents as allies, where he reaches out to work with them, where he encourages participation, not only do *they* respond, but the children do, too. The atmosphere in the building is different. There is an openness that the visitor feels immediately. In other situations, where parent-educators work diligently in making home visits, in reaching out into the community, the game is lost if the parent approaches the door of the school building and finds some written sign, or act on the part of a clerk, that lets him

know he is really not welcome, that he is a trespasser.

The principal sets the tone. Indeed, he is the key person in setting the tone in this shift toward mutual cooperation and mutual respect in the educative process. The principal, however, is under the gun. He is still responsible to people in the system above him. He must still operate within the laws of the state and school board regulations, and he is never quite sure who really speaks for the parent. What complicates life even more for him is that within the parent community there are pressure groups, demagogic leaders, who wish power for its own sake and not necessarily for the sake of the education of children. Thus, the principal is caught very often between his old allegiances to the system and the new requirements of the parents.

Furthermore, in many cities in the Southeast, busing to achieve integration has led to a change in the concept of the neighborhood or community school. Under the old system, theoretically the elementary school served a small neighborhood, and if there were parents involved, they could identify readily with the nearby school. This was actually more myth than reality, for the organization of schools was such that the school was not necessarily responsive to the people who lived in the neighborhood. The teachers, particularly, did not live in the neighborhood, and there really was no neighborhood school except in a geographical sense.

With busing, however, the community has to be viewed differently and cannot be seen even in a geographical fashion. The organization of parent groups may be more difficult because of distance. The mix of classes and ethnic groups may lead to value splits and power struggles over the control of these parent councils. To whom, then, will the principal listen? Who will speak for the parent?

In the large urban centers of the North, the problem of the principal *vis à vis* his community is equally troublesome. If the system is decentralized and power passes to local boards, a principal, even one who is perceived by many parents as a good educational leader, may be removed because of ethnic reasons. Nothing in his training or experience has equipped him for the type of power struggle in which he finds himself.

I see the principal as the key agent in the effective implementation of family-oriented and family-responsive early childhood education. He faces several major tasks in carrying this off. First, he will be working with parents who possess various degrees of sophistication in education decision making. It is a farce to create a parent council and assume that by its creation it possesses all the skills necessary to act. This is as bad as building a campus, labeling it a university, and assuming, therefore, that it is. Parents need considerable help in learning the language in order to deal with budgets, to understand the laws, to negotiate with the system. If you have ever tried to follow a federal guideline in your own field, you know how difficult it is. Coming into education from the lay community, the parent faces the same difficulties. Second, the principal faces the task of educating his teachers and his colleagues to learn how to listen and how to share. If his teachers adopt the view long taught to them that they are the possessors of all educational wisdom, he has a difficult teaching job ahead in bringing his own faculty around to learning how to work in an egalitarian fashion with the parents of the children they teach.

A basic need in professional education—both for teachers and administrators—is for information and experience in working for and with parents. Courses in colleges of education ill-equip the professional for this new role. Unfortunately, it has to be learned on the job and requires considerable unlearning of bureaucratic notions about schools and schooling.

Parent involvement and parent education mean professional involvement and professional education so that all recognize that a sound learning environment is not restricted to the classroom or the street or the home. Professionals need to learn that effective education and warm human relationships go hand in hand and can occur at any place. Parents and school people need to discover that, in the long run, they share a set of common goals for children. They need to learn to emphasize and assess which of their behaviors help children to achieve these.

I recently asked a mixed group of parents and professionals working with young children what it was they hoped for these children when they reached adulthood. The answers were amazingly simple. They wanted children to be able to "make it." They wanted them to be able to earn a living and provide for themselves, to be capable and competent people. They wanted them to value themselves, to have high self-esteem. And finally, they wanted them to live better and more effective lives than they had lived.

If these are common goals, the path toward them begins at birth. There is no arbitrary day when responsibility shifts from home to school. My hope is that, especially in the field of early childhood education where we are perhaps most open to the new, we can truly begin the effective partnership between parent and principal in the common task of enabling children to reach their full potential.

Learning from Each Other

Earl S. Schaefer

ed'u·ca'tion . . . the act or process of rearing or bringing up . . . the process of providing with knowledge, skill, competence or usually desirable qualities of behavior or character . . .
Webster's *Third International Dictionary of the English Language,* unabridged.

FROM CURRENT RESEARCH on early child development and early education there is emerging a major change in perspective on how best to help children grow. The result may be no less than a complete revolution in the way we think about the educational process—one that enlarges rather than destroys existing structures.

It is still quite common today, when we talk about education, to mean what happens to a school-age child in a classroom, under the supervision of a professional educator who seeks to help him learn academic skills through formal instruction, usually within a graded sequence. When we refer to the U. S. Office of Education, we really mean the U. S. Office of Schooling. If this restricted model of education was ever functional, it no longer is.

I agree with Ivan Illich that learning is not to be equated with schools or professional teachers, any more than health is equated with clinics or hospitals or doctors. Our new perspective on child development is not going to be a child-centered one of "What can the teacher do for the child?" or "What can the doctor do for the child?" Instead it is going to be a family-centered perspective and, going beyond that, a community-centered perspective, which will ask, "How can we provide support for *families* so that they, in turn, can care for and educate their children?"

Every Home a Learning Center

Secretary Elliot Richardson of the U. S. Department of Health, Education, and Welfare recently stated that the challenge of the seventies will be to make every home a learning center (1971). Well, in a sense all homes are learning centers. But some obviously are more effective than others. When we start to think of *families* as well as schools as educational institutions, we need to begin to devote our attention and resources to families and how they function—not just to schools and how schools function. Too many professionals see the family as the problem rather than as part of the solution. I think we're going to have to look instead at the strength in families, at the skills they already possess, the supports they need.

In a total integrated model of education we will have to challenge the idea that education is finished at some set point and will have to seek ways of developing people who are students throughout their lifetimes. This concept of education as a process that begins at birth and ends with death will demand a different role from the professional educator. Historically he has been a *doer*. Now he must become more a leader, who supports and supplements the role of the parent educators, rather than supplants them.

I would like to share with you some of my own experience that has led me to this point of view. Back in 1963 I became engaged in a review of literature on intellectual development. This led me to evidence that socioeconomic groups appear to reach their level of intellectual functioning before they enter school. The mean level of intellectual development tends to be established as early as three

CHILDHOOD EDUCATION, 1971, Vol. 48, pp. 2-7.

years of age (Schaefer, 1970), and the schools don't change it; they merely educate at the level to which the family and community have initially developed the child's skills. I found that most socioeconomic groups test at their own level by the age of three.

The Infant Education Research Project in Washington, D. C.

This review led me and a group of associates to the idea of designing an infant education project (*Preschool Breakthrough,* 1970; *"It Works"* report, 1970). Since differences in mental test scores appeared to emerge between approximately fifteen months and three years, we began tutoring children at fifteen months. An experimental group of 28 black male infants and a control consisting of 30 black male infants were selected by door-to-door surveys from two lower socioeconomic neighborhoods in Washington, D. C. The tutors were college graduates, both black and white, who had varied experience in working with young children. They went into homes for an hour a day, five days a week, to work with infants. We welcomed the participation of mothers, but did not insist on it, nor did we do much to encourage it.

Evaluation during the tutoring period showed success in terms of gains made in mental-test scores. Our initial thesis, the need for early education, was confirmed. But when we stopped tutoring the children at three years of age, their IQ scores began to decline.

In retrospect, we feel that in our infant education study we made a number of crucial errors. Basically, we started too late and we stopped too early (Schaefer, 1969, 1970). We now feel that education of the child in the home should begin at birth and continue through the school years. Another error was that we ourselves (i.e., the tutors) worked directly with the infants of our experimental group. Now we feel that we should not have been working directly with the children, but with their parents. (Implicitly we were telling our "experimental" parents: *we* are the experts; *we* have the skills and the competence; *we* will take the responsibility for educating your child. The control parents, on the other hand, not having seen anyone tutor their children, appeared to become themselves interested in taking a more active role in the children's intellectual development.) As a result of our experience in infant education we moved from an emphasis upon the need for early education to an emphasis upon the need for continuing education. We also moved from a child-centered approach to education to a parent-centered approach.

Related Studies from Abroad

Several other research studies have confirmed our developing views about the importance of the family's role:

1. In the book *The Home and The School,* J. W. Douglas (1964) reported research on a national sample of 5,000 children in England, Scotland and Wales. His conclusion was that the quality of parental involvement in a child's education had four times as much influence on test scores at eleven years of age as did the quality of the school attended.

2. A longitudinal study by another Englishman, T. Moore (1968) sought to correlate measures of the quality of children's home environments at two and a half years of age with their IQ scores at ages three and eight, and with their reading success at age seven. He sent investigators into the home to quantify

such factors as the amount and nature of verbal interaction between parent and child; the extent to which conversations were encouraged and participated in by the parents; the kinds of toys, books and experiences provided. Even when social class was statistically controlled as a value, he still found a high correlation—suggesting that the key to improving reading skills may not so much lie in what happens in school as in what happens in the family.

3. Similar data was obtained by Rupp (1969) in a study done in the Netherlands. Again focusing on the cultural-pedagogical atmosphere of the home and concentrating on the lowest socioeconomic group, he found that variations in the home milieu—the extent to which parents talked with the child, played games with him, provided enriching experiences for him, felt themselves effective educators—were highly related to reading success.

Some Family-centered Approaches in the U.S.A.

In the United States several examples of family-centered early childhood intervention programs give further emphasis to the importance of working with parents to increase their effectiveness.

Ira Gordon, Director of the Institute for Development of Human Resources, College of Education, University of Florida at Gainesville, has developed a pioneering program involving the use of paraprofessionals in parent education (1970). David Weikart's work (1969) with the cognitively centered curriculum study in Ypsilanti, Michigan, where he carried on an intensive nursery school program and also worked with parents one day a week to encourage them to continue to support the child's education, has been highly effective. Susan Gray (1968) found that in a nursery-school program in which she worked with parents in the early years she too got great gains in IQ, but that over a period of years, after the intervention ended, the mean IQ's of the experimental group declined ten points. She concluded that improved performance results from the *continued* interaction of the infant with his environment—again stressing the need for continuing education. Elsewhere she contrasted a preschool program for young children with a program in which the teacher went out and worked with the mother, once a week, on the education of her children. In terms of immediate gain on the part of the children, working with the mother once a week proved as effective as bringing them into the preschool—and *cost one-fifth as much.* Moreover, Gray has reported evidence of vertical diffusion down to the younger children who subsequently were born to the mothers, and horizontal diffusion through the neighborhood. I think this study has profound implications for what we need to do about early education. Are we going to bring children into preschools and fix our entire attention on what goes on in the schools? Or are we going to try to improve the competence, the adequacy and the sense of power on the part of parents who are with their children from birth to maturity?

A recent study in New York by Phyllis Levenstein (1969) fascinates me, mostly because of her very sharp focus on parent education. She chose about a dozen books and a dozen toys that could be used to promote verbal interaction between a parent and a child. She then took these books and toys into homes,

226

demonstrated their use to mothers, had the parents try them under the supervision of the demonstrator, and left them with the mother. Levenstein reported that with thirty-two visits over a seven-month period, she had a seventeen-point IQ gain in her child population. That's equivalent to the effects of our child-centered infant-education project over a twenty-one month period with over 300 visits!

Levenstein's program sounds to me socially feasible. Is it possible that we could really enroll children in the educational process at birth and that educators could move out to work with parents on early education from that point onward? I realize this would take manpower. It would take money. But if we really feel we should move in this direction, perhaps we'll start to work on it.

Recapitulation

To summarize the conclusions I have come to from my own research:

1. Experience with lowest socioeconomic status black families shows that the genetic potential is there for higher levels of intellectual functioning. The challenge to society is to develop it.

2. The quality of family care, as well as supplementary tutoring, significantly influences early intellectual development of young children. The low IQ child in our infant-education study typically had a hostile, neglecting, distant mother.

3. Research suggests that varied, increasingly complex experience, accompanied by language stimulation, in the context of positive parent-child relationships, supports early language development and intellectual growth. These early experiences also foster the development of interest and curiosity, as well as of task-oriented behavior, all related to later reading success.

4. To maintain and increase levels of intellectual functioning, *continuing education* is essential.

5. Perhaps above all else there is need for training and experience in child care. We must prepare parents and future parents for their roles as educators.

6. The task is to strengthen the whole network of relationships that foster the development of the child. One of the challenges of the Seventies will be to bring fathers back into the home-education picture. Our concern must go beyond parent-child relationships; the mother-father relationship is also vitally important.

Today some people are proposing that we extend academic education down to three, for all children. Others are talking of extending education upward by having open-university enrollments for all. We can extend academic education downward and upward and still continue to do the same old thing. But doing that may consume all our educational resources, all of our money and our manpower for the next twenty years.

I wonder if we couldn't take a different tack, if we couldn't say education is going on in the family, it's going on in the community. Children can help educate one another. And schools can help prepare children as future parents.

The new model of basic education I have given the label of "Ur-education," "Ur" meaning basic, primitive, early. The model goes like this: a parent develops a positive relationship with a child, who reciprocates and in the context of this relationship is led to share activities, to develop interests. As the child develops language, the relationship is reinforced; and he also develops task-oriented skills: the ability to listen, concentrate, attend, focus, persist. This Ur-education model of the parent and child engaged together in an activity or exploring materials is the basis of all subsequent education.

Next Steps

Finally, I would like to suggest a few ways to implement this kind of thinking. We have been paying lip-service too long to thinking we are doing something about parent education. To strengthen and support family- and community-centered education we must

☐ Develop techniques of enrolling children in "school" at birth, by providing training for parents in child care and education—through summer workshops, home visits, and more effective use of mass media.

☐ Prepare teachers who see themselves as leaders of an educational team, with special focus on supporting the parental role of Ur-education. Building on the programs of Gray and Levenstein, we may need new training programs which prepare family educational consultants, teachers without classrooms, who visit families regularly on an inservice basis. *All* teachers would benefit from courses on the family as an educational institution.

☐ Establish a library of toys and materials on child development in each school that children can be taught to use with their younger siblings. We need to help children, boys as well as girls, develop roles and responsibilities as future parents—teaching them to teach each other.

Our ultimate goal will be a comprehensive, integrated system of education in which everyone is a student, everyone is a teacher throughout his life-span and throughout his life-space.

References

Coleman, James S., et al. *Equality of Educational Opportunity*. U.S. Printing Office, Washington, D. C., 1966.

Douglas, J. W. *The Home and the School: A Study of Ability and Attainment in the Primary School*. Mcgibbon and Kee, London, 1964.

Gordon, Ira J. "Reaching the Young Child Through Parent Education." CHILDHOOD EDUCATION, 46, 5 (February 1970): 247-253.

Gray, Susan W. and Klaus, R. A. *The Early Training Project. A Seventh Year Report*. John F. Kennedy Center for Research on Education and Human Development, George Peabody College for Teachers, 1969.

Hess, Robert D. *Parental Behavior and Children's School Achievement: Implications for Head Start*. In Grotberg, Edith (Ed.) *Critical Issues in Research Related to Disadvantaged Children*. Educational Testing Service, Princeton, 1969.

Illich, Ivan. "The Alternative to Schooling." *Saturday Review*, 54 (June 19, 1971): 44-48.

Levenstein, Phyllis. "Cognitive Growth in Preschoolers Through Stimulation of Verbal Interaction with Mothers." Paper presented at the 46th Annual Meeting of the American Orthopsychiatric Association, New York, April 1969.

Moore, T. "Language and Intelligence: A Longitudinal Study of the First 8 Years." *Human Development*, 11 (1968): 88-106.

National School Public Relations Association. *Preschool Breakthrough: What Works in Early Childhood Education*. An *Education U.S.A.* Special Report. Washington, D. C., The Association, 1970.

Richardson, Elliot. Speech before Council of Chief State School Officers, Miami Beach, Florida, November 16, 1970.

Rupp, J. C. C. *Helping the Child To Cope with the School: A Study of the Importance of Parent-Child Relationships with Regard to Elementary School Success*. Wolters-Noordhoff, Groningen, 1969.

Schaefer, E. S. "Home Tutoring, Maternal Behavior and Infant Intellectual Development." Paper presented at the meeting of the American Psychological Association, Washington, D. C., September 1969.

———. "Need for early and continuing education." In Denenberg, Victor (Ed.), *Education of the Infant and Young Child*. Academic Press, New York, 1970.

U.S. Department of Health, Education, and Welfare/ Office of Education. *"It Works" Series: Summary of Selected Compensatory Education Research Projects*. OE 37069. Washington, D. C. 1970.

Weikart, D. P., Lambie, D. Z. et al. "Ypsilanti-Carnegie Infant Education Project Progress Report." Department of Research and Development, Ypsilanti Public Schools, Ypsilanti, Michigan, 1969.

PIAGET'S TASKS: THE EFFECTS OF SCHOOLING AND INTELLIGENCE

JACQUELINE J. GOODNOW AND GLORIA BETHON

What is the effect of schooling on Piaget's tasks? And what is the relation between these tasks and others more widely used as measures of intelligence? The two questions, normally separate, became intertwined in an unusual result from a previous study (Goodnow, 1962), a result that led to the gathering of data on both variables within the single study reported here.

The result to be unraveled was obtained in Hong Kong. A group of Chinese boys with no schooling did as well as European schoolchildren on

This study was supported by a grant from the National Institutes of Health (MH 06740). For wholehearted cooperation, we are deeply indebted to the principals and teachers of several schools in Montgomery County, Maryland. We are especially indebted to members of the Educational Services Section—Mr. Maxwell Burdette and Dr. Elizabeth Wilson—and to Mrs. Frances Bentzen. In addition, our thanks are due to Magali Bovet, Bärbel Inhelder, and Mimi Sinclair for a valuable discussion of results; to John Brun for assistance in testing; and to Dr. H. Goldstein for the loan of stimulus material.

CHILD DEVELOPMENT, 1966, Vol. 37, pp. 573-582.

tasks for conservation of weight, volume, and surface. In contrast, the un-schooled Chinese boys were markedly poorer than the schooled Europeans on another Piaget task, one of combinatorial reasoning. (The latter task demands that the child, after making pairs of three and four colors, work out in advance a system to cover all possible pairs of six colors. The conservation tasks require that the child see one property of an object—its weight, for instance—as remaining invariant in spite of a change in the shape of the object.) In addition, the unschooled Chinese were much poorer than the Europeans on Raven's Progressive Matrices, usually regarded as a measure of general intelligence but perhaps unreliable for the unschooled children.

The discrepancy between the conservation and the combinatorial tasks raised the question: are the conservation tasks insensitive to lack of schooling, or are they insensitive to differences in intelligence? One could argue that the Chinese boys were actually average in intelligence and that the lack of schooling depressed performance on the Matrices and on the combinatorial task but left the conservation tasks intact. Or one could argue that the Chinese boys were actually dull, but the conservation tasks, in contrast to the combinatorial task, were insensitive to this dullness. The available literature could be used to support either argument. In support of the first hypothesis, for instance, is Inhelder's (1943) early conclu-sion that the conservation tasks for amount, weight, and volume differen-tiate between dull and average children. Inhelder's (1943) conclusion, however, is weakened by the lack of a reported control group and by the use of children with emotional problems as well as low IQ scores. It also does not fit with a subsequent finding by Dodwell (1961) of no dif-ferences among three groups varying in IQ on tasks for conservation of amount and quantity.

The present study rules out the hypothesis that the tasks for conserva-tion of amount, weight, and volume are insensitive to differences in in-telligence. The tasks differentiated, first of all, between dull and average schoolchildren in the United States. This positive finding prompted us to make some additional comparisons: between "average" and "superior" boys of the same CA and between children with the same MA's but different CA's. Both Feigenbaum (1963) and Hood (1962) have suggested that the young, bright child may be better than the older, duller child on Piaget's tasks. The results presented here argue instead for equal performance with equal MA.

TESTING FOR THE EFFECTS OF SCHOOLING

This section deals with a combination of Hong Kong and American data.

230

In all, six of Piaget's tasks and one other were used. The main Piaget tasks were conservation of amount, weight, volume, and surface, and the combinations of colors. For all but the conservation of amount, the standard procedure has been described in Goodnow (1962). The description given here is accordingly restricted.

1. Raindrops.—The child guesses the pattern of raindrops falling onto a squared sidewalk (from Piaget & Inhelder, 1951, pp. 62–68). This task was used only as an introduction.

2. Conservation of amount.—Each child starts with a new bar of clay, marked at the center. The *E* says: "Break this in half for me as evenly as you can. You'll be taking half, and I'll be taking half. Let's make sure, first, that it's fair and even." The two pieces are compared, and, with the child's agreement that the division is fair, *E* says: "You roll your half into a ball. I'm going to take my half and make it like this [pressing it into a pancake shape]. Is it still fair and even? Do I still have as much as you do, or does one of us have more?" If the child says "the same" or its equivalent, *E* asks: "Can you tell me why?" If not, *E* asks: "Which one of us has more? Can you tell me why?" Then follows a short inquiry, intended as a check on the correct answer or as an opportunity for the child to review his answer. If the original answer is correct, *E* takes a piece away from the pancake-shaped clay and asks: "How about now? Do I still have as much as you do, or does one of us have more? Can you tell me why?" If the original answer is incorrect, *E* asks: "How much do I give you (or you give me) so that I'd have as much as you do? Show me." If the difference is quite small (the amount that can be scraped or pinched off with a fingernail, for instance), *E* says: "Sometimes a little bit of difference is important, but in this game a little bit of difference doesn't really matter." The child is scored as correct if he judges the two pieces to be the same after the change in shape and can give an adequate reason, either on the check or on the first-time round. Adequate are such reasons as: "You didn't take any away; you just flattened it; you just changed the shape; we had the same before, and you haven't done anything."

3. Conservation of weight.—The child starts with two balls of clay, weighs them on a balance to check that they weigh the same, watches while cne piece is changed into a pancake shape, and is asked if the two pieces of clay still weigh the same. The child's answer is followed by a check similar to that given for conservation of amount.

4. Conservation of volume.—The task again uses two balls of clay, with volume in terms of the amount of water displaced in two identical jugs of water. After an incorrect answer, *E* asks the child to estimate where the water level would be on the two jugs. The task yields two scores. Volume 1 allows as correct the answer: "They push the water up the same because they weigh the same." Volume 2 scores as incorrect any answer which contains a reference to weight.

5. *Combinations of colors.*—The child is asked to make pairs of colors with no repetition of pairs. With corrections and promptings, he makes pairs for three and four colors. He is then given six colors and asked to think for a while, to try and find a system or a trick that will make it easy to find all the pairs. The task yields two scores. Combinatorial 1 requires only that the first five pairs should be in a systematic order (one color held constant). Combinatorial 2 requires that all 15 pairs be found systematically.

6. *Incidental memory.*—This task was patterened after Goldstein and Kass (1961) and designed as a break between the conservation tasks when the combinatorial task was not used.

7. *Conservation of surface.*—The child starts with two equal-sized fields, each containing a horse. The child watches as E adds houses to the fields, placing one on each field at the same time until each field contains 12 houses. In one field these houses are scattered; in the other, they are to the side of the field in two back-to-back rows of six. The child is asked if each horse has as much grass to eat as the other or if one horse has more. As a check, houses are removed from the fields. For Ss who give the correct answer immediately, one house is removed, and the child is asked, "How about now?" For incorrect Ss, houses are taken away from the scattered field until the child judges the two horses to have the same amount of grass.

Tasks were given in thre order 1, 2, 3, 4, 5 or 6, and 7. All tasks were given individually and at school.

Design

Since unschooled children are rare, and their intelligence scores suspect, it is hard to test directly the hypothesis that the conservation tasks are not upset by the lack of schooling. We tested instead the alternate hypothesis, that is, sensitivity to intelligence differences, by comparing two groups (32 pairs) of 11-year-old schoolboys: a "dull" group (IQ 64–88, median 81, scores from the California Test of Mental Maturity, administered by the school system), and an "average" group of the same age (IQ 101–120, median 111).

For each boy in the dull group, there is a boy in the average group with the same CA, a higher IQ, and a scholastic record in keeping with his IQ. (The mean difference between pairs in CA is 1.8 months, the range 0–7 months. The mean difference in IQ is 30 points, the range 21–40 points.) All dull Ss had to have IQ scores below 90 and to be recognized by their teachers as slow, but they also had to be still within the local school system, rather than in special schools, and to have no referrals for emotional problems.

With a few exceptions, pairs were drawn from the same school, with a total sample of five schools. The range of school grades was restricted to grades 4 and 5. The selection and matching of Ss was done by one person, the testing by two others who did not know to which group a child belonged.

Both groups were given, in the first session, the tasks for conservation of amount, weight, and volume, followed by incidental memory, and conservation of surface. At a later date, 25 of the 32 pairs were given the combinatorial task.

Results

Figure 1 puts together two American groups with two Hong Kong groups of the same CA and makes it clear that we can rule out the hypothesis that the conservation tasks are insensitive to differences in intelligence. The average and dull groups of American school children are quite distinct. We can accept, instead, the hypothesis that the conservation tasks are relatively insensitive to a lack of schooling, an insensitivity not shown by the combinatorial task. (An additional group of Chinese, reported in Goodnow [1962], rules out the possibility that the effect is due to differences in socioeconomic class rather than in schooling.)

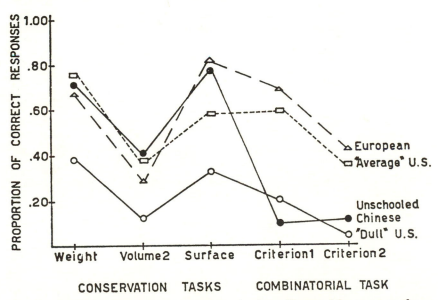

Fig. 1.—The interaction of task and schooling, illustrated by a group of unschooled children (Chinese) and three groups of schoolchildren (U.S. "dull," U.S. "average," and European "average plus").

The tasks are the same as those used in the first set of comparisons.

Design

To the two groups already described (groups 1 and 3 in the list below), we added four more, giving the following six groups as a final sample:

1. Dull 11-year-olds (IQ 64–88).
2. Average 8-year-olds, matched to group 1 for MA. The match was generally within 3 months.
3. Average 11-year-olds, matched to group 1 for CA, but with IQ scores about 30 points higher.
4. Superior 8-year-olds, unmatched (IQ 129–157).
5. Average 11-year-olds.
6. Superior 11-year-olds, matched to group 5 for CA (within 4 months), but with IQ scores about 30 points higher.

Details of MA, IQ, and CA for these groups are given in Table 1

TABLE 1

GROUPS OF SUBJECTS COMPARED FOR MA, IQ, AND CA

	MA		IQ		CA	
GROUP	Median	Range	Median	Range	Median	Range
1. Dull 11....	8:7	6:8 −10:1	81	64–88	11:0	10:3 −11:7
2. Average 8..	8:8	6:11− 9:11	110	93–119	7:9	7:5 − 8:7
3. Average 11.	12:1	11:0 −14:2	111	101–126	10:9	10:3 −11:7
4. Superior 8..	11:3	9:11–13:0	135	129–157	8:4	7:8 − 8:6
5. Average 11.	12:1	11:5 −14:6	108	101–128	11:1	10:7 −11:6
6. Superior 11.	15:11	14:2 −18:7	139	129–168	11:2	10:10−11:6

Note.—Groups 1, 2, and 3 are formed by 32 triads; groups 5 and 6 by 32 dyads; group 4 ($N = 20$) is unmatched.

Matched groups are matched by *subject*. Groups 1, 2, and 3 are formed by 32 triads, groups 5 and 6 by 32 dyads. Group 4 is the only unmatched group. Matching was, as far as possible, within the same school, and the range of school grades was restricted. Testing was blind for IQ level. Further details of matching, for groups 1, 2, and 3, are given in Bethon (1964).

Results

The proportion of correct answers, by task, is given for all groups in Table 2. The general order of results indicates the increasing proportion of success with increasing MA, on all tasks.

TABLE 2

PROPORTION OF CORRECT ANSWERS AMONG SIX GROUPS OF BOYS

| | | CONSERVATION TASKS | | | | | COMBINA- TORIAL TASK | |
GROUP	MEDIAN MA	Amount	Weight	Volume 1	Volume 2	Surface	Criterion 1	Criterion 2
1. Dull 11.....	8:7	.88	.38	.28	.12	.34	.20	.04
2. Average 8...	8:8	.72	.47	.44	.31	.38	...	...
3. Average 11..	12:1	.97	.75	.62	.38	.59	.60	.36
4. Superior 8...	11:3	1.00	.65	.65	.50	.65	.50	.25
5. Average 11..	12:1	1.00	.78	.56	.31	.84	.62	.38
6. Superior 11..	15:11	.97	1.00	.75	.56	.94	.91	.72

We shall consider, first, the role of the conservation tasks in differentiating among groups 1, 2, and 3. Groups 1 and 2, matched for mental age at 8:7 and 8:8, are not significantly different from one another, even though one group is "dull 11" and the other "average 8." Both are significantly different, at the .01 level, from group 1 (11 years, MA 12:1). These statements are based on an analysis of variance summing across tasks—amount, weight, volume 2, and surface—and on Duncan's Multiple Range Test. Since this analysis tells us nothing about the contribution of any one task or how well any single task differentiates, separate χ^2s were also computed for each task in a comparison of groups 1 and 2. The χ^2 values are as follows: amount, 0.87; weight, 7.68 (.01 level); volume 1, 6.3 (.05 level); volume 2, 4.05 (.05 level); surface, 3.1 (N.S.).

Still staying with the conservation tasks, we may ask next if the tasks differentiate as well at another part of the intelligence range, between average and superior. In the Hong Kong study (Goodnow, 1962), a number of boys with very high scores on the Matrices were oddly poor on conservation tasks. The question can be answered by a comparison of groups 5 and 6. Between these groups the conservation tasks again differentiate, at the .01 level. The analysis-of-variance sums across the tasks weight, volume 2, and surface, omitting amount. (Amount was given to these groups only to keep the experimental procedure standard.) No one conservation task by itself, however, yields a significant difference. The combinatorial task does yield such a difference, both between average and dull (groups 2 and 3), and between average and superior (groups 5 and 6). All χ^2s for the combinatorial task are at the .05 level or better.

Despite all the indications of a strong tie to MA, the suspicion remains that a point may come when a young child with a high MA will be held back by the sheer lack of experience that CA provides. It was to allay this doubt that we added group 4 (superior 8-year-olds). This group may be roughly compared with the two groups of average 11-year-olds, groups 3 and 5. The superior 8-year-olds hold their own quite well, in line with their MA, and clearly their degree of sheer youth is no handicap.

DISCUSSION

It will be simpler to discuss the two issues separately: the effects of variations in intelligence and the effects of lack of schooling.

Variations in Intelligence

The results make it clear that variations in intelligence are to be seriously considered in any comparison of children by way of Piaget's tasks. The results also indicate the levels of success one might expect at various MA's.

The results provide a substantiation of Inhelder's (1943) argument that the conservation tasks of amount, weight, and volume will differentiate between dull children and children about 30 points higher on an IQ scale. In short, her conclusion is not to be set aside for the lack of a direct control group or for any confounding of low IQ and emotional disturbance.

The results do not support the idea of significant differences between older dull Ss and younger bright Ss, as suggested by Feigenbaum (1963) and concluded by Hood (1962), although there may well be limits to this lack of difference. Certainly our results are not in line with Hood's, who used a similar design of same MA and different CA and concluded that the dull Ss were much poorer on tasks of seriation, correspondence, and conservation of quantity. The discrepancy in findings may be the result of a change in tasks. It is more probably the result of a difference in sample. Hood's dull and average Ss were not directly matched; the dull Ss were in special schools or training centers, all with "IQ's below 75" (1962, p. 274); and the range of CA differences is much greater (Hood's normal sample ranged from 3 to 8 years, his retarded from 9 to 41 as against a restriction of CA differences to 3 years in the present study).

Variations in Schooling

When we put together the Hong Kong and American data, the conservation tasks for weight, volume, and surface emerge as insensitive to lack of schooling. A similar finding has been reported by Sigel and Mermelstein (1965) for Negro children deprived of schooling in Prince Edward County, Virginia. This does not mean, however, that the conservation tasks cannot be upset by particular kinds of schooling. A poor science course and an attitude of down-playing the evidence of one's own experience created difficulties for one group of Chinese schoolchildren (Goodnow, 1962). What is suggested is that in the normal course of events children acquire the skills they need for these conservation tasks without benefit of schooling.

In contrast, the combinatorial task is definitely sensitive to the lack of schooling. The question then arises: what is the difference between these tasks? One difference is in the demand for working things out "in the head," by thought rather than by hand or by eye. The critical part of the combinatorial task demands that the child do most of the work in his head before he places down any colors. This may put the unschooled child at a disadvantage if his preferred mode of learning and thinking is by way of moving things around and observing perceptual patterns. Such a preference has been commented on by Maistriaux (1955, pp. 430, 450). On construction tasks that he gave to unschooled Africans, he was impressed by the extent to which his Ss consistently estimated length by the direct placement of a piece rather than by eye or by a reference length. In short, one of the effects of schooling may be a shift from approach by hand or by direct test, an effect suggested also by some of Hanfmann's (1941) results on education and a manipulative approach to the Vygotsky blocks.

In contrast to the combinatorial task, the conservation tasks have more direct counterparts in the experience of the child. Within the experimental task, the child can refer back to the fact that he divided the clay and he weighed the pieces to check that they were equal. Outside of it, he can draw on past experiences with changes in shape. As one Chinese boy explained, a catty of rice may come in different-shaped bags, but it is always a catty; he has carried them and he knows. Such action backstops to reasoning may be especially important to children who have not had a great deal of schooling.

REFERENCES

Bethon, G. D. The effects of chronological and mental age on Piaget's tasks of reasoning in children. Unpublished Master's thesis, George Washington Univer., 1964.

Dodwell, P. C. Children's understanding of number concepts: characteristics of an individual and of a group test. *Canad. J. Psychol.*, 1961, 15, 29–36.

Feigenbaum, K. Task complexity and intelligence as variables in Piaget's problems of conservation. *Child Develpm.*, 1963, 34, 423–432.

Goldstein, H., & Kass, C. Incidental learning of educable mentally retarded and gifted children. *Amer. J. ment. Defic.*, 1961, 66, 245–249.

Goodnow, J. J. A test of milieu differences with some of Piaget's tasks. *Psychol. Monogr.*, 1962, 76, No. 36 (Whole No. 555).

Hanfmann, E. A study of personal patterns in an intellectual performance. *Charact. & Pers.*, 1941, 9, 315–325.

Hood, H. B. An experimental study of Piaget's theory of the development of number in children. *Brit. J. Psychol.*, 1962, 53, 273–286.

Inhelder, B. *Le diagnostic du raisonnement chez les débiles mentaux*. Neuchatel: Delachaux & Niestle, 1943.

Maistriaux, R. La sous-évolution des noirs d'Afrique. Sa nature—ses causes—ses remèdes. *Rev. Psychol. Peuples*, 1955, 10, 167–189, 397–456.

Piaget, J., & Inhelder, B. *La genèse de l'idée de hasard chez l'enfant*. Paris: Pr. Universitaires, 1951.

Sigel, I. E., & Mermelstein, E. Effects of nonschooling on Piagetian tasks of conservation. Unpublished paper presented at A.P.A. meeting, September, 1965.

Emily Kernkamp and Eleanor Price

Coeducation May Be a 'No-No' for the Six-Year-Old Boy

Long taken for granted as a responsible school practice, coeducation may be detrimental to some children's early school adjustment, especially that of first-grade boys.

In our school we experimented to find out if separation would make a difference academically, personally, and socially. We separated all first-grade children into one all-boy and one all-girl group for one year. As a control, the next year we grouped the new first-grade class coeducationally. The same teachers taught the two first-grade classes both years, trying to plan for and share similar enrichment experiences for both boys and girls.

Pre- and post-test data assessed cognitive and affective outcomes for both the experimental and control groups. The problem was: Does grouping make a difference in academic achievement, classroom behavior adjustment patterns, and social acceptance of the isolate for first-grade boys and girls? We found there were certain significant differences related to grouping.

Standardized test scores at the end of the year, compared with initial group differences, revealed that same-sex grouping had a very favorable effect on first-grade boys in the areas of spelling and total reading. First-grade girls out-performed first-grade boys in arithmetic, regardless of treatment.

Other findings revealed differences in classroom behavior adjustment. The all-girl group tended to be less distractible and better able to concentrate than all the boys and the girls in coeducational classes. They were found to be less verbally expressive and more gregarious than all the others, too. In the task-orientation dimension, the all-boy group and the girls in coeducational classes were significantly higher than the other two groups.

Sociometric data revealed that there was a higher level of isolationism at the end of the year for both groups, regardless of treatment or sex. Neither the all-boy nor all-girl groups showed an advantage over the coeducational classes in lessening the total number of isolates.

The population of children was small (77 in all), but responsibly controlled and analyzed with covariant procedures. Teacher and counselor formed the basis of certain intuitive reactions reported here.*

Boys in an All-Boy Class

We found that the characteristic learning styles of boys get diluted or overlooked in a coeducational group, but in the all-boy class teacher horizons were widened. Without the presence of

EMILY KERNKAMP is a teacher and ELEANOR PRICE is a counselor on the staff of the University Laboratory School, Northern Illinois University, DeKalb, where they conducted this study.

*A more detailed report of the statistical treatment and results is scheduled for publication in a coming issue of the Journal of Experimental Education.

PHI DELTA KAPPAN, 1972, Vol. 53, pp. 662-663.

239

girls, boys were freer to be themselves. Their leadership qualities emerged when they had the opportunity to use them. The results can best be summarized this way:

1. *Boys were investigative and manipulative.* Boys responded to an open or investigative environment, and wanted to touch, handle, and manipulate whatever intrigued them. They touched first and found out the facts later. They were "here and now" people with little patience for postponement of an activity or idea until a later time. Pets, especially, had tremendous meaning for them. Their freedom to observe, handle, and feed frogs and rabbits living in the classroom provided acceptable outlets for many needs.

2. *For boys, physical activity was a powerful concomitant to mental activity.* Individualized instruction was a natural and necessary mode for boys' learning. Having little patience with someone else's reading or discussion, they moved out mentally and physically. Their need to release physical energy was very evident. In the reading lesson, for example, they rocked and crawled all over their chairs and twisted and turned throughout the lesson.

With their wriggling and ready comments, the use of headsets was important for good auditory discrimination during listening activities with record player and tape recorder. Frequently a boy would shout a comment to his neighbor about what he was hearing or thinking. Eyes, ears, and fingers were all at work. Boys would scribble on the table while at the listening station, or get up to peer through the window at something that caught their eye. They even chewed through some of the cords on the headset.

When they were allowed to "do their own thing," mental activity was often accompanied by motor noises and comments. The teacher observed one independent worker who verbalized about whatever he was doing. At first restrained from talking, the boy's work virtually ceased. But later, when his particular learning style was accepted, his work improved and his talk soft-

ened. Even in motion, the boys were able to make many astute and valuable comments and to attend to the lesson when it interested them.

3. *Boys needed to be involved in decision making.* The boys wanted transaction with the teacher and seemed to manage academics best when they had some input. They were very outspoken, telling the teacher frankly when they didn't want to do something, and capable of offering good alternatives. There was a fresh, free-flowing energy in the all-boy class. They refused to stay in a narrow channel, always communicating in their candid, insistent way that there was more than one route to go.

4. *Limits for boys were a creative challenge.* The creativity of boys thrived with reasonable limit setting. They liked a little latitude and responded well to an open structure. For example, on the playground they found many solutions to the limit: *Keep your shoes clean and dry.* They made a game of pretending that there were alligators in the huge mud-puddle at the foot of the slide – an innovation which gave spice to their need for precaution and kept their shoes clean.

5. *In peer relations boys could settle differences with dispatch.* Their messages were open, direct, and swift. There was much physical contact – hugs for friends and blows when provoked. The boys tended to strike out when displeased, but there were few verbal taunts and a great deal of sympathetic understanding.

Boys in a Coeducational Class

But something seemed to happen to both boys and their teacher when they were in a coeducational setting. This was evident the next year with a new group of children composed of boys and girls. We observed these changes:

1. *Boys were less willing to extend themselves when they shared a classroom with girls.* The boys were "turned off" in the coeducational setting. Their quick activity and frankness often interfered with teacher goals. Their fresh nonconformity and originality offended

240

the girls' values of industry and conformity. Girls swiftly reacted with criticism and prescriptive remarks. And the teacher was pressured by the girls to do something about the boys!

A natural hesitancy and shyness of boys about success with academic tasks became dramatically clear in the coeducational class. They became easily discouraged, dropped their tasks quickly, and left their seats to socialize or investigate somewhere else in the room.

2. *Boys became more of a behavior problem as the girls dominated the classroom scene.* Sometimes they were uncooperative and uncontrollable. Boys delighted in teasing the girls and reveled in the response it provoked. The teacher remarked, "Last year the boys did much more imaginative play . . . this year they need kindergarten equipment to create a happy play period. . . . It's extremely difficult in a coeducational class to give the boys the support and latitude they need when you have the girls. . . ."

3. *Seatwork and handwriting seemed to be particular problem areas for boys in a coeducational class.* Boys were less willing to do much with paper and pencil and became easily bored. The girls, on the other hand, got more satisfaction out of writing and made their figures and letters more carefully and legibly, a discouraging state of affairs to the boys. In the mixed class, the teacher observed, "The boys have lost some of their zest for writing. . . . We wrote so much more last year that was of interest to them. Last year the boys were free to be themselves. They had a lot more fun with animals, handling them, experimenting, and wanting to write stories about their new discoveries. There is not the camaraderie and willingness to help each other. This year the girls kind of take over."

4. *Playground activity was often a time of conflict.* The girls insisted on conformity to higher standards of playground management. They became coercive and punitive, constantly reprimanding the boys. The teacher believed that the same boys would not have presented behavior problems in an all-boy class

and would have dealt with each other "in a more honest and open way."

Our findings enabled us to see young children better as individuals when they were not under the influence of the opposite sex. Our data offer the first-grade teacher a new picture of what the six-year-old can be. They suggest new goals for children in her classroom. What can she expect?

1. Girls in first grade will probably do better than boys in arithmetic, regardless of grouping.

2. Boys will have some difficulty with spelling and total reading if she continues coeducational grouping.

3. Boys will want active participation and an open structure, with little concern for time . . . except for savoring, investigating, and expressing their reactions.

4. Girls in a coeducational class will be more positively task-oriented. Teacher observations suggest that these girls, with boys in the class, may be more apprehensive about conformity. Girls seem to need more structure. They want the teacher to say what comes next.

However, it seems to us that it is not enough to have these new understandings if we are unwilling to make some real changes in our first-grade programs. There may be a better way of grouping young children in their early school life than the traditional mixing of the sexes. Coeducation may indeed be a "no-no" for boys, because it has failed to adapt itself to the natural qualities of the boy learner. But educators have failed to look critically at the traditional role expectations they have made acceptable for the girl learner. Coeducation may be a "no-no" for the six-year-old girl too. And for all fours and fives! Perhaps girls need help in stepping out to go adventuring in their school world. Instead of being little mothers and overpowering the boys, they may need encouragement to savor and explore with the abandonment of the boys.

What's good for girls is not necessarily good for boys. It may not necessarily be good for girls either!

K. EILEEN ALLEN
KEITH D. TURNER
PAULETTE M. EVERETT

A Behavior Modification Classroom for Head Start Children with Problem Behaviors

HEAD START programs across the country represent a diversity of educational models. Klein (1969) described a number of these: the traditional nursery school approach exemplified by the Bank Street program, the Deutsch-type programs based on sequential programing with heavy emphasis on listening, the autotelic-discovery approach espoused by Nimnicht and the Far West Laboratory, the cognitively oriented programs modeled after

K. EILEEN ALLEN *is Coordinator, Early Childhood Education and Research, Experimental Education Unit, Child Development and Mental Retardation Center, University of Washington;* KEITH D. TURNER *and* PAULETTE M. EVERETT *are Teachers, Experimental Education Unit. The research reported herein was performed in part pursuant to a grant from the King County Mental Health-Mental Retardation Board.*

EXCEPTIONAL CHILDREN, 1970, Vol. 37, pp. 119-127.

Weickart's work at Ypsilanti, and the "pressure-cooker" approach of Engelmann and Becker, to name a few. These programs have demonstrated, in varying degrees, their effectiveness in ameliorating the accumulated deficits of young poverty children.

But what' about the children with severe behavior disorders who seem to profit little or not at all from a head start program? Although they are relatively few in number, perhaps only one or two in a head start class (about the same ratio as in middle-class nursery schools), they do exist, regardless of the educational model upon which the class is based. These children exact a heavy toll of teachers' time and energy, often to the detriment of the other children.

The Demonstration Project

It is imperative that effective programs be created for these children. One possible approach is described in this paper. The project, entitled the Demonstration Head Start Classroom (Haring, Hayden, & Nolen, 1969), has three major goals: (a) to furnish remedial services for children with marked behavioral excesses or deficits; (b) to provide a training program for the teachers of these children; and (c) to conduct research in behavior modification procedures through analyses of teacher-child interactions.

Twelve to 15 children are enrolled in the class at one time with individual enrollment periods varying from 3 weeks to 6 months. The children are referred by head start teachers in consultation with a head start interdisciplinary team. Some of the reasons given for referral include severely disruptive, excessively withdrawn, lacking in communication skills, hyperactive, incontinent, schizoid, echolalic, and brain damaged.

The ideal program for each child study contains four phases:

1. Observation of the child and his teachers and the accumulation of baseline data in the home classroom prior to the child's entry in the demonstration class.

2. Enrollment in the demonstration class for a period of time adequate to ameliorate the child's problems.

3. Involvement of home classroom teachers in an in-service training program.

4. Return of the child to his home classroom with collection of followup data and guidance for the teacher.

Behavior Modification Procedures

The overall philosophy of the demonstration class is based on the application of behavior modification techniques derived from principles of reinforcement. An abundant literature attests to the effectiveness of such procedures in dealing with the aberrant behaviors of preschool children. A few examples include: regressive crawling (Harris, Johnston, Kelley, & Wolf, 1964), hyperactivity (Allen, Henke, Harris, Baer, & Reynolds, 1967), operant crying

(Hart, Allen, Buell, Harris, & Wolf, 1964), and mutilative self scratching (Allen & Harris, 1966).

A single unifying theme is apparent in each of these experimental analyses: The common, everyday social behaviors or responses of preschool teachers are powerful determinants of child behavior. Therefore, the child behaviors that teachers respond to will increase while the child behaviors that teachers fail to respond to will decrease. If a teacher wishes to eliminate the isolate tendencies of an excessively shy child (Allen, Hart, Buell, Harris, & Wolf, 1964), she withholds her smiles, nods, conversation, suggestions, and presentation of materials as long as the child isolates himself from the group. But the moment the isolate child moves toward a peer or a peer group activity, the teacher immediately directs attention to him, reinforcing (providing consequences for) his first approximations to social behavior. By controlling the timing of responses, that is, holding responses contingent on the child's emission of appropriate rather than maladaptive behaviors, preschool teachers have demonstrated that beneficial behavior changes can be effected (Harris, Wolf, & Baer, 1964).

Individualized Programing

In accordance with the principles of systematic application of behavior modification procedures, the demonstration class emphasizes an individualized program for each child within the context of a typical preschool program. The daily schedule, though flexible, has a basic structure which enables children to acquire skills in self-management. Such skills are, or should be, one of the major educational goals of a well-designed preschool program. However, the program is also organized to promote each child's acquisition of social, verbal, preacademic, and motor skills. To this end, a variety of quiet, sedentary activities are balanced by vigorous play activities; child-initiated activities are balanced by teacher-structured and teacher-directed activities. Regardless of the activity in progress, the teachers are continually on the alert to reinforce target behaviors peculiar to each child's individual needs.

During outdoor play, for example, when the overall emphasis is on free play and vigorous large motor activities, a dozen different programs may be in effect: for one child, the teachers may be reinforcing appropriate peer contacts; for another, constructive use of materials; for a third child, more creative use of the equipment. Several different verbal development programs may be in progress: reinforcement of one child for more audible verbal output, of another for simply joining two words, of a third for asking for instead of grabbing. Span of attention, sharing, concept development, visual and auditory discriminations—all of these skills and many more, a teacher can teach (reinforce) in the context of a free play situation if she has carefully specified in advance the target learning or behaviors for each child.

Part of the daily program is devoted to a more formal, preacademic work time when the children sit at tables in small groups. The tasks consist of activities designed to extend attention span, increase perceptual-motor skills, refine visual and auditory discrimination skills, and develop basic concepts of size, shape, color, equivalence, seriation, and spatial relationships. Again, the program is individualized and is based on the skill levels of each child at the time of his entry into the class. Materials used are those found in every preschool classroom: puzzles, pegboards, matching cards, color cubes, formboards, and a variety of teacher-made materials. The materials are carefully sequenced, however, so that each child acquires specific learning in gradual increments. Correct responses and error rates over time are recorded by the teacher on each task for each child (Nolen, Hulten, & Kunzelmann, 1968). These data provide the teachers with a basis for preparing individual lesson kits so that maximum success comes to each child as he acquires the basic school performance skills.

Natural Contingencies

The natural reinforcers in the environment are also carefully monitored by the teachers. For example, receiving a snack is contingent on completion by each child of his preacademic tasks. However, for a new child or an excessively active child, material may be so programed that he is required to attend to academic tasks for as little as 3 minutes at first (30 seconds has been a beginning requirement in some cases). The time depends entirely on the individual child's behavior. The crucial factor is that the teacher set the first approximation in accordance with the target behavior.

Another example of the monitoring of the natural reinforcers in the preschool environment is the opportunity to go out of doors. Going outside to play is always contingent on the child's putting away blocks, housekeeping materials, or whatever else the child was playing with at the time. Thus, in the demonstration class, all activities and teacher attention are devoted to molding appropriate behaviors, and nothing is expended on attending to maladaptive responses. Three adults effectively manage and provide a sound educational program for 12 to 15 children who only a short time before were causes for grave concern in their home classrooms. To illustrate individual behavior modification programs, two case studies are presented.

Case Study 1

Townsend was 4½ years old when he was transferred to the demonstration class. Collection of data (according to the system described by Bijou, Peterson, Harris, Allen, & Johnston, 1969) continued after his transfer to the demonstration class, where the teachers were instructed during the baseline period to replicate as nearly as possible the homeroom teachers' methods of handling Townsend: rechanneling his disruptive activities, comforting him during outbursts, and physically restraining him when he attacked other children. Maladaptive behaviors continued at a high rate during baseline conditions.

Tantrum Behavior

On Townsend's eleventh day in the demonstration classroom a first step in behavior modification was initiated. All tantrums, regardless of duration or intensity, were to be ignored, that is, put on extinction. Absolute disregard of the tantrum, no matter how severe it might become, had to be thoroughly understood by the teachers inasmuch as there are data (Hawkins, Peterson, Schweid, & Bijou, 1966) which indicate that when tantrums are put on extinction, extremes of tantrumming may temporarily ensure. Townsend's data were no exception to the classic extinction curve. His first tantrum under the nonattending contingency lasted 27 minutes (average duration of previous tantrums had been 5 minutes), becoming progressively more severe up to the 20-minute point. When it became obvious that the tantrum was going to be lengthy, the other children were taken to the playground by a teacher and a volunteer while the second teacher stationed herself immediately outside the classroom door. When Townsend quieted down, the teacher opened the door to ask in a matter-of-fact voice if he was ready to go to the playground. Before the teacher had a chance to speak, Townsend recommenced his tantrum. The teacher stepped back outside to wait for another period of calm. Twice more Townsend quieted down, only to begin anew at the sight of the teacher. Each time, however, the episodes were shorter (6, 3, and 1 minutes, respectively).

On the second day of tantrum intervention there was one tantrum of 15 minutes with two 2-minute followup tantrums when the teacher attempted to re-enter the room. On the third day there was one mild 4-minute tantrum. No further tantrums occurred in the demonstration class nor was there a recurrence when Townsend returned to his regular head start class.

Disruptive Behaviors

Modification of generally aggressive and disruptive behaviors such as hitting and kicking children, spitting, and running off with other children's toys was instituted on the sixteenth session. On the first day of modification the teachers were instructed to give their undivided attention to the child who had been assaulted, while keeping their backs to Townsend. Nine episodes of aggressive behavior were tallied on this day. During the next 11 sessions, there was a marked decrease (an average of three per session). During the twelfth session, there was an upswing to seven episodes, then a gradual decrease until finally, no more grossly aggressive and disruptive acts occurred. A zero rate was recorded for the remainder of the sessions.

Bus Program

Another behavior modification project with Townsend involved the use of consumable reinforcers. Townsend had been banned from the head start bus for failing to sit in a seat with the seat belt fastened, attempting to open the doors while the bus was in motion, playing with the instrument panel, and throwing himself upon the bus driver while the latter was driving. Staying buckled in the seat was the target behavior.

On the first day of the program Townsend's seat belt was fastened, and the teacher immediately put a peanut in Townsend's mouth commenting, "Good, you are sitting quietly, all buckled up snug in your seat belt." She then quickly dispensed peanuts to every child on the bus with approving comments about their good bus riding habits. Rounds of peanut dispensing and approving comments were continued at 30 to 90 second intervals throughout the 15 minute bus ride. The peanuts were dispensed at longer intervals for the next 4 days. On the following 3 days the peanuts were saved until the children got off the bus.

On the ninth day, Townsend rode the bus without a rewarding adult other than the bus driver who had been instructed to praise the children for their good bus riding behavior as he let them off the bus and to ignore Townsend if he had not stayed buckled. When the teacher and social worker, waiting at the bus stop, heard the bus driver praise Townsend, they voiced approval and gave him a small sucker as they accompanied him to his house. Gradually all consumable reinforcement was eliminated and only occasional social reinforcement, in the form of praise for Townsend's independent bus riding, was used.

Shaping Play Skills

Establishing appropriate behaviors incompatible with his maladaptive behaviors was the area on which his teachers concentrated the greatest time, energy, and planning in Townsend's program. Data from the home classroom indicated that he had few play skills and also, that he had a low rate of interaction with other children. It seemed futile to attempt to build cooperative play with children until Townsend had acquired some play skills. Therefore, the teachers began a step-by-step program of teaching play with each of the materials considered important in a preschool program. For example, a teacher helped Townsend to duplicate what at first were simple block models. If he refused to participate in a play lesson he forfeited the attention of all adults in the classroom. The moment he returned to the play materials, the attention of the teacher was again forthcoming. He was also reinforced for all divergent or unique uses of materials and equipment as long as the divergence was within the broad limits acceptable to preschool teachers.

Between sessions 6 and 26 Townsend acquired a functional repertoire of play skills with a variety of materials and equipment. It was decided, therefore, to change reinforcement contingencies: Adult social reinforcement would be available only when Townsend engaged in constructive use of play materials and interacted appropriately with another child. The change in contingencies appeared to have a positive effect. Between sessions 26 and 32 (Figure 1) there was a steady increase in the rate of cooperative play.

Return to Home Classroom

Analysis of the data at this point indicated that it was an appropriate time to return Townsend to his home classroom.

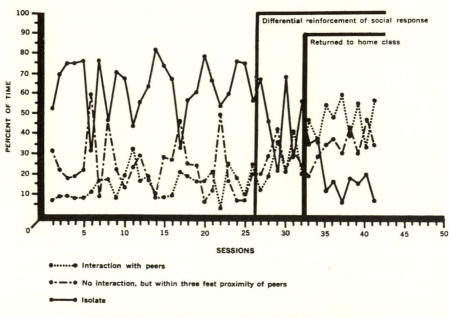

FIGURE 1. Case Study 1—Townsend: Social behavior with peers.

●········● Interaction with peers

●·—·● No interaction, but within three feet proximity of peers

●———● Isolate

Townsend's original teachers had had 3 days of in-service training in the demonstration classroom and had worked with the staff person who had been assigned to Townsend's home classroom. The staff person provided coaching on sessions 33 to 36 (Figure 1), at which point the data indicated that Townsend's teachers were able to continue the contingency management procedures on their own. Not only were there no incidents of disruptive behaviors, but Townsend's social skills continued to hold at a high stable rate as measured by the amount of cooperative play (Figure 1, sessions 37-41). Several postchecks were made throughout the remainder of the school year. These indicated that Townsend continued to function in an acceptable manner.

Case Study 2

Doreen was 4¾ years old when she entered the demonstration class. The reasons for referral were many: immaturity, incessant crying, frequent physical attacks on other children, excessive dependency on adults, severe deficits in large motor skills, little interaction with peers, and speech that was either echolalic or unintelligible mumbling. Data taken for six sessions in the home classroom prior to her transfer to the demonstration class confirmed referral reports.

Shaping Motor Skills

Where does one begin with a child displaying so maladaptive and deficient a repertoire? As with Townsend it was reasoned that a child needs play skills to participate even minimally in the preschool program. However, in Doreen's case, basic motor skills had to be developed first. Therefore, a program was planned beginning with very simple skills such as walking a low, wide board and progressing to more complex activities like climbing on the outdoor equipment, riding the wheel toys, and pumping on the swings. A teacher's hand and other forms of physical contact were forthcoming only when Doreen was making an effort to engage in a motor task. At all other times the teachers disengaged her hands and turned away when

she clung to them or to their clothing. Within 5 weeks Doreen was using all the outdoor equipment competently and independently. One data photography sequence shows her going up and over a 6-foot climber without assistance. Concurrently, the teachers ignored totally her repeated attacks on children. They gave their attention to the child who had been attacked, inserting themselves between Doreen and the other child, with their backs to Doreen. Attacks on children became infrequent, occurring only once or twice a week.

Differential Reinforcement of Verbal Behavior

Doreen's verbal behavior continued to be of a low order. The verbal data were broken down into two categories: (a) appropriate verbalizations as specifically defined, e.g., intelligible words relevant to the situation, and (b) inappropriate verbalizations or vocalizations as specifically defined. The latter included her whimpering cries, echolalic or parroted responses, and unintelligible monologues. The baseline data taken in the classroom indicated that the teachers tended to respond more to her inappropriate verbalizations than they did to her appropriate ones (Figure 2, sessions 1-6). When Doreen entered the demonstration class, the teachers were instructed to attend as frequently as possible to her appropriate verbalizations and to attend as infrequently as possible to her inappropriate ones. As can be seen in Figure 2, the teachers rarely succeeded in totally ignoring the inappropriate verbalizations. Nevertheless they did, for the most part, give a proportionately greater share of their attention to the appropriate responses. Under this regimen, appropriate verbalizations began an irregular increase with inappropriate verbalizations slowly declining at an irregular rate; the latter eventually constituted a relatively small percentage of the child's total verbal output (Figure 2, sessions 34-39). Six days of data taken after Doreen's return to the home classroom indicated that appropriate verbalizations continued to dominate her verbal output and, further, that her teach-

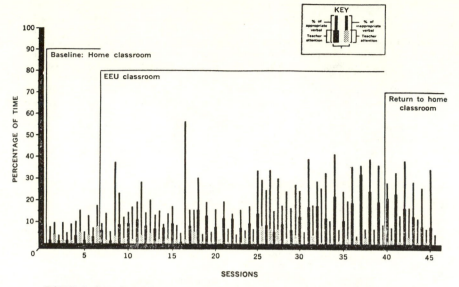

FIGURE 2. Case Study 2—Doreen: Proportion of appropriate to inappropriate verbal behavior; ratio of adult social reinforcement for each category.

ers were responding in an appropriately differential fashion.

No specific program to increase Doreen's social interaction with peers was instituted though the question was posed: Will amelioration of the major behavior disorders be accompanied by improved social interaction with peers? The data indicate that cooperative interaction with peers did increase from an average of 10 percent of each session during baseline in the home classroom to an average of 26 percent (Figure 3) in the demonstration class. It seems probable that as assault behaviors decreased, verbalizations became less bizarre and improved motor skills enabled her to use the play equipment, Doreen became a more desirable play companion, thus making peer as well as adult social reinforcement available to her.

Conclusions

These behavior modification projects have been described in detail in order to illustrate the application of reinforcement principles by preschool teachers in a field setting. The principles and techniques as they relate to these specific case studies follow:

1. Preschool teachers can readily employ reinforcement procedures to produce desired changes in children's behavior. To do so effectively, a teacher must assess children objectively, select specific target behaviors, keep continuous records, and use these records as a basis for program planning and continuous assessment.

2. Modification of only one or two of a child's behaviors at a time is essential to a successful program. A teacher's responses may become scattered and unsystematic if too many contingencies must be kept in mind for each child.

3. Every adult involved in a child's environment is potentially a powerful social reinforcer. Thus, every adult who interacts with children in the preschool situation must carefully monitor his responses to each child.

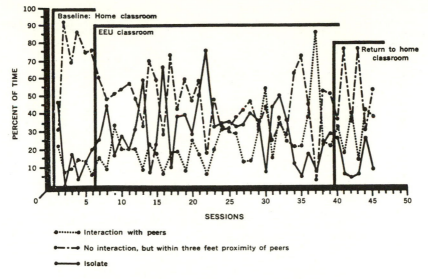

FIGURE 3. Case Study 2—Doreen: Social behavior with peers.

Legend for figure:
- Interaction with peers
- No interaction, but within three feet proximity of peers
- Isolate

When strict monitoring is not exercised, progress will be slower and more irregular.

4. The preschool environment abounds in natural reinforcers—play materials, snack time, outdoor play, special games and activities. Preschool teachers must make these reinforcers work for the child by making them available contingent on responses which will enhance the child's progress.

5. Though the extinction process (withholding reinforcement) is a highly effective means of freeing a child of his maladaptive response it does not automatically provide an alternate set of appropriate behaviors. Therefore, it is critical that teachers give their attention to desired behaviors so that the child may acquire a functional response repertoire.

6. Reinforcement of successive approximations to the target behaviors (shaping) is essential to achieve successful behavior modification. Reinstatement of Townsend as a bus rider is one

example of shaping procedures.

7. A careful step-by-step reduction in the amount of reinforcement (leaning the schedule) is necessary if a response is to be self-maintained. The bus riding sequence is again cited as an example.

8. Elimination of maladaptive behaviors simultaneous with shaping of appropriate behaviors often correlates with other favorable changes in the child's behavioral repertoire. The concurrent changes in improved cooperative play patterns in the second case study demonstrate this effect, an effect which has been noted previously (Allen, Henke, Harris, Baer, & Reynolds, 1967).

It would appear from this demonstration project, as well as from many other experimental analyses of behavior, that the teacher's differentiated responsiveness is the crucial variable in determining what and how the young child learns. No educational model, no preschool curriculum alone can insure optimum progress for a child. The deciding factor is the teacher's behavior and appropriate reinforcement techniques. Successful behavior modification depends on correct teacher-child interaction.

References

Allen, K. E., Hart, B. M., Buell, J. S., Harris, F. R., & Wolf, M. M. Effects of social reinforcement on isolate behavior of a nursery school child. *Child Development*, 1964, 35, 511-518.

Allen, K. E., & Harris, F. R. Elimination of a child's excessive scratching by training the mother in reinforcement procedures. *Behaviour Research and Therapy*, 1966, 1, 305-312.

Allen, K. E., Henke, L. B., Harris, F. R., Baer, D. M., & Reynolds, N. F. The control of hyperactivity by social reinforcement of attending behavior in a preschool child. *Journal of Educational Psychology*, 1967, 58, 231-237.

Bijou, S. W., Peterson, R. F., Harris, F. R., Allen, K. E., & Johnston, M. S. Methodology for experimental studies of young children in natural settings. *Psychological Record*, 1969, 19, 177-210.

Haring, N. G., Hayden, A. H., & Nolen, P. A. Accelerating appropriate behaviors of children in a Head Start program. *Exceptional Chidren*, 1969, 35, 773-784.

Haring, N. G., Hayden, A. H., & Allen, K. E. *Building Social Skills in the Preschool Child.* 16mm color film. Experimental Education Unit, Child Development and Mental Retardation Center, University of Washington, 1968.

Harris, F. R., Johnston, M. K., Kelley, C. S., & Wolf, M. M. Effects of positive social reinforcement on regressed crawling in a preschool child. *Journal of Educational Psychology*, 1964, 55, 35-41.

Harris, F. R., Wolf, M. M., & Baer, D. M. Effects of adult social reinforcement on child behavior. *Young Children*, 1964, 1, 8-17.

Hart, B. M., Allen, K. E., Buell, J. S., Harris, F. R., & Wolf, M. M. Effects of social reinforcement on operant crying. *Journal of Experimental Child Psychology*, 1964, 1, 145-153.

Hawkins, R. P., Peterson, R. F., Schweid, E., & Bijou, S. W. Behavior therapy in the home: Amelioration of problem parent-child relations with the parent in a therapeutic role. *Journal of Experimental Child Psychology*, 1966, 4, 99-107.

Klein, J. W. Innovative approaches in project Head Start. Paper presented at the Council for Exceptional Children, Special Conference on Early Childhood Education, New Orleans, December 1969.

Nolen, P. A., Hulten, W. J., & Kunzelmann, H. P. Data diagnosis and programing. In John I. Arena (Ed.), *Successful programing: Many points of view.* Boston: Fifth Annual International Conference of the Association for Children with Learning Disabilities, 1968, 409-418.